THE GIFT BEST GIVEN

A Memoir

Edward Di Gangi

The Gift Best Given – A Memoir

Copyright © 2020 by Edward Di Gangi

All rights reserved. No part of this book may be reproduced or used in any manner without written permission of the copyright owner except for the use of quotations in a book review.

Unless otherwise noted, all images contained in this book are from the author's collection and are believed to be free from copyright restrictions.

For more information, address:
edward.digangi.author@gmail.com

First edition May 2020
By Beddington Court Press

Edited by Jessica Holland
Book design by Polgarus Studio
Cover Design by Wes Flanary

ISBN 978-1-7347572-0-0 (paperback)
ISBN 978-1-7347572-1-7 (ebook)
ISBN 978-1-7347572-2-4 (kindle)

Library of Congress Control Number: 2020904719

www.digangiauthor.com

To My Parents
Nina and Jim Di Gangi
Who I Am and What I Am
I Owe to Them

Contents

CHAPTER ONE: *A Story Was Never Intended* 1
CHAPTER TWO: *A Young Woman's Dream* 15
CHAPTER THREE: *Leaving Home* 33
CHAPTER FOUR: *Traveling West* 45
CHAPTER FIVE: *Pickers* 73
CHAPTER SIX: *The Other Side of the World* 83
CHAPTER SEVEN: *Traveling Home* 115
CHAPTER EIGHT: *Gerry Verden* 129
CHAPTER NINE: *Teddy Roman* 145
CHAPTER TEN: *Ice Follies* 153
CHAPTER ELEVEN: *Difficult Decision* 175
CHAPTER TWELVE: *An Unexpected Discovery* 199
CHAPTER THIRTEEN: *Parting Ways* 217
CHAPTER FOURTEEN: *Alone in New York* 231
CHAPTER FIFTEEN: *A Decision Made* 259
CHAPTER SIXTEEN: *The First Weeks of May* 281
CHAPTER SEVENTEEN: *The Home Stretch* 301
CHAPTER EIGHTEEN: *Kin* 321
CHAPTER NINETEEN: *Pieces of the Puzzle* 339
EPILOGUE 351

Acknowledgements 353
About the Author 355

CHAPTER ONE
A Story Was Never Intended

St. Vladimir's Cemetery
Jackson, New Jersey

February 1, 2017

This story was never intended to begin as it did. In fact, a story of any sort was neither intended nor anticipated. On the first Wednesday of February, we had come to New Jersey to bury my father-in-law's remains. The ten pounds of his ashes contained in the faux marble urn were the remnants of a larger than life character's eighty-three years.

He would be buried the next day, Thursday, in a different cemetery not far away. The space between he and I had been too small for too long, and his need to rely on us—my wife and me—on a daily basis had been for him, I imagine, too great. Sadly, at a time when the opposite would be hoped for, it had frequently left us both intolerant and impatient with one another. Yet, the next day, as others would come to his gravesite, having been removed from him by time and by miles, and wistfully recall that he was "quite a character," I would smile. There would be no purpose in disagreeing.

But, on this day, this Wednesday, chilly and cloudy, the air redolent of the smell of smoke from fireplaces in nearby homes, we stood among an expanse of mostly gray granite headstones that had stood for fifty years or more. Like pieces of broken glass tossed by the sea and left on the beach as the tides receded, each one had been polished by seasons of swirling winter snows, sandy New Jersey soil blown by March winds, and the heat of the scorching summer sun on this bare, unprotected hillside. One after another, each monument displayed the name of some immigrant family from Russia or Poland or Ukraine, and many were engraved with a three-pronged Russian Orthodox cross like the one that could be seen on the small whitewashed church with its gold onion domes that faced Route 571, Cassville Road, by which we had arrived.

They had come in waves to this place midway between New York City and Philadelphia beginning in the 1930s. They were refugees and immigrants escaping wars already fought and wars yet to come, famine, poverty, and ruthless dictators' efforts to extinguish them. They were survivors of treacherous journeys and denizens of overcrowded city tenements. Those who could, those who had skills that would support them, moved to this place and built pastel-colored cottages on parcels of land purchased on installments from the Russian Benevolent Society. They lived in the midst of New Jersey's Pine Barrens, a million acres of sparsely populated land covered with pines dwarfed by harsh weather and poor soil perforated by man-made cranberry bogs, which were flooded and the fruit gathered every autumn since the middle of the eighteen hundreds.

Living in close proximity to one another, they attempted to preserve their culture. The ones who earned their meager livelihood in the city would travel by bus on weekends to stay with friends. Late into the night, in the pavilion beside the lake, they would sing and dance to Ukrainian folk tunes played by men on their banduras.

Nearby, Jewish immigrants who had fled Eastern Europe in the 1930s and 1940s, subsidized by relief agencies, had established chicken farms numerous and large enough to distinguish New Jersey as the country's largest producer of eggs. I'm less naïve now than I was in my youth. Then, all the Jewish families I knew on my block of tract homes in a New York City suburb were the second or third generation in America and were pharmacists or furriers or drapery manufacturers. Today, I smile with embarrassment when I recall how incongruous I found the thought of Jews farming and raising chickens.

We had come to visit, my wife, my son, and I. James and Linda knew only one of the people buried here, my mother's cousin, my Aunt Fay, who lived to be eighty-nine and was smiling, gentle, soft-spoken, and uncomplaining to the end. She had been returned here from California several years before to be with her husband, my Uncle Johnny, who had loved sports and bowling and golf. He had worked for years at Esso's Bayway refinery, where the noxious fumes escaping as gasoline was produced belied the notion of New Jersey ever having been the Garden State. He had passed years before. A company man through and through, I remember him calling out, "Happy motoring!" Esso's advertising slogan at the time, as we would back out of their driveway after spending a weekend visiting. On that gray, chilled, windy day, they lay together beneath a blanket of evergreens, silver-painted pine cones, and red velveteen bows placed there at Christmas. To their left were Uncle John's parents. In writing this, I realize now that we had somehow missed Aunt Fay's father and her mother, who was my own mother's aunt, buried nearby.

Down a sandy, rutted path was the grave of Aunt Fay's brother Bill, a large man—a very large man, I recall—known simply as Brother or Willie, who had served in Korea, given me bags of scarred golf balls that I would later methodically hit into the lake in front of our home in Queens, and who, when we spent weekends with Aunt Fay and her family (likely our visits were not the only time he did this) would arrive early on Sunday morning with a bag of donuts still warm from the fryer. His weight—and the donuts, I suspect—stopped his heart before he reached his fiftieth birthday. His wife, Sophie, a petite woman who I knew as Aunt Sue, though I had never felt a particular connection to her, lived another thirty-four years before she joined him here.

And beside Brother and Aunt Sue, to the left of their gravestone, stands a monument more imposing than the others. Broad-shouldered and of polished red stone, it stands on a thick red base. This garnet red marker bore the names of my grandparents—Buchanok, Peter and Anna—my mother's parents. Immigrants from Ukraine at the beginning of the twentieth century, they lived first in a four-story walk-up apartment on Manhattan's Lower East Side (the building still exists, today housing a Starbuck's on the ground floor. A one-bedroom apartment in it recently rented for $3,000 per month). Afterward, they moved to the Bronx, then finally to Long Island, from where my grandfather commuted to his job in a coat factory on Twenty-Third Street in Manhattan. On Thanksgiving Eve of 1950, the 6:09 p.m. express from Penn Station, the train on which he was returning home, collided at high speed with a second train inexplicably sitting stopped outside a station along the way. I suspect that the meaning of Thanksgiving for the other seventy-seven families whose loved ones also perished that night was changed forever too.

While those who knew him would fondly recall my grandfather and his friends disappearing on weekends aboard someone's less than seaworthy little boat to drink homemade vodka and angle for weakfish in Great South Bay or would all nod in agreement speaking of his kindness, they would talk about my grandmother in hushed tones. Each would agree, "She was never the same after the accident."

In private, some would dare to confide that she had never been "quite right." In both respects, perhaps they had been correct. But, for all the obstacles that stood in the way of she and I being close, her maybe not being "quite right," the fact that she spoke little English, and the fact that she was, for the most part, a stern and solitary woman, on some level I think we shared a bond. I loved walking down the rows of her big vegetable garden and climbing on the tarpaper roof of the shed beside a long-unused outhouse. As we arrived for weekend visits, I would jump from the car and hurdle her picket fence with its peeling white paint to pick the impossibly sweet raspberries that grew along her property line. I recall inhaling the damp, musky cool of her cellar and running my fingers through the silky grains of winter wheat she sowed in her garden every fall and kept in a large pottery container there in the dark.

Each of these memories is part of a mosaic. Even today, when I go to our porch in the evening to call Kitty, a magical little cat who appeared from nowhere one day, hungry and bedraggled and who decided we were the family she was going to adopt, I shake my head in amusement at the high pitched "kit, kit, kit" that comes from the back of my throat when I call her, or the "puss, puss, puss" that slips from between my lips. I remember that Grandma had called her own cats to dinner the same way.

Despite the fond memories brought alive on that bare New Jersey hillside, the cold wind and the dwindling daylight of a February Wednesday discouraged a lengthier stay. Linda, James, and I left them there—those and others from my childhood—the three of us knowing that we might not ever return. We live far away now, and there are few alive of the generations to whom this place would call. There were things still to be accomplished that day and the next. As we laid Linda's father to rest, I would regret not having had the benefit of a child's forgiving eyes and the two of us not having had the gift of greater space and time. But, from it all—the wishes, the regrets, the confrontation with our inevitable mortality—unexpectedly came a need to explore a part of my past of which I then knew little.

The Box
Orange County Public Library, Hillsborough, North Carolina,

February 22, 2017

Many years ago, my parents purchased an ostensibly fireproof metal box in which to store their important documents. When I write of years, I think of "many" in terms of party lines, of Fuller Brush salesmen walking door-to-door, of being awakened in the early morning by the clink of glass milk bottles being delivered to the back door, butterfat clogging their necks, or of seeing Dr. Jacoby's black 1955 Sedan de Ville parked at the curb in front of a neighbor's home as he made house calls.

With a chrome locking clasp, the box was silver-gray and was large enough to hold multiple letter-sized manila folders, each labeled in my mother's meticulous printing. One bore her name, one my father's, and another my name. Over the years, "House", "Car", "Insurance", and still other folders were added. With time and use, they became dog-eared as they were opened and closed and their contents changed and swelled.

I recall secretly rummaging through this box sometimes when my parents were out, examining ancient birth and baptismal certificates, diplomas for elementary schools that no longer exist, papers discharging my father from the army after fighting the Second World War with the Signal Corps, and fuzzy carbon copies of resumes typed on translucent onion skin paper from an era before copy machines. In the folder marked with my mother's name was a white, legal-sized envelope the contents of which I removed and examined only once before carefully replacing them, though they would call out to me periodically in the years to follow.

After my father's death in 1975, then my mother's twelve years later, the box became ours. A folder was added with Linda's name, and when James was born in 1991, another was inserted for him. Each folder is a time capsule chronicling the important events in our lives; in my parents' case, a narrative of lives full and rich but too quickly lived.

Late in February of last year, I found myself examining the contents of the box again. Linda was working, and with James having a place of his own, the house was quiet. I recalled the secretive explorations I had made as a boy. It had been three weeks since we'd returned from visiting the cemetery where members of my mother's family were buried. In the interim, I'd finished reading Daniel Mendelsohn's book, *The Lost*, for the second time, which is at once a mystery thriller, a lesson in the Old Testament, and a frightening reminder of the closeness of evil as he searched for what had become of six of his relatives who had vanished in the Holocaust. The two events—the cemetery visit and reading Mendelsohn's book—had suddenly compelled me, after almost seventy years, to want to know more about where I had come from. To truly know.

My cousin Ann, once the matriarch of my late father's side of the family and now sadly no longer alive, had completed a comprehensive search of their family's Italian roots. Still, I quickly examined the documents in the folder with my father's name printed on the crumpled tab and jotted down names and places. I did the same with my mother's folder, which, after her own mother had died, had swelled with still more documents and names and locations. A small spiral-bound notebook contained place names that, until recently, I couldn't locate, no matter whether I searched for them in Ukraine or Russia or Poland. I added the names and the places to my notes. Beneath all the documents was the white, legal-sized envelope with my mother's name on it, the contents of which I had viewed only once as a child. I understood later that it was this envelope and what it contained that had compelled me to take the box from the shelf to begin with, but I chose to leave them unexamined. I replaced the folders and returned the box carefully to its place in our pantry.

Carrying a speckled composition book with faceless names and distant, unknown places in hand, I went to our local library. I had determined that it would provide me with access to Ancestry's genealogy software, something of which I knew little at the time but have learned a great deal about since.

The second-floor area contained a dozen computers in two facing rows of six and was quiet, save for a woman propped against the wall, cocooned in a purple, goose down coat that looked like a sleeping bag, her eyes closed, the insistent thud of a hip-hop baseline escaping from the headphones tethering her to one of the computers. At the other end of the same row, one of the librarians attempted to connect to an online Department of Motor Vehicles safety program, working to maintain his composure as he found himself having to explain to a patron why the six-hour program couldn't be completed in two hours that afternoon.

Seated in front of a computer in the middle of the opposite row, I found the program I was looking for. Spreading out my list of names and places, opening my book in hope that there would be meaningful bits of information to capture, I began to enter names and dates for my mother's parents into the search window. Details emerged, some expected, some surprising. I puzzled over why tenement dwellers from Manhattan's Lower East Side would have moved to the Bronx. I made notes. I looked for a deceased infant, the deed for whose grave I'd inexplicably found in my mother's folder. No information. I turned to the information for my father's family but found nothing not already known. Perhaps if I had looked harder I would have found more, but I was distracted. I sat and stared at the computer screen understanding that there were other things that it might reveal, questions that it might answer. As I sat there, I confronted the fact that, after waiting so many years, I hadn't been looking for what I truly wanted to know. There was something else, and I had avoided what I might discover. I gathered my papers, shut down the computer, left the cocooned woman and the librarian with his frustrated charge behind. I returned to my car and made the short drive home.

Back in the house, again I took out the metal box and opened it. Deliberating only briefly, I retrieved my mother's folder. Again, I slowly spread it open on the table in front of me and once again carefully removed its contents, though I knew precisely what I sought. I removed the white legal-sized envelope that bore my mother's name. As I had done so many years before, I carefully opened it and extracted the two sheets of paper it held. I unfolded them, smoothed them, and although I was sure I knew what they would tell me, I read both pages carefully. It was a legal document to which the names and signatures of my parents, of Francis E. Carberry, Attorney at Law, and of one other individual whose name I hadn't recalled since examining the decree so many years before were all affixed. In the speckled composition book, I carefully wrote down the name that accompanied the final signature—given name, middle name, surname—before returning the papers to the envelope from which they had come, placing the envelope back in the folder and the tattered folder back in the box. As if there was a decision to be made, I looked again at the name I had written down, but I had already decided what I would do.

Save for one person who briefly stopped in to check his email, the bank of library computers was quiet on this visit. More confidently this time, I opened Ancestry and stared at the blank boxes. From my open notebook I entered the name I had transcribed. Letter by letter, I slowly typed the first name, the middle, and the last: GENEVIEVE IRENE KNOROWSKI. I sat for a moment and wondered what the program would tell me once I pressed the search button. What would I learn? Who would I find? Would I find record of anyone at all?

A deep breath followed by a single deliberate tap of my forefinger answered my questions as a page filled with responses was returned. I scanned the screen, and though logic would seem to dictate opening the first listing that appeared, I slowly scrolled down the page and stopped at an item titled Rio de Janeiro, Brazil, Immigration Cards, 1900-1965. With curiosity, I clicked. An official document printed in Portuguese appeared—an application for a visa or perhaps it was the visa itself—dated March 25, 1949, and while I don't read Portuguese, I could discern her name, her birthdate, January 26, 1925, her parents' names, and an address in Flushing, New York. Adjacent to the text was a picture of a young woman, her hair done, makeup applied, and a serious look on her face. Though there was no reason that anyone should care, I looked around me to see if anyone else was seeing what I was. I looked again. Her profession, her *profissao*, was listed as "artista." Artista? Artist. What kind of artist? I was as perplexed by that as I was excited by my discovery. I found that I could email a copy of this document to myself. I quickly examined census enumerations for 1930 and 1940. Same person, same birthday, same parents; she had two older sisters and an older brother. Feeling as if, uninvited, I was peering through a window into the life of this previously unknown woman and her family, I made quick notes in my composition book, dated them February 22, 2017, and left for home trying to digest what I had discovered.

Linda was home when I returned, and I attempted to sound nonchalant when she inquired about what I had done that afternoon.

"Oh, not much, I went to the library," I replied. I opened my laptop and retrieved the image of the document I had emailed from the library. I examined it one more time before asking, "Would you like to see a picture of my mother?"

Understandably puzzled, Linda responded, "We have lots of pictures of your mother. What makes this one special?"

Turning the computer to Linda, I said simply, "This is my mother—my birth mother."

CHAPTER TWO
A Young Woman's Dream

Ice Revue '42

February 28, 1942

The photograph came to me unexpectedly. Found on a scrap of newsprint at the bottom of a carton of other ephemera, neither the date nor the source of the picture remained attached to it. More than likely it had been cut from the publication by someone who, living in the moment, knew both these things well. Breathing in the acidic smell of the newsprint, ink smudging their fingertips as they wielded their scissors, they would never have considered that, decades later, someone interested as I am would again hold the faded clipping in his hands. They would never have considered that this newspaper clipping, brown and brittle, from a newspaper that published for the last time more than half a century ago could survive.

The photograph appeared on the first page of the second section of the *Long Island Daily Press* on Saturday, February 28, 1942 and is of six teenage girls on ice skates. All of them are wearing simple matching outfits made of satin, with lace trim around the sleeves and necklines, likely sewn at home by the girls themselves or by one of their mothers. The image is black and white—it would be four decades before color was introduced to newsprint—but surely their dresses are pink or powder blue.

The six are positioned in a diagonal line, left to right, back to front, under the headline "They Starred in Victory Ice Revue." My research reveals that all the girls were from the neighborhoods surrounding the New York City Building, the venue for the Revue. The massive, low-profile structure of glass, brick, limestone, and granite in Flushing Meadow Park had been constructed for the 1939 World's Fair and housed a 200-foot by 80-foot ice rink at one end of the building and a smaller, roller-skating rink at the opposite end.

On that day in 1942, the crowd entered through the New York City Building's massive bronze doors, paid their admission, and turned to their left to the ice rink at the south end of the building. As the spectators seated themselves to witness a skating exhibition, turning up collars, buttoning coats, and tightly crossing arms against their chests to ward off the unexpected cold of the arena, volunteers circulated through the crowd selling war bonds to support the United States' involvement in World War II. Numerous skating professionals were scheduled to appear that night, but it was this picture of these six local girls that was used to promote the event. The girls would perform twice during the evening, first as an ensemble and then, in the finale, with the entire cast.

From the left of the photo, at the rear of the line, is Yvonne Arnold, who is seventeen. Next is Sharlee Munster, one of the oldest of the group at eighteen. Sharlee would go on to appear as a cast member in hotel ice shows in New York City, as well as in Sonja Henie ice skating productions at the Center Theater. In front of her is Gloria Abbott, the youngest at only fourteen, and then Anita Stamm, another eighteen-year-old. Jo-Ann Axtel, sixteen-years-old, placed second from the right and in front of Anita, fills the picture with a smile that attempts to draw every eye immediately to her. While each of the four behind her smile shyly for the camera, Jo-Ann's smile seems to say, "Look at me." Referred to later in her family's records as having been an "Ice Follies Starlet," Jo-Ann skated professionally for a time before she married, though only in roles supporting featured performers. The last of the group, Genevieve Knorowski, barely a month past her seventeenth birthday, appears at the front of the line. Of the six, she displays a natural presence, an effortless smile, and a confidence that those who knew her over the years would always recall.

Genevieve came from a talented family. Her father, Leonard, along with his mother and sister, arrived in New York from what is now eastern Poland early in the 1890s at the age of two. Her mother, Josephine, the eldest daughter of farmers who were recent immigrants from Austria, had been born in the United States. But it was the encouragement and support of Genevieve's paternal grandfather that nurtured the talents of Genevieve and her siblings.

Aleksander, a piano maker, emigrated from Poland to the United States in 1890 and settled his new family in Astoria, Queens, just outside of Manhattan, in close proximity to where he worked at the newly built Sohmer & Co. piano manufacturing facility that loomed over the East River. Genevieve's oldest sister, Eleanore, was a gifted soprano with early, though ultimately unfulfilled, aspirations of joining the Metropolitan Opera. A brother, Alexander, older than Genevieve by eight years, was a talented violinist who played with a local symphony orchestra but never pursued the heights others thought he might attain. Her next sister, Lucille, artistically gifted and later recognized for her acting in theatrical productions, was older than Genevieve by only two years. After completing eight years in the structured and sheltered environment of Catholic parochial schools, Genevieve, the youngest of the four siblings, chose to commute by subway to Washington Irving High School in Manhattan, a girls-only public school with a curriculum centered on the arts.

After leaving school every day, Genevieve would rush to the Union Square station and take the subway to Iceland, an ice skating facility adjacent to Madison Square Garden. It was home to the prestigious Skating Club of New York as well as the haunt of many professional skaters, and it was a natural place for an aspiring performer to observe, emulate, and practice the techniques they had observed. It was Genevieve's natural grace, her studious approach, and the way she would relentlessly practice her skills that ultimately attracted the attention of Phil Hiser, an older skater who earned his living traveling with various ice shows. He gave her tips on how to improve her skating, until one day he asked Genevieve if she had ever considered skating professionally, telling her he thought she had the ability. Genevieve blushed and laughed, thinking that he was simply being encouraging.

Ballet on skates was an intriguing feature of the "For Victory Ice Revue of 1942," presented at the Flushing Meadow Park rink. These dancers-on-skates are, left to right, Yvonne Arnold of Elmhurst, Sharlee Munster of Flushing, Gloria Abbott of Flushing, Anita Stamm of Jackson Heights, Jo Ann Axtell of Flushing and Genevieve Knorowski of Flushing.

THE GIFT BEST GIVEN

At the New York City Building, W. Carl Snyder stood beside the rink wrapped in an expensive woolen top coat and wearing a fedora as he watched appraisingly throughout the performance. Hiser had mentioned Genevieve to him and suggested that, "She might be worth a look." A principal at Frederick Brothers, a talent agency based in Chicago, Snyder was constantly on the alert for new talent to fuel the recent rapid growth of ice shows in night clubs, hotels, and the remaining vaudeville houses around the country. One can only imagine the excitement Genevieve must have felt when Snyder approached her as she came off the ice, introduced himself, and asked to speak with her. Not realizing that this would be only the first of a number of times that her nascent career and Snyder's would intersect, Genevieve, with her parents now beside her and the other five girls curiously, enviously, looking on, listened. He told her that Phil Hiser had recommended that he come to see her skate. He explained the nature of his work and then, repeating the same question Hiser had asked, inquired if she had ever considered performing professionally. Sensing that a door might be opening on her dreams, Genevieve's heart skipped a beat.

Less than three years prior, when she was still in eighth grade, a teacher had entered her classroom with a pair of used, black ice skates. Holding them up, she said that if anyone wanted them and fit into them, they could have them. The boots were a size too small, but Genevieve squeezed her feet into them and exclaimed that they fit perfectly. She had often thought of Cinderella and the glass slipper since that moment. Though Mr. Snyder was not quite Prince Charming, he had asked questions that suggested the fondest of her aspirations could become a reality. Looking from her mother and then to her father, she told him that she had often thought about it and that there was nothing she wanted to do more than to be a professional ice skater.

Snyder smiled at her enthusiasm, but he cautioned her about the demands of such a career and of the sacrifices it would require. He warned her that for every skater who reached any level of prominence, hundreds of other young women like her would become discouraged and give up on their dreams. Seeing that she was not dissuaded, he told her that the McGowan and Mack Ice Revue, an ice show that he represented, was currently performing nearby. He suggested that before Genevieve made any decisions, she should see their show, meet the principals, and then decide if performing on a piece of ice the size of a postage stamp amidst a dining room full of patrons would be as interesting to her as this night's performance on a significantly larger stage had been.

The Boulevard Tavern

Rego Park, New York

Nearby, in what is now Rego Park, Queens, was a Spanish-style stucco-walled building suggestive of one found in Las Vegas. The structure was illuminated by bright exterior lighting and a red canopy extending from the curb on Queens Boulevard to its double entry doors, which were tended by a doorman. Valets in smart burgundy uniforms would open car doors for patrons and then park their vehicles beneath a massive red-and-blue painted marquee that towered over the building and advertised * 3 * Complete * Shows * Nightly *.

After Prohibition was repealed in 1933, the Boulevard flourished as a restaurant, a night club, and as a gathering place for political and entertainment industry notables. The enterprising owners built their business on liquor sales and nightly floor shows. When ice shows became popular in the late 1930s, they installed a twenty by twenty foot ice rink purchased from one of the half dozen manufacturers in the business at that time, becoming one of the few small venues to do so. The ice could be quickly covered by a dance floor, which ushered in an era of live bands and accompanying ice shows featuring well-known performers in the tavern's large dining room three times a night.

Following Snyder's suggestion, Genevieve arrived at the Boulevard three evenings later, well before the first scheduled show at eight o'clock. She was accompanied by her sister, Eleanore, and Eleanore's husband, Charles, a large man who had assumed an almost paternal concern for Genevieve's best interests from the first time they met. As they walked through the main entrance and then past the lobby coat room, Genevieve was struck by the pungent smell of cigar smoke, the sounds of chatter punctuated by bursts of laughter, and of ice cubes clinking in highball glasses. They walked past the bar and lounge area and then through the arched entryway to the partially filled dining room in the rear of the facility. She surveyed the room. A small stage for the band was positioned in the room's far left hand corner, and thirty or perhaps forty tables—Genevieve could not quickly count them all—each set for dinner, ringed the square sheet of Freon-chilled ice that glistened in the center of the large room under the ceiling's recessed lighting. It certainly was different than the huge ice rink on which she had performed just days before. The patrons, a few of whom looked curiously toward her, were seated at tables situated within only a few feet of the ice's edge. As she recalled Snyder's cautionary words, Charles, who was watching her, asked her what she was smiling about. Genevieve matter-of-factly responded that she could see herself there on the ice; that she knew she could perform in a place like this.

BOULEVARD TAVERN. The Boulevard Tavern in Rego Park, New York. One of the first clubs to install a permanent ice surface.

BOULEVARD TAVERN. Advertisement for McGowan and Mack at the Boulevard. Postcard and ad from author's collection.

At that moment, a woman approached them and introduced herself as Ruth McGowan. She was attractive and dressed in skater's attire far more elaborate than that which Genevieve and her peers had worn three nights prior. She suggested that Eleanore and Charles take one of the tables and pointed Genevieve in the direction of the curtained archway through which she had emerged. Ruth watched the aspiring young skater's movements as they walked to the dressing area to meet her husband, Everett, and other members of the cast. Genevieve moved confidently, and Charles looked to his wife, smiled, and said, "She'll be fine; they're going to love her."

As relaxed as Genevieve had been, as she observed the layout of the dining area and imagined performing there, her heartbeat quickened as she entered the dressing area just off the kitchen. Waiters hurried past on one side. On the other, orchestra members tuned their instruments. Four attractive girls already wearing skates—two older than her, two her own age, she estimated—smoked and idly watched as she entered a private room, looking as bored as Genevieve was excited. Inside was Ruth's husband, Everett, with whom she had formed the Revue several years earlier, and their ten-year-old daughter, Joann, who was spotlighted in the first show each evening, delighting patrons with flips and somersaults and her precise single-skate dancing.

Everett, though most knew him by his nickname, Mack, was cordial, but Genevieve felt goosebumps unpleasantly break out as he stepped back and slowly looked her up and down. He briefly smiled and said that he had spoken with Carl Snyder. "Mr. Snyder said you're good ... very good ... lots of potential."

Genevieve quickly forgot the goosebumps and the uneasy feeling. She was floating.

"But we don't have a place for you now. And you're still in school. Maybe we can use you later. Stay for the show," he said. "Decide if this is what you really want. If it is, stay in touch with Mr. Snyder."

Each phrase was curt and clipped. As quickly as the conversation began, Mack, with one more unhurried head-to-toe look of Genevieve, turned his attention back to the papers he had been reviewing when she entered the room with his wife.

Ruth led Genevieve back out of the room and into the bustling area outside. The four girls, cigarettes finished, had not moved. As Myron Hanley's orchestra began to play in the dining room, she introduced Genevieve to them one by one: Shirley, Grace, Eileen, and Ruth. Each extended a friendly if unenthusiastic hand, and Eileen, one of the two older skaters, asked, "Comin' to skate with us, hon?"

Remembering how her grandfather had admonished her to make a good impression with everyone she met, Genevieve summoned up a confident smile. In her most determined voice, she said, "Not yet, but soon."

Ruth was impressed by Genevieve's interaction with the girls. "My husband liked you, I can tell. He trusts Carl's judgment. But we've already got a full show, and you're still young. This is hard work. It's fun, but trust me, it's not as glamorous as it looks, and it doesn't last forever. Keep skating and finish school, and then if you still think that this is what you want, let Carl know. Mack will make a place for you."

The dining room had filled during the brief time that she had been with the McGowans, and Genevieve returned to sit with Eleanore and Charles. She recounted the brief conversation with Mack, but she didn't share that she wasn't sure what she thought of him; their conversation had been so short and the way he'd looked at her made her nervous. But she liked his wife, and Ruth had said her husband was serious: finish school, keep skating, and call Carl Snyder when she was ready. At that moment the lights in the dining room dimmed and the four girls, now displaying enthusiastic smiles, emerged from the rear and took the ice. Nodding toward them, Genevieve stated firmly, "That's what I'm going to do. By next year, I'll be there with them."

Genevieve's grandfather was the only one still awake when they returned home from the Boulevard Tavern. Both more than eighty years old, he and his wife, Wanda, lived with their son Leonard's family. Aleksander smiled as Genevieve eagerly described what had happened. More than ever, she told him, her dream of becoming a professional ice skater seemed real. He smiled and nodded, patiently waiting as she recounted every detail of the evening. Reaching out, Aleksander patted his granddaughter's hand. In his thick Polish accent, he cautioned her. "If this is what you want, do not just dream about it. Every day, you must see yourself there. You need to have a plan." With his words in mind, still filled with excitement, she kissed her grandfather goodnight and climbed the three broad flights of stairs to her bedroom.

Washington Irving High School

40 Irving Place, New York City

Genevieve slept fitfully before waking at six a.m. to quickly prepare to leave for school. Leonard had already departed for work, and her mother was in the kitchen as the first signs of daylight began to appear through the east-facing window above the sink. Genevieve walked the one block to the corner of Union Street and Thirty-Fifth

Avenue, passing towering homes with gables, turrets, and porte cocheres, constructed on large lots at the turn of the century. There she waited for the same city bus, painted gray and green that she boarded each day. Smiling at the driver's "Good morning, sunshine," the same words he had greeted her with since school had started the previous September, she showed her student transit pass that allowed her to ride for free and stood among the other commuters for the ten minute ride to Main Street Station, where she would board the number seven Flushing Line train.

The first part of her daily journey would take her across northern Queens and then under the East River to Manhattan. At the station beneath Grand Central Terminal, she would transfer to another train that would take her to school downtown. Her mind filled with thoughts of the previous night, Genevieve was oblivious to the stifling heat pumping from beneath the car's tightly woven rattan seats. The coaches, still in their faded orange and blue World's Fair livery, clattered across the borough on their elevated tracks.

High above the roofs of the single-family homes and the four and six-story apartment buildings built close to the streets below, she felt like she was floating. Genevieve pondered Everett McGowan's promise of making a place for her in his ice revue once she was ready, but her excitement was tempered by the cautious advice received from his wife and the wisdom provided by her grandfather. As Aleksander had reminded her, she knew that becoming a professional skater would require talent and a plan to realize that dream. "Keep skating and finish school," Ruth McGowan had said. Skating was easy; Genevieve skated every moment she had the opportunity. Finishing school was more of a challenge. It was March, and she was a high school junior, and if she did no more than adhere to her current curriculum, she would not be out of school until the following June. She was sure she didn't want to wait that long.

Genevieve was a serious and bright, if not extraordinary, student, pursuing a curriculum focusing on the visual arts—its history, the study of light and color, landscape and anatomical drawing, as well as her core of academic subjects. She arrived at school that morning, entering through the large lobby with its well-worn marble floor. Washington Irving High School had been architected as much a museum as a public high school. A massive fireplace with its *Legend of Sleepy Hollow* artwork over the mantle stood opposite the entrance doors. Above the oak-paneled walls, historic, hand-painted murals depicted the early history of New York State.

Genevieve sought out her guidance counselor to make an appointment for later in the day. When the two met, he was impressed, though guarded, about Genevieve's desire. The plan she presented, to graduate no later than the coming December, was one that was both ambitious and unusual. Genevieve suggested that not only would she willingly attend summer school, something typically reserved for students who failed courses the previous academic year, but also that she wanted to take the equivalent of a full term's classes to move her toward earning her diploma earlier than her classmates. Genevieve asked if it could be done. Her counselor told her that he was not aware of anyone having done it before and that it was not something he would normally recommend, but yes, it could be done. He wondered if her parents would agree to her proposition, but if they signed a written authorization, he could begin to help her schedule the required classes. Genevieve smiled. She was certain that her parents would agree.

The Ice Pond

Rockefeller Center, New York City

"Every day, you must see yourself there." Genevieve repeated her grandfather's words. She treasured her grandfather. He listened to her. He encouraged her. On the piano in their living room, he had taught her to play Chopin, the music of the great composer and pianist who was from Warsaw, like he was.

Now, on the last Saturday in April, the day that the Skating Pond—the ice skating rink that had become the focal point of Rockefeller Center—was to close for the season, Genevieve laced and tied her skates and stepped onto the ice. Crowds of tourists lined the walls above the rink looking down at the circling skaters. The massive, gilded bronze statue of Prometheus loomed over the ice. She listened to the sharp blades of her skates cut into the frozen surface as she slowly and gracefully circled the rink counterclockwise, repeating her grandfather's words. "Every day, you must see yourself there."

Genevieve was little aware of the other skaters on the ice as she looked up at the tourists watching from above. In her mind, they had become her audience. She smiled at them as she skated. Then, as she looked ahead, she saw the diners enjoying lunch behind the glass wall of the Café Francais restaurant at the south end of the rink. She slowed and circled, spinning in a small, self-measured square of ice in front of the restaurant's floor-to-ceiling windows. As she performed the intricate moves she had practiced over and over, she remembered how close the tables were to the ice at Boulevard Tavern. She wished these people were closer. She wished there was no glass separating her from them. At that moment, she imagined that she was on stage.

The diners smiled at one another, nodding their approval. Those at one table silently applauded, and Genevieve gleamed. Skating to the opposite end of the rink, the north end, other diners were enjoying the view as they were seated at the window walls of the English Grill. Genevieve circled another small patch of ice before them, and as she had moments before, she imagined herself on stage, providing unanticipated entertainment for them as she silently repeated to herself, "Every day, you must see yourself there." At that moment, she was there.

CHAPTER THREE
Leaving Home

The Telephone Call

Flushing, New York

After dinner, the family moved from the dining room to the living room as they did every evening. A fireplace was centered against the wall facing the window, with a mantle adorned with framed photographs of the four children. Leonard assumed his usual spot in the wing chair to its left, close to the arched entrance to the room. He picked up the evening edition of the *World Telegram*, unfolded it, and began to read. Aleksander sat in the matching chair on the other side of the fireplace while Lucille, Genevieve's sister, perched on the bench at the upright piano against the wall to the left of the two men. She idly touched its keys as she looked over her shoulder to the couch in front of the window where Genevieve sat nervously with her mother. Other than the hiss of the steam coming from the radiator under the window and the sound of Leonard smoothing the pages of his paper, the room was quiet. Genevieve stared at the Chesterfield cigarette advertisement on the back page of Leonard's newspaper and then glanced at her grandfather. Aleksander silently raised his eyebrows and nodded toward Leonard as if to say, "Go on. Tell him."

Genevieve swallowed, wet her lips, and said to her father, "Mr. Snyder called today." Leonard didn't respond, though he heard his daughter's words. Behind his newspaper, he closed his eyes for a moment and he felt his five feet ten inch, 160-pound frame shrink a little. He had known that the call would come, but still, he wasn't prepared for the invitation to his daughter, not even eighteen, to leave home to travel with an ice show. When he said nothing, Genevieve took a deep breath and continued. "Daddy, he heard back from Mr. and Mrs. McGowan; they want me to come and skate for them."

Leonard swallowed and then closed his paper, folding it in half and then in half again before putting it down. "Where are they?" he asked.

Lucille, watched, looking first to her father, then to her sister, then again to her father. Genevieve, trying to sound as confident and as sure of herself as she could, answered, "Vancouver." After a pause, she said, "British Columbia," sounding not quite as certain.

There was a silence as Leonard stared at a gardenia on the slipcover of the couch on which Genevieve and her mother sat. He had never been farther west than New Jersey, although he had traveled back to Poland fifteen years prior. He tried to place Vancouver and was angry at himself when he realized he had no idea where British Columbia was. The family sat in silence.

Finally, Aleksander said, "It's in Canada, Leonard."

"Canada," Leonard repeated as he continued to stare at the gardenia. "Montreal is in Canada and Toronto is in Canada. I know where those places are, but I don't know where Vancouver or British Columbia are."

Josephine wanted to reach out, but knew he would not have welcomed her touch. Leonard was a strong man, not prone to displays of emotion, and such a touch would be an acknowledgment of his vulnerability.

Genevieve went to the bookcase recessed into the wall a few feet to her father's right and removed the last volume of the *Encyclopedia Britannica*, the atlas. Leonard had purchased the twenty-five black, leather-bound volumes when the family moved to Flushing. They were as much a sign of his family's upward mobility as they were intended for their educational value to his children. She flipped the pages and then leaned over her father, pointing at a map of Canada that covered two facing pages. "This is where Vancouver is, Daddy. Look."

Leonard placed his finger where his daughter was pointing and held it there for a moment. Then he drew it back across the map from left to right, west to east. "This is New York," he said. Then, once again addressing the gardenia, "Vancouver ... British Columbia ... it might as well be the other side of the world." Once more, silence filled the room the same way the heat coming from the radiator did, and the quiet seemed endless.

Finally, Genevieve began to speak. "Daddy—"

But Leonard interrupted her, speaking to no one in particular as if trying to convince himself. "No, it's too far. What if she doesn't make it as a skater?"

Genevieve, feeling helpless, looked to Aleksander for support, but it was Josephine who spoke. Leonard and Josephine had been married for thirty years, and during that time, because she respected her husband—and because it was expected of her—she had almost always deferred to his judgment. This time, however, she spoke up. "Leonard ... Leonard," she said, "look at me." His eyes were sad as he turned his face to her. "What if she does make it as a skater? We need to let Gennie go."

Leaving Home

Flushing, New York

In the days that followed Leonard's reluctant acquiescence, Genevieve felt like she was caught in a whirlwind. A second call with Carl Snyder confirmed that she would join McGowan and Mack in Vancouver, and the details of when she would need to depart and when she would be expected to arrive were discussed. Travel plans were made and tickets purchased. Snyder had cautioned, "Things get lost in transit. Make sure to carry your skates with you." She had received a new pair for Christmas, so she packed her old ones—skates an eager boyfriend had given her as a gift a year before—in the newly purchased footlocker that would be shipped ahead. She would carry the new ones in the luggage that would accompany her on the train. There was an air of excitement and anticipation in the house. Leonard did his best to hide the discomfort he felt as his youngest daughter prepared to leave home.

Thursday afternoon, a Railway Express Agency truck, painted in shining dark green with black fenders, pulled up to the house. Genevieve's footlocker would be shipped ahead of her to a boarding house in Vancouver. If all went as planned, it would be awaiting her when she arrived there the following week. In a statement that this was all finally real, that it was truly happening and not just a dream, the truck pulled away from the house, and a part of Genevieve was on its way across the country. But after the truck left, the whirlwind slowed, and time seemed to suddenly stand still. As much as she loved her family—as much as she knew she would miss them and as much as leaving home unnerved her—Genevieve wished that she was on that truck along with her trunk. But she would have to wait until the following Monday to be on her way.

On Sunday, Genevieve's mother and grandmother prepared a massive family dinner. Eleanore and Charles, along with Lucille and her fiancé, Ed, joined them for the meal. Away from the rest of the family, Charles confided to Leonard that over the past week he had spoken to both Snyder and to Everett McGowan about the family's concern for Genevieve's well-being. McGowan had assured him that he understood their apprehension and that she would be watched over as if she were part of their family. When Leonard asked Charles if he truly believed what they said and Charles said that he did, his mood brightened. With a handshake and a word of thanks, Leonard led Charles back to the family in the dining room, and for the first time, he was able to share in his daughter's excitement.

Genevieve was scheduled to travel on New York Central's Pacemaker, an all-coach train making only limited stops between New York and Chicago. It would depart on Monday at three o'clock in the afternoon. How she wished it left earlier. The tension in the house that morning—the anticipation—seemed unbearable. Finally, at noon, Leonard announced that it was time to go. It would take time to make the drive to midtown Manhattan, and they needed to allow still more time once they arrived.

Leonard backed the family's maroon, 1940 Buick Super sedan from the large garage behind their home. Six of them, Genevieve, between Lucille and their mother in the rear, Leonard and his parents in the front, settled onto the car's gray Bedford cloth seats. A large suitcase that would be checked in the train's luggage car and another smaller bag holding Genevieve's precious skates were both placed in the trunk.

Genevieve knew the route and had driven it countless times before with Leonard between home and his plumbing business in Long Island City. They drove slowly past the other imposing, single-family homes lining Thirty-Fifth Avenue, turned left at the corner of Union Street, where Genevieve had waited for the bus so many mornings as she commuted to school, and then turned right on Northern Boulevard. At the next corner, they passed Flushing's old town hall and then the service station with its whitewashed walls, where her father bought his gasoline. The RKO Keith Theater was farther down the street at the foot of Main Street. The building was plain on the outside, but patrons walking through the doors beneath the large marquis entered a wonderland of gilded arches, waterfalls, fish ponds, and the smell of popcorn. Genevieve thought about how she had sat with her mother and sisters and her friends among the three thousand seats to watch just-released movies like *Gone with the Wind*, *Snow White and the Seven Dwarfs*, and *The Wizard of Oz*. She recalled the nights that she and Lucille had stood in the crowd when celebrities like Bob Hope and Judy Garland and the Marx Brothers arrived in chauffeur-driven limousines and strolled down a red carpet to perform there.

Leaving downtown Flushing, the road took them over the cement bridge that spanned Flushing Creek. The last book she had read while still at Washington Irving High School was F. Scott Fitzgerald's *The Great Gatsby*, and she recalled how he described that same creek as "a small foul river." Looking down at its polluted waters that slowly wound through what Fitzgerald had called the "valley of ashes," she smiled slightly, feeling quite sophisticated and well-read. Their ride continued through areas that had been rural ten years before. Josephine reminded them that she had grown up on a farm nearby. Now the land crisscrossed with newly paved streets lined with single-family homes and low-rise apartment buildings. The World's Fair of 1939 had brought attention and lots of people to Queens County.

As the family came closer to the city, factories began to appear, and traffic became heavier. Shortly they were at Queens Plaza, where Northern Boulevard met Queens Boulevard, and three subway lines all converged at the foot of the Queensboro Bridge. As they traversed the span over the East River, Genevieve looked out the window to the right, leaning forward to see around her mother. She could see the red brick Sohmer & Co. Piano Company building with its impressive tower on the river's Astoria side. She saw her grandfather staring that way as well, probably recalling all the many years he had worked there. Then, below them was Welfare Island, with its array of municipal hospital buildings. Someone had once told her that there had been an insane asylum and a prison there, but the inmates of both had since been moved. As Genevieve wondered where they had all gone, still another hospital, one to isolate people with tuberculosis, appeared. Welfare Island had never been a good place to be.

Ahead, Manhattan loomed, and Leonard turned left off the bridge onto Second Avenue. Traffic moved slowly in the middle of the day, and policemen wearing white gloves stopped them several times at intersections to allow pedestrians and cars to move across the city. The ride from Fifty-Ninth Street to Forty-Second Street seemed endless to Genevieve, but finally, they made a right turn. As Genevieve was looking to her left at the Chrysler Building, for a short time the tallest building in the world, Leonard stopped the car and announced solemnly, "We're here."

They were parked on Forty-Second Street opposite the entrance doors to Grand Central Terminal. Overhead, automobiles passed on the viaduct that took Park Avenue around the perimeter of the building. Genevieve was used to the city and its din, but she had never felt it as loud or had seen it as congested as it did as she stood on the curb. People were everywhere, some entering the terminal, others hurrying past on their way to other places, pushed down the wide sidewalk. As Leonard removed her suitcases from the trunk, Genevieve retrieved the smaller of the two as a red-capped porter took the larger one. Checking her ticket, he gave her a claim stub, and before the man disappeared with Genevieve's possessions, Aleksander tipped him a dime. Leonard left to park the car, shouting to his father over the blowing horns of taxis, "I'll meet you at the clock."

Genevieve was confused, but her grandfather took her by the arm. "Come, I will show you," he said.

Aleksander and Genevieve walked ahead. Lucille was followed by

Wanda, who shuffled slowly holding onto Josephine's arm. The five of them entered the terminal through the wide doors, walked down a large sloping entry hall, and came to the south side of the terminal's main concourse. Genevieve's eyes widened as she looked around. It occurred to her that she had transferred trains in the tunnels deep beneath this building but had never been in the terminal itself. It seemed everything was constructed of marble or brass. She felt like she was in a palace.

She looked around the concourse. She was sure it was at least the size of a football field. On the north side of the concourse was a row of gleaming brass doors—too many to count—leading to the station's upper-level departure tracks. To her left was a grand granite staircase sweeping upward to a mezzanine level and the opulent Commodore Hotel opposite the terminal. She recalled that one of her art teachers at Washington Irving had spoken of the painting on the ceiling of the terminal, and she looked up. The ceiling was more than 100 feet above and was painted a deep blue, which had darkened by degree each year since it was painted in 1912, stained by rising cigarette and cigar smoke. Still, she could see the stars and constellations painted there.

Genevieve jumped when there was a sudden clatter like cards being shuffled behind her. She looked around and saw mechanical boards above the ticket windows constantly changing to reflect the ongoing departures and arrivals of the trains on the almost 100 tracks that the station served. She watched as the boards turned and changed. Genevieve saw her train, The Pacemaker, listed for its three o'clock departure time from track twenty-four on the terminal's upper level.

Once more, Aleksander gently took her by the elbow and led her toward the center of the concourse, the rest of the family following. An information booth shaped like a pagoda, crafted of marble and brass, stood there. On its roof were four clocks housed in a single polished brass enclosure, fluted at its base and topped by an acorn finial. The four clocks faced north, south, east, and west, allowing travelers to see them from anywhere in the concourse. The faces of the clocks, made of opalescent milk glass, were illuminated from behind, and the numbers for each hour and the ticks for each minute were carefully painted in black to match their hour and minute hands. "The clock," Genevieve said to herself. She understood now and was no longer concerned that Leonard might not find them. At that moment, as Leonard appeared from the Forty-Second Street passageway at the south end of the concourse, they saw Charles hurrying toward them from the Lexington Avenue side.

Genevieve was grateful to have her family around her. Soon she would be alone, traveling across the country and spending her next several days on a train. They moved together and joined the crowd of people around the brass door beneath the arch with Gate 24 carefully painted on it in black. Aleksander and Wanda stood to the side. Her grandmother looked solemn, and her grandfather beamed with pride. Lucille had teased all week that she was going to take over her sister's bedroom for her craft work, and both smiled and cried as they embraced. Josephine, who was always serious, a woman who seldom found a reason to smile, was busy giving Genevieve last-minute instructions about eating well and traveling safely and calling when she arrived and then calling every Sunday. "You know what time we get home from church. Call then. Call us collect."

Lucille let Genevieve go so Charles could embrace her. Genevieve had never realized just how big a man he was. At only five foot two and weighing less than 100 pounds, she disappeared in his hug. In his best Humphrey Bogart voice, he told her, "You'll do great, kid."

Leonard stood outside the circle of family around Genevieve. As the announcer called all passengers to board the Pacemaker, the brass doors to the platform smoothly slid open. Genevieve went to her father and hugged him. "Thank you, Daddy. I love you."

Leonard stiffened his jaw. His eyes were wet as he hugged his youngest daughter. "I love you too. Now go be a star."

The family craned their necks, their eyes on Genevieve as she walked down the ramp to the platform and disappeared into the mass of passengers boarding the train. They stood there watching, Leonard still behind them all until no one remained on the platform. Suddenly, the brass doors slid shut. No one said anything as they turned back toward the information booth. Josephine went to her husband and took his hand between hers, with no words spoken between the two. Again he clenched his jaw, and with eyes still wet, he placed his other hand on hers.

CHAPTER FOUR
Traveling West

New York Central Railroad's Water-Level Route

New York City to Chicago, Illinois

Genevieve didn't look back. She knew that if she did, she would cry, and she didn't want her father to see her like that. But, as she walked away with her small leather suitcase in hand, she felt suddenly alone, a young girl swallowed up in the swarm of travelers. She walked down the ramp to the platform and showed her ticket to a uniformed man who directed her to one of the heavyweight coaches painted in the New York Central's two-tone gray paint scheme. As she stood waiting to board, she inhaled and thought that the air smelled of electricity. She wasn't sure if electricity actually had a smell, but no other explanation came to her. The scent wafting up from the tracks below the platform made the fine pale hairs on her arms stand on end.

Her seat was in the first of nine coaches. Both in front of it and behind it were numerous other cars of different types. Each coach was painted so that the band of light gray on the side of each car perfectly met the same ribbons of gray on the ones in front and behind it. As she boarded, Genevieve stepped from the platform to the vestibule and imagined the train looking serpent-like as it wound down the tracks. She located a pair of empty seats on the left side of the coach—having been told that the views were better on that side of the train—and slid into the seat against the window.

The car was well lit and smelled of tobacco. It was a familiar smell, not unpleasant to her. Her father smoked Pall Malls, and her grandfather, almost magically, could make one cigar last all day. The coach was only about half full, mostly with couples and a few older businessmen. Genevieve was grateful that the seat next to her remained empty. A woman who appeared to be her mother's age was seated across the aisle. Genevieve had noticed her standing alone with her suitcase inside the terminal and had thought that the woman looked weary, her eyes heavy and sad.

From a distance—someplace outside the coach—she heard a voice call, "All aboard," as a conductor quickly walked through the car. With an abrupt jolt and the harsh clank of the couplers between cars pulling tight, the train began to move forward. Genevieve looked across the aisle, past the woman sitting there, and watched through the window as they passed the few people remaining on the platform before the train slid into darkness. She had studied the route the train would take, and Genevieve knew that they were exiting the terminal's cavernous structure on tracks that ran north under Park Avenue. She watched as the train passed illuminated signals briefly glowing bright green in the dark of the tunnel.

As she used to do when she rode the subway to school, Genevieve attempted to guess what numbered street they were passing beneath. The train began to gather speed. She guessed that they were beneath Fifty-Seventh Street. She counted silently and tried to picture landmarks, now guessing they were at Seventy-Second Street. Eighty-Sixth Street, she thought next, when suddenly the train emerged from the tunnel and the car was flooded with daylight, already at Ninety-Seventh Street. Genevieve watched out the window as the train moved on elevated tracks above Harlem with street after street of brownstones, once fine residences, some retaining their previous elegance as others beside them showed neglect. Girls at school who came from here had told her that Harlem had the best music in the city. Her parents had told her that people like her didn't go to Harlem. She never questioned them.

The train continued through upper Manhattan before crossing the Harlem River into the Bronx to snake along the river's other shore. She saw the grand sandstone arches of Yankee Stadium out the window on the opposite side of the car, as well as the Polo Grounds, smaller and painted dark green, across the river to her left. Her father and grandfather had begun the long winter wait until baseball season resumed in the spring. Leonard was a Yankees fan and was still smarting over their loss to the Cardinals in the World Series. Aleksander rooted for the Dodgers—from Brooklyn—because when he first came to America that was where he and Wanda had briefly lived. The Dodgers had made it to the World Series the year prior, but Leonard's Yankees had beaten them. Genevieve smiled thinking of how the two of them argued endlessly about baseball.

The shoreline was lined with wharves and warehouses. Just before the river and the tracks parallel to it curved to the left, a long freight train, moving slowly in the opposite direction, passed. In minutes, the afternoon sun reflected off the surface of the Hudson River. She stared out the window, looking across the river to New Jersey and the vertical rock cliffs known as the Palisades. They were austere and gray, but fading splashes of autumn foliage remained as they cast their shadows on the water, and the sun began to sink lower in the western sky.

Something made Genevieve turn to the other side of the coach. The lady seated across the aisle was looking past her at the river. Their eyes met briefly—Genevieve decided it was sadness in them—and they offered one another brief, guarded smiles. A moment of awkward silence followed, and then softly, the woman offered, "I'm going home. Rochester."

In her mind, Genevieve quickly retraced the map that she had studied of the train's route then asked, "Have you been visiting family?"

The lady sighed. "My daughter-in-law and my new grandson. He's two months old. They live in Brooklyn." Then, as if not sure whether to say it, she added, "My son's in the army. He's in France, we think. He's been gone four months. We've only heard from him once." She whispered the last sentence and Genevieve immediately understood both the tiredness in the woman's eyes and the sadness. Other than the sound of the coach's metal wheels on the steel rails beneath them, it seemed the car was momentarily silent, and the lady stared past Genevieve out the window. "What about you, dear? Are you going to visit someone?"

Quietly but confidently, Genevieve said, "I'm an ice skater. I'm on my way to join an ice revue."

Her sad eyes widening, the woman said, "My goodness, you're so young! How old are you?"

"Seventeen," Genevieve responded matter-of-factly.

The woman seemed to ponder the response, perhaps trying to remember being seventeen herself, or thinking about her own son who was also young—a husband, and a father, and a soldier not heard from in months. Seemingly still in thought, she asked, "And where is this ice revue you're joining?"

Genevieve smiled, thinking about how her father had asked the same question. This time she didn't hesitate. "Vancouver, in British Columbia." She stated this in a way that would suggest everyone might take a train across the country to join an ice show.

Nodding her head as if she had just reached a conclusion, the woman said, "You must be very good at what you do, or your parents would never have let you go." A couple walking through the coach to the dining car at the front of the train had stopped so as not to interrupt their conversation. The woman looked up at them and announced, "My friend here is going to Vancouver." She then stated with certainty, "She's going to be a star."

They smiled politely, nodded, and continued on. The woman turned, shaking her head, to again look out her own window. Genevieve was sure she heard her say, "British Columbia. It might as well be the other side of the world."

The train rolled along the east bank of the Hudson as the sun, in streaks of orange and red and purple, set over the mountains to the west. When it reached Albany, it crossed the river, its tracks running in close proximity to the Erie Canal. It was almost six o'clock and Genevieve took down and opened the suitcase she had placed in the rack above her seat. In it, she had carefully placed the cloth drawstring bag in which her mother had packed her dinner. From it, she removed a cotton napkin and a package wrapped in butcher paper. She spread the napkin out on the seat beside her and then unfolded the paper in which her food was wrapped. Inside were three slices of chicken breast from the previous night's dinner, a slice of black bread, and a slice of pound cake, both of which her mother had baked early that morning before they left the house.

Genevieve looked up and caught the attention of the woman across the aisle. At that moment, she appeared sad, small, and lost in thought. They had not spoken since she had been proclaimed a star more than an hour before, and Genevieve asked if the lady would like to share some of her dinner. The woman smiled graciously and declined, saying that she had some crackers and was soon going to walk up to the dining car for a cup of tea, and besides, it wouldn't be too long before they reached Rochester. Genevieve nodded and looked back out the window into the darkness. She knew that Rochester was still almost four hours away.

Genevieve stayed awake until the train reached Rochester. Although they had not spoken much, she wanted to say goodbye to the lady and to tell her that she would say a prayer for her son. In return, she received a hug, a sincere, whispered, "Thank you," and another assurance that she was destined to become a star. Genevieve watched the woman as she walked down the platform, carrying her small suitcase, and disappeared into the station. She hoped that someone was inside to meet her.

As the train departed Rochester, Genevieve took out Louis Bromfield's most recent book, *Night in Bombay*. She had read several of his other books, and her mother had taken her to the Keith's in Flushing to see *The Rains Came*, a movie that had been made from one of them. One page, two pages, three ... and propped in the corner between the window and her seat back, covered by her woolen coat, she drifted into sleep. She woke briefly as the train stopped in Cleveland in the middle of the night and then again when it reached Toledo. She squinted and saw the clock on the platform: 3:50 a.m.

It was 5:30 and Genevieve awoke as the train lurched forward after its brief stop at the station in South Bend, Indiana. The sky was still dark, but she was now awake. Everyone else in the coach appeared to still be asleep. She took out the half slice of pound cake that she had saved from the night before. She didn't usually eat sweets this early, but she was hungry and it was all that remained of her food. She ate it bit by bit, and then, looking around to make sure no one was watching, carefully touched her fingertip to her tongue, dabbed up the crumbs, and licked them from her finger, savoring them as well. The cake would hold her until she reached Chicago. Genevieve opened her book, hoping it would help her pass however much time remained until the train reached its destination. As if reading her mind, the conductor—one she had not seen before this morning—stopped at her seat on his way through the car and told her they were two and a half hours away from Union Station, where Genevieve would change trains to continue her trip to the West Coast.

The book remained open in her lap, but Genevieve looked out the window as the train passed farms and countless towns too small to warrant more than a blast of the locomotive's horn. In about an hour, the train slowed as it approached a small city, gray and sooty in the half-light of early morning. "Gary, Indiana," the conductor called. "Next stop Chicago—Union Station." Genevieve spent the next ninety minutes with her face pressed to the glass as Gary disappeared and the rural farmland of the Midwest reappeared.

As the train turned north, returning to its water-level route along the western shore of Lake Michigan, she moved to the vacant seat across the aisle to look out the window. The lake was huge; it looked like an ocean. Genevieve recalled how in summer her family would sometimes visit her maternal grandparents, Joseph and Mary, who were farmers in St. James on Long Island, and they would spend the afternoon at Long Beach on nearby Long Island Sound. Lake Michigan looked easily as large and much more foreboding. "Lake" didn't seem a word big enough to describe it.

She watched as scattered houses along the route turned to more densely built residential neighborhoods. As the train began to distance itself from the lake, the neighborhoods soon turned to warehouses, factories, and coal and scrap yards. Then, almost at once, stores and tall office buildings appeared as they entered downtown Chicago.

Union Station

Chicago, Illinois

Impatient to be off the train—she had been on it for almost seventeen hours—Genevieve stood in the aisle putting on her hat, slipping into her coat, and gathering her pocketbook and suitcase as the train slowed and entered the station. She was in the vestibule as the coach door opened, allowing her to step onto the platform. She walked purposefully toward the baggage car. Beyond it, the engine hissed, steam escaping in a white cloud. Two baggage handlers were already removing passenger luggage, and Genevieve was pleased to see her large suitcase was among the first pieces placed on the platform.

A red-capped porter approached her as she reached for it. He was an older man, large and muscular, dark-skinned, and with a broad smile and kindly face. He asked Genevieve if Chicago was her destination or if she was traveling on. When Genevieve showed him the ticket for the remainder of her journey, he placed the bag on a triangular-shaped wooden cart that looked like a wheelbarrow without sides. He gave her another claim check like the one she had received in New York and assured her that the suitcase would be placed on the right train. Genevieve reached into her purse, and as Aleksander had done at Grand Central, and as he had instructed her to do, she gave the man a dime.

He walked alongside Genevieve and directed her to enter the station through the doors at the end of the platform. He told her that once she was inside, there was a large hallway from which every platform could be reached, and beyond that was a waiting room. She should look for the sign for the women's waiting area, which would be much more comfortable and much less noisy. Before they reached the doors, Genevieve saw a train painted in olive drab and marked United States Army. Seeing her curiosity, the porter said, "That's a troop train, miss. Gonna take the boys to boot camp and make soldiers out of them so they can go to the war." She nodded at him as she thought about the sad-eyed lady on the train and her son who had only written once and had not yet held his baby.

The area beyond the platform was teeming with people. The porter, still beside her, said, "There hundreds of trains a day that leave here. From morning to night it stays busy just like this. They say a hundred thousand people a day come through here." Turning to his left as he pushed the cart with Genevieve's bag on it, he motioned for Genevieve to continue straight ahead. "You keep walking, miss. Follow the signs and you'll find everything you need out there. Make sure you find the ladies' waiting room. You'll be more comfortable than in the big one."

Genevieve smiled, grateful for the short bit of company and the direction that this kindly man had offered. She followed the signs and soon found herself in the Great Hall, Union Station's main waiting area. Row after row of heavy wooden benches, their surfaces polished by countless thousands of people who had sat on them over the years, lined the massive space. She stepped aside, her small suitcase and handbag still in hand, aware of the constant sound of footsteps and the clattering of heels on the marble floors, attempting to avoid the rush of arriving and departing travelers as they moved through the waiting room.

Looking around her, she saw that the walls, like the floors, were marble. Round fluted columns supporting the roof high above. The ceiling must have been at least as high as the one in Grand Central Station, Genevieve thought. She wondered why this one, a massive glass skylight, was painted black, allowing no sunlight to enter the building. It was later that she overheard a conversation in which one man explained to another that it was a precaution taken due to the war. The concern was not about denying light from entering the station; it was about keeping light from escaping at night. Even in Chicago, eight hundred miles from the Atlantic Ocean, there were concerns about offering a potential target to aerial enemy bombers.

Genevieve began to look for a place to sit on one of the long benches, but then recalled that the porter had told her to find the ladies' waiting area. She looked along the wall behind her and then the one to her right. Then, on the wall opposite where she was standing, etched into the rose-tinged marble and highlighted with black paint, she saw Ladies' Waiting Room over an arched entry. She carefully made her way across the crowded room and tentatively walked through the portal. One sign directed travelers left to the waiting area, another straight ahead to the ladies' restrooms, and another, indicating a nursery, pointed down a marble staircase. Genevieve walked into the waiting room and was surprised to see that it was illuminated by soft-lit lamps, and instead of hardback wooden benches, there were upholstered chairs and couches. Floral murals adorned the walls, painted in muted pastel colors. As she had in New York, she felt more like she was in a palace than in a train station.

Genevieve was standing in the entryway when a middle-aged woman, wearing a matching skirt and jacket of a blue material so dark that it was almost black, approached her. She explained to Genevieve that she was a representative of the railroad, and if there was anything she could do to make her more comfortable, that was her job.

She asked Genevieve where she was going.

"I've come from New York, and I'm going to Vancouver, umm, British Columbia."

The woman smiled and said, "You've already had a long trip, and you have a still longer trip ahead of you. You have more than three hours before your train leaves. You can freshen in the ladies' room if you like. It's very comfortable and private. There are sinks and dressing rooms and even showers. Then, when you're done, I will be happy to store your suitcase for you. If you'd like to walk through the tunnel from the waiting room to the concourse, there are a number of places to eat. You must be hungry." With that reminder, Genevieve realized how hungry she was—she had not thought about it until then. All she had had to eat was the small piece of pound cake that morning when it was still dark.

She was grateful for the lady's kindness and followed her directions to the ladies' restrooms. The area was enormous, the floors of marble, and the walls of shining black and white tile. A long row of sinks lined one side of the room. Lights reflected off the mirrors placed above each basin. On the other side of the room were stalls of highly varnished wood, the doors with bright polished brass handles and locks. She looked around and saw another sign for Dressing Rooms and Showers, pointing to an adjacent room. Genevieve followed the sign and an attendant dressed in white and pale blue announced, "Ten cents to use the dressing rooms, miss, twenty cents for one with a shower—towel included." Genevieve reached into her purse and decided to indulge in what felt like a bit of luxury.

When she was finished, she returned to the Great Hall. The steaming shower and the opportunity to change her clothes had revived her. The lady tending the women's lounge had secured Genevieve's suitcase as she had offered. It felt good to be unencumbered as she walked through the terminal. The main waiting area had grown more congested than it had been when she had arrived earlier. She saw the steady stream of people either hurrying toward or emerging from the end of a walkway in the center of the wall to her left. The sign above indicated Tunnel to Concourse.

At the other end of the walkway, Genevieve entered a large room that was only slightly smaller than the concourse at Grand Central. Similar to the station in New York, an information booth was in its center, ticket windows ran down one side, and a double staircase was at its far end. A huge Buy War Bonds for Them banner was suspended over the stairway, and when she turned around, she saw another banner, equally as large, saying Buy War Bonds for Us, above the tunnel from which she'd just emerged. Instead of marble columns, steel beams, looking like oversized parts from the Erector Sets advertised every year at Christmas, stood on end and supported the roof. Netting had been stretched high above the concourse floor, and hundreds, perhaps even a thousand miniature models of military aircraft grouped in squadrons were suspended from it as if in flight.

Genevieve thought of the troop trains outside between the platforms, the banners advertising war bonds, the constellations of aircraft overhead, and the porter's mention of boys going to boot camp to become soldiers before going into combat. Then she thought of the lady who got off the train in Rochester who didn't know where her son was.

Genevieve walked the perimeter of the concourse and then down the adjacent passages. There were newsstands, gift shops, and a variety of restaurants. Through a window, she looked into a formal wood-paneled restaurant, still closed, and then passed a large utilitarian looking one with both tables and counters. Waitresses scurried between tables bringing food from the kitchen. Across the hall from it, she found a self-serve cafeteria and went in.

Beneath the heat lamps were mountains of breakfast foods that reminded Genevieve of just how hungry she was. She walked down along the lengthy steam table and watched as the servers filled her plate. She paid and sat at a small table close to the place where she had entered the cafeteria. Despite how hungry she was, she ate slowly as she looked around the cafeteria and watched the other patrons. She wondered where they were all going.

It suddenly dawned on her that she was eight hundred miles from home and among all these strangers. Feeling lonely for a moment, she took a deep breath and reminded herself that she was following her dream. Genevieve finished her breakfast, using the crust of her toast to swab up the little bit of egg still remaining on her plate, and then took the last sip of her tea. She looked at her watch, realizing that it was time to return to the lounge to collect her things.

The concourse was filled with people in constant motion, and arrival and departure announcements filled the space as she walked back to the tunnel to the Great Hall. She looked one more time at the hundreds of tiny airplanes overhead before stepping into the walkway. She emerged at the other end and, now knowing where she was going, went directly back to the women's waiting area. The dark-suited woman retrieved Genevieve's suitcase and told her that her train would be departing from gate eighteen. She would be on a train called the Empire Builder to which, with so many military men and tradesmen traveling to the West Coast, a car exclusively for women had been added. Genevieve thanked the lady, stepped out and walked through the Great Hall. Through the doors beneath a sign that read To Departing Trains, the next stage of her journey began.

The Rosie the Riveter Girls

Chicago, Illinois to Seattle, Washington

Genevieve heard shouting as she entered the boarding area. She saw at least two hundred young men in civilian clothes at the other end of the rotunda. They were mostly in their twenties, though some seemed no older than her. Older men wearing khaki uniforms topped by wide-brimmed hats were forming them into columns and barking orders. These were boys about to board the troop trains that she had seen earlier. It had been less than a year since the United States had entered World War II. Aleksander had been impatient for the United States to become involved ever since Germany had overrun Poland three years before. He constantly fretted that they had distant family who were in danger, and he could not understand why President Roosevelt had not entered the war against Germany earlier.

In just months, it seemed to Genevieve that almost every young man was being called to go to Europe or to Japan to fight. Charles was involved in work he couldn't discuss for something called the Office of War Information. Lucille's fiancé, Ed, had enlisted in the coast guard, and her brother was planning to enlist in the army. Even her father, who was fifty, had needed to register along with the other men too old to fight. "The Old Man's Draft," they called it; an inventory of every man's skills in case their expertise was needed. Leonard, a plumber, laughed wryly. "When the toilets get stuffed, they'll know who to call." In March, when Genevieve had skated with her friends to help raise money for the war effort, she had understood that the country had gone to war. But now, after seeing these boys on the way to basic training, and after listening to the lady on the train the day before, the war had become real.

Genevieve stepped onto the platform when passengers were called to board her train. Even early on a sunny afternoon, the Chicago air carried a chill that made Genevieve grateful for her woolen coat. The train on which she had traveled from New York had been painted in conservative gray tones. The cars of this train were painted in brilliant bands of orange and green, and Great Northern was emblazoned in gold block letters beneath the roofline of each car. She was directed down the platform and passed a buffet and lounge car and a large-windowed observation car before reaching the coaches. Shrouded in a cloud of steam, Genevieve could see the profile of the massive steam engine that would propel them west.

    She lined up behind a handful of other women who were climbing a short flight of steps to board the train. She handed her suitcase to a man on the vestibule as she ascended the steps and then reclaimed it as she entered the coach. It was much the same as the one she had ridden in from New York, but it was already more crowded, and it was filled with the hum of multiple, animated conversations. She found a vacant seat against the window halfway down the length of the car. As she placed her things in the overhead rack, Genevieve surveyed the carriage. The seats were all occupied by a variety of women. Some were older, dressed in tailored suits or dresses, but the majority were younger and in plainer clothes—worker's clothes—and appeared to be traveling together in small groups. She was curious about where they were all going.

    Settling herself, Genevieve was once again grateful that no one had come to sit in the vacant seat beside her, and she waited for the now-familiar jolt as the train moved forward and for the screech of metal as its steel wheels searched for traction against the tracks. The train left the station at a crawl then slowly began to gather speed, leaving Chicago behind and traveling along the western shore of Lake Michigan before bearing north and then west. They would reach Minneapolis in approximately eight hours. From there, Genevieve knew the train would travel directly west through the Rocky Mountains, which she estimated were a day away. Genevieve yawned unconsciously. She hadn't realized how tired she was. The shower and the good meal she enjoyed in Chicago had revived her, but she had slept restlessly the night before and had awakened early. Looking through the window at the passing farms, their fields of annual crops already harvested and at pastures full of dairy cattle, the gentle rocking of the coach lulled her to sleep.

Genevieve awoke as the train rumbled past the platform of a simple station without stopping. She saw a sign for the Wisconsin River flash by, and as she looked out the window, she saw that the train was following the river's bank. Formations of red sandstone towered over both its shores. As the sun began to set, she watched the flowing waters slip by as the train made its way toward Minneapolis. Unexpectedly, the car plunged into darkness as the train entered a tunnel. It emerged, following the Wisconsin River and then the La Cross River to its confluence with the Mississippi, which it would follow for 140 miles before reaching Minneapolis.

The car had grown quieter. The atmosphere, excited when the train departed Chicago, now diminished. Some of the passengers were napping while others quietly chatted. Listening, Genevieve could make out fragments of their conversations.

"Portland."

"No, we're going to Seattle."

"The shipyard at Swan Island."

"Ryan Point."

"Yeah, Kaiser paid for us."

"Flying Fortress."

And then she was certain someone exclaimed, "We're going to be Rosie the Riveters!"

At 5:30 that evening, Genevieve walked to the dining car for dinner. She had not eaten since morning, and she was very hungry. As she would be for the rest of the trip, she was asked to share a table with other women from the coach that she was seated in. Traveling along the banks of the Mississippi, she finally learned who these women were and where they were going.

Most were young, but some were a good deal older. They had enlisted themselves in the war effort and were on their way to the

West Coast—to Seattle and to Portland in particular. The government, together with private industries, had created factories in those places for the emergency production of ships and aircraft for the military. With almost every able-bodied young man fighting the war in Europe or the Pacific, the companies managing the massive effort had started recruiting women from places like Chicago to support their production. More and more often, they paid for the women's transportation and provided housing for them once they arrived at their destination. Genevieve realized that she was not the only one traveling far from home for work. She asked lots of questions and listened attentively. She determined that almost all the women were traveling out of a sense of duty, though some said it was to find a job better than the one they had at home. All of them laughed and nodded as one of their group said, "Maybe I can find a man!"

Listening to them talk about the work they would be doing when they arrived at their destinations made Genevieve feel like ice skating was unimportant in comparison. But then one of the women asked Genevieve where she was traveling and why. When Genevieve shyly told them that she was an ice skater and that she was traveling to become part of an ice show, they showered her with questions. The women told her about how they had seen Ice Follies at Chicago Arena, or how someone had once taken them to a show at the Sherman Hotel and how she had to be the luckiest girl in the world.

Shortly after the first night's dinner, the train reached St. Paul, and then fifteen minutes later, around 8:00 p.m., Minneapolis. The conductor walked through the car announcing that this was a brief stop to service the engine and that passengers were welcome to depart the train if they cared to. Genevieve slipped into her coat and stepped out onto the platform. She welcomed the feel of the cold night air on her face and the opportunity to stretch her legs for a bit. She made her way through the crowd of people who had exited the coaches and sleeper cars and walked toward the newsstand on the platform. As she read the headlines on the *Minneapolis Star Tribune*'s evening edition, she saw more war news. "Overland Military Supply Route to Alaska Opened" and "Cathedral City of Canterbury, England Suffers Extensive Damage in Retaliatory Raid."

"Not much in the way of good news these days," the newsstand attendant said, seeing the frown on Genevieve's face. He absentmindedly jingled the coins that filled the pockets on the front of his newsprint-stained canvas apron. "Anything I can get you, miss? Chewing gum? Candy? It's a long, flat ride you'll be making tonight."

"No," Genevieve said, smiling politely and shaking her head. She returned to the train, and they resumed their journey.

When the train stopped in Fargo, North Dakota sometime after midnight, Genevieve was still awake. She had watched from the window as the train crossed seemingly endless miles of flat farmland, the occasional silhouette of a barn or a light from a farmhouse vanishing as quickly as it had appeared. For the last five hours, her mind had been filled with thoughts about her family and home. She wondered what would be expected of her when she finally joined with McGowan and Mack in Vancouver, and she thought about the war that was going on and of all the people who were affected by it. She saw a handful of people on the platform, white puffs of vapor escaping them as they breathed in the chilly night air. They were there to meet the few passengers who disembarked. Before the train departed the station, the platform was empty.

Genevieve arranged her things around her, making herself as comfortable as possible. She fell asleep as the train's stuttering departure from the station turned to the now-familiar rhythmic rocking as it glided over the cold metal rails beneath. She slept hard, not stirring as the train made another service stop in Minot before crossing the half-mile long, one hundred-foot high trestle as it approached the Montana border. Genevieve did not wake up until the train slowed and then stopped. She opened her eyes and saw a sign for Wolf Point.

The women who were traveling to the shipyards and aircraft factories had amicably divided themselves into the Seattle girls and the Portland girls. Two of the latter, passing Genevieve's seat as she blinked herself awake, offered a bright "good morning, sleepyhead. We're going to breakfast. Come meet us in the dining car." They continued on as Genevieve offered a sleepy nod.

By the time she freshened and joined them, everyone in the dining car was looking out the windows to the right. One of the waiters, assuming the role of tour guide, announced, "That's the new Fort Peck Dam. More than ten thousand men been workin' on it since 1936. It two hundred and fifty feet high and four-mile-long. It goes across the Missouri River. They say the lake above the dam gonna be two hundred feet deep once it all fills up. The dam gonna be making electricity starting next year. Now you all enjoy your breakfast. Best part of the trip is comin' up." From their table, the girls continued to watch out the window as the train crossed the river, the dam below, and high-tension power lines stretched overhead.

The girl who had invited Genevieve to join them looked at her watch. "Eight o'clock. Just one more day on this train; it can't come soon enough." All nodded in agreement.

Unexpectedly, on the side of the train across from which the passengers had viewed the dam, there was a sudden blur of orange and green as another long train sped by, traveling in the opposite direction. The same waiter called out, "That the other Empire Builder. It goin' back to Chicago." The three women nodded and ate slowly as they chatted and watched the passing scenery. Until the next day, they had no place to be.

After they had paid for their breakfast and were ready to return to the coach, the train slowed and then came to a stop at a station marked Havre. Passing them in the aisle, the conductor told them, "Service stop, ladies. You have some time to get off for some fresh air if you like." Genevieve and the women returned to their seats, got their coats, walked to the vestibule, and stepped out. The morning was cold, but the sun was beginning to warm the air. Genevieve was certain she had never breathed air so clean and pure. The colors around her were all vibrant. The golden leaves that still clung to the aspen trees late in the year, the blue of the sky, and the mountains, tipped with snow on the Canadian border twenty-five miles to the north.

Enthused for what the rest of the day would bring, and knowing that she was getting closer and closer to her destination, Genevieve returned to her seat. By early afternoon, her expectations were rewarded. As the train approached Shelby, she caught her first glance of the snow-covered, knife-edged peaks of the Rocky Mountains. Through the windows on the other side, the mountains to the north continued to increase in height. The train continued its progress, and with each mile, the mountains grew closer and the views became more dramatic.

By mid-afternoon, they were traveling through Glacier National Park, surrounded by mountains nine and ten thousand feet high. Genevieve—none of the girls, apparently—had ever seen such sights. The car was hushed with only occasional "oohs" and urgent commands like, "Come to my side, look out my window," punctuating the silence. The tracks twisted and turned between the spectacular mountains, first to the south as the train left the west entrance to the park and then almost due north along the rushing Flathead River, with the steep mountains above on either side.

The setting sun reminded Genevieve that she had lost track of time, and she happily accepted an invitation from three of the Seattle girls to go to the dining car with them. She had not eaten since breakfast. As their food was brought to them, the train stopped at the station in Whitefish. Then it continued north, almost to the Canadian border. As the girls anticipated arriving at their destinations the next day, excited conversations were interrupted as the train entered a seemingly endless tunnel. Sensing everyone's curiosity, the waiter who had provided information about the dam that morning announced, "We in the Whitefish Tunnel—seven miles long. It one of the longest in the country."

The four women returned to the coach as the train zigzagged its way south, then west, then north and then south again through mountain valleys as it left Montana and entered Idaho. The Portland girls had their suitcases open on the seats next to them and were repacking the things they had taken out over the past two days. The train would be reaching Spokane late that evening, where they would depart to board another that would take them across the high desert to Portland. Genevieve took down her bag and began to do the same thing. She had taken things out during the trip and returned them, but still, straightening and organizing her suitcase would help pass the time. Once the Portland girls departed the train, it would be another twelve hours until she reached Seattle. Because she wanted to say goodbye and wish them well, she would wait up until the women left the train. Then, Genevieve would try to sleep, although she worried that her building excitement would keep her awake. She listened to everyone else's nervous patter. It was the same excitement she had sensed when everyone boarded in Chicago. She was not alone in her anticipation.

After crossing so much of rural America, Genevieve was surprised as the train crossed the border from Idaho into Washington and entered Spokane in the dark. While it certainly was not the size of

New York or Chicago, it was a city with illuminated, densely clustered buildings. When the train stopped, she stepped out of the car to wish the departing girls goodbye. There were hugs all around, and one girl shouted over her shoulder, "We'll look for you if you come to skate in Portland." Genevieve smiled and waved as she looked around. There were multiple tracks, some vacant, some with darkened trains on them. She looked up to see a clock tower looming over the station. The clock's hands were stopped at six o'clock. She wondered how long it had been since they had moved. She returned to the train and waved one last time to the girls on the platform as she settled into her seat.

The car was quiet save for the occasional whispered conversation. Genevieve quickly fell asleep, her concern that her excitement would keep her awake unfounded. The train glided through Ephrata, south of the Grand Coulee Dam, which had only recently been completed after almost ten years of construction. Then it passed through the Columbia River Basin, where apple, pear, and cherry orchards were being established to take advantage of the fertile soil, the mild climate, and the irrigation opportunities that the new dam would offer. After three hours, the tracks began to lead steeply upward as the train entered the Cascade Mountains. Genevieve never heard the engine straining or felt the train slow and then come to a halt as the steam engine was exchanged for an electric one to pull the train through the eight-mile-long Cascade Tunnel at Stevens Pass. At the tunnel's other end, the electric unit was once again replaced with a steam engine for the steep descent to Seattle, still four hours away.

Genevieve awoke to the squeal of the wheels and the hiss of its brakes as the train stopped in Everett, a modest-sized port town. While she slept, the scenery had changed from mountainous to coastal, and Genevieve realized she was getting close to her destination. After quickly grooming, Genevieve went to the dining car, not knowing if there would be food available on the four hour trip to Vancouver once she changed trains in Seattle. As she ate, the Puget Sound came into view, and the train turned south along the shore toward Seattle. She hurriedly finished her meal and returned to the coach, where many of the Seattle girls were impatiently looking out the windows. After about thirty minutes of travel along the Sound, Seattle appeared ahead, and the train entered a tunnel that would take it under the city. In a matter of minutes, the train returned to daylight and slowly skirted the city's edge. The terminal appeared shortly, a large building of red brick with a massive, classically proportioned tower so tall it could be seen over the trees and rooftops of other buildings for blocks around. Genevieve could not believe that she had finally arrived. She had been traveling for two and a half days.

The Seattle girls and the regular passengers, like Genevieve, were scurrying, getting ready to depart the train. Coats were slipped on, bags were taken down from the overhead racks, and last checks were made for things left behind. Soon everyone was in the aisle waiting to step out onto the platform, which all at once became crowded as all the cars emptied. There were hurried hugs, goodbyes, and well wishes as the passengers found their way to those who were there to greet them, relatives with arms extended, the waiting representatives of the aircraft and shipyard facilities, or out to the curb for taxis. Genevieve walked toward the baggage car to retrieve her large suitcase, and when it was brought to the platform, a porter was waiting to help her. He guided her past several other tracks to the one where the train she would take to Vancouver was waiting, timed to depart shortly after the arrival of the one from which she had just disembarked.

EDWARD DI GANGI

Just Four More Hours

Seattle to Vancouver, British Columbia, Canada

"Just four more hours," Genevieve thought as she found a place on the new train. Painted in the orange and green colors of the Great Northern Railway, this one was neat and clean though not nearly as long or as modern as the one she had just departed. In the coach, there were couples and men who appeared to be traveling for business. Genevieve was the only woman traveling alone, and she was aware of some of the men's curious glances. Avoiding their looks, she watched out the window as the train moved out of the station to retrace the route by which the other train had entered Seattle.

Moving slowly, the train entered the tunnel beneath the city and then exited, gaining speed as it traveled northward along Puget Sound, once again heading toward Everett to follow the tidal marshlands. Genevieve was awestruck watching flocks of waterfowl taking flight as the train passed. She watched fishing boats trolling the waters dotted by the San Juan Islands and then looked out the window across the aisle to see the range of steep mountains in the distance. She had been thinking of her family back at home and recalling her father's words: "It might as well be the other side of the world." Genevieve smiled. He was right—this was different than anywhere she had ever been.

She had been staring out the window of the coach for almost three hours, mesmerized, when the conductor called out, "Next stop, Bellingham." Before she started her trip, Genevieve had read that Bellingham was the last city in the United States and that there were coal mines there as well as canneries to dress and package the fish brought in by the boats. She overheard someone say that this was the beginning of an inland waterway; that you could get from Bellingham to Alaska without ever going into the Pacific Ocean. The stop at the station there, a one-story brick structure with a Spanish tile roof and large arched doors leading inside, was brief. As the train pulled out, Genevieve's heart began to beat more rapidly as she realized that in an hour, she would be stepping out of the carriage in Vancouver.

With more than a quarter of a million residents, Vancouver was bigger than Genevieve had anticipated. As the train entered the city, she saw substantial buildings out of both sides of the coach. As it came to a halt, she was surprised by the size of the station. The Pacific Central Station was a multi-storied rectangular building constructed of granite, with numerous tracks between covered platforms extending from it. A crowd of people was on the adjacent platform, boarding a long passenger train marked Canadian Pacific Railway. Behind her, as she stood in the aisle, she heard someone say, "That's the train that goes to Toronto and then Montreal."

Recalling her own journey, Genevieve rolled her eyes thinking, "I'm glad it's not me making that trip."

Everett McGowan had told her that a member of the troupe would meet her at the station when her train arrived. As she stepped out onto the platform, she was surprised to see Mack standing there himself. He smiled when he saw her and said, "Welcome to Vancouver. How was your trip? You must be tired."

"It was a long trip," she responded, "but it was magical. There was so much to see."

Mack nodded. "You're going to be seeing lots more. We have more dates planned after we leave here—California, Las Vegas, and we'll even be going to Mexico."

CHAPTER FIVE
Pickers

Pickers
Cumberland, Cobb County, Georgia

March 25, 2017

I can recall only once, when I was a small child, my mother mentioning that I was adopted. It came as a confusing and incomplete explanation, and I sensed that it made her uncomfortable, so I didn't question it. There was never a subsequent mention.

As a child, I spent little time wondering about where I had come from. Perhaps I'd taken that awkward mention of adoption and shelved it in the recesses of my mind from where it would now and again remind me that there was an important question to be answered. I recall asking my father what hospital I was born in. This may well have been before I had processed the thought and understood that I was adopted. He told me that it was a small hospital in Manhattan that no longer existed. At the age I was, it seemed a strange, maybe even an evasive answer that added to my confusion. In my child's eyes, everything in Manhattan was large, and certainly, hospitals just didn't cease to exist. Recently, however, I found the name of the hospital, and it had, indeed, been small, and by the early 1950s, it had ceased to exist. As curious as I may have been about the hospital, I gave little thought about who my birth mother was. I never stopped to consider what she looked like or what she might have done for a living or even why I was where I was and not with her. Totally absent in my thoughts was the obvious fact that someone had fathered me.

The bottom line was that those things mattered little to me. I was who I was, and I was where I was, and I lived in the moment—safe, loved, and with no inclination to look in any direction but forward. Later, when I understood more, perhaps there was some subconscious thought that the effort involved in trying to learn more wouldn't be worth the result. It would be too much work. Records were sealed. There was no Ancestry, no online databases. "Online" was an unknown term for most of this time, anyway, and would I have known what to do with what I found if my search was actually successful?

The visit to the hillside cemetery in New Jersey and Mendelsohn's book, which I was then reading for the second time and have read again since, convinced me that the results of a search for my biological beginnings might, in fact, be worth the effort. The rising popularity of television shows researching the family histories of celebrities or locating and reuniting everyday people's missing families added to this conviction. The emergence of affordable DNA testing, the availability of numerous online databases allowing you to look into the lives of others with almost disturbing ease encouraged me further. All of these things caused me to finally become curious about my birth mother.

The few random times I thought about the person who had given birth to me, my images were in the grainy black, white, and gray of the early days of television and were so out of focus that there wasn't a discernible face attached to the person. I pictured an ordinary woman who lived a useful but ordinary life. For some reason, I decided she may well have spent her life serving food to ungrateful students in a high school cafeteria. I could picture a hair net and an apron, but still not her face. Or perhaps she had worked the counter in a local variety store, selling needles and thread to housewives and lucky rabbits feet died pink or blue to children who had saved their allowance for the purchase. Useful and meaningful jobs they were, but nothing out of the ordinary. Get up, go to work, return home and repeat again tomorrow. I never imagined that she had a family, though I never assumed that she hadn't. Such details never entered my thoughts. I did the calculations, thinking she had been fifteen, or sixteen, or seventeen, or maybe eighteen years old when she gave birth to me. So, by the time I began to seriously consider all this, she would at least have been in her mid-eighties. I wondered if she was still alive.

Having removed the two sheets of paper from the envelope that had always been there, and having spent an hour on a library computer, the obscured picture began to clear and questions began to be answered. I was rewarded with the face pictured on the Rio de Janeiro travel papers. She had been born in 1925, so she was older than I assumed she would have been when she gave me up for adoption. If she was still alive, she would be in her nineties. My birth mother had not spent her working life in a high school cafeteria or standing behind a counter in a variety store after all. She was, according to her travel document, an artista. I needed to find out what that meant.

More time at the library, more searching, and I found Genevieve Knorowski's name on a 1950 passenger list aboard the Queen Mary, en route to Cherbourg, France from New York City. Her anticipated time out of the country was indicated to be seven months, but there was no mention of the trip's purpose. Certainly, she seemed to be well-traveled. And then a marriage license appeared, dated November 16, 1955, issued in Norfolk, Virginia, joining Genevieve Norris Knorowski, listed as a "performer," and Ted Sebastian Meza as man and wife. I was certain that Norris was not her middle name. It hadn't appeared elsewhere. I assumed that she had taken it as a stage name, and hoping to find legal documents that might provide me more information about the name change, I searched further. I was surprised to find out that there were no papers or court proceedings necessary to adopt a new name, so long as the purpose of that change was not to defraud.

The marriage license offered no new clues, so I then entered "Genevieve Norris performer," and at that moment, the blurry picture became clear. A blog, written by a woman who identified herself as a "picker," appeared. The post contained numerous pictures of a woman, along with other ephemera, and it explained that Genevieve Norris had been a prominent ice skater in the 1940s and 1950s. This was my birth mother, the artista, the performer—a star.

The blog's author, the picker, explained that although she knew nothing of Genevieve or her career, she had purchased a box of memorabilia at an auction in Atlanta a few years prior, simply out of interest in a different time and a young woman's exciting and glamorous career. I read the text of the blog several times. I looked at each image repeatedly. A door felt like it had opened for me, and I wondered if the owner of this treasure still had the items or if she had sold them, as a picker would typically do. If she had them, if she would sell them to me, I wondered what price she might ask. I didn't want to publicly post on her blog, so I set about locating the author by searching for her name via social media. I found several people with the same name, but one living in Marietta, a suburb of Atlanta, and with associations to an antiques mall jumped out.

It seemed a logical match so I messaged. "I saw your blog. I'm exploring a family relationship. Do you still have the items?" Almost immediately I received a reply. She still had them but was busy and would get back to me "later." I waited impatiently, and then I waited still longer. Days passed. Everyone's definition of "later" is different, I guessed, trying to be patient. Finally, I messaged again, and this time I gave a phone number. I added that I thought Genevieve Norris was a quite close relative. Almost immediately my phone rang. "Oh my God, I'm so sorry, I totally forgot." The words were spoken in a woman's kind-natured voice. Abandoning the coy approach of, "I'm exploring a family relationship" or that I was searching for a "quite close relative," I told her that the pictures she had posted—the documents and diplomas and promotional items she had included—all of them were of my birth mother. Another, "Oh my God" was followed by a, "Yes, I've still got them." Finally, she suggested, "You need to come here and see them."

I laugh now, realizing how quickly Linda and I responded to the urgency of "Come here and see them." From memory, I would have said that we traveled to Atlanta a month later. Looking back over my notes, however, we were anxious to make this important trip before Linda underwent already scheduled knee replacement surgery. We arrived seven days later on a Friday evening, after a seemingly endless drive across South Carolina which was—still is, it seems—under construction from the North Carolina border to the Georgia line, only to then sit in stalled traffic when we reached Atlanta.

At ten the next morning, as agreed, we were waiting in the hotel lobby when a woman, Tobey, eyes bright and a smile on her face, came through the door carrying a large tattered carton. There was no question as to who this was, and I recall rising to my feet to meet her. Though I can't remember how we managed with the carton still in her arms, we shared a hug. It was the kind of embrace shared between close friends. She, Linda, and I were sharing greetings when Dan, her husband, came through the door, attracting some degree of attention from other guests as he carried a shield and a sword, a la Teenage Mutant Ninja Turtles. We learned that these were props that had been created by my mother and her husband after their skating careers were over.

The lobby was not a convenient place to spread everything out, so we went upstairs to a separate sitting area in the suite we had rented. The carton held too many things to list and to describe, but they represented a cross-section of Genevieve's life: her diploma from St. Michael's Catholic school in Flushing, New York; her first professional skating contract at the Netherlands Plaza Hotel in Cincinnati —$100 a week plus room—huge money for anyone, let alone a young woman in the 1940s; a scrapbook of press clippings, and another of publicity stills. The personal nature of the items caused the four of us to question why such things would be discarded, and it would be several months before I was able to find an answer to this. As we went through the items, turning the pages of the albums and sifting through the loose documents, the image of my birth mother that was once lost in that grainy black, white, and gray and that had only recently begun to sharpen now came into winter-crisp focus. I'm not one to show great emotion, but it was overwhelming not just to see but to touch all these pieces of her life.

As I slowly paged through the album containing her publicity photographs, I came across a series of similar portraits of other women, all young and beautiful and in costume, each signed with a note to my mother recalling good times, wishing her well or telling her that she was the best roommate ever. These were obviously fellow ice skaters. I went to get my notebook. I wanted to record each of the names, hoping that I would later be able to find information on them. With luck, I thought, I might find one or two still alive with whom I could talk to learn more about my mother.

The author, left, with pickers, Tobey Olson and Dan Frey

I had begun making notes when Dan interrupted me and asked what I was doing, a quizzical look on his face. I explained. Looking to Tobey and then to me, he shook his head and said that notes weren't necessary; that the photos, all the things they had brought with them that day, now belonged to me. What were the chances that Tobey would still have these things years after she had purchased them and not have sold them? And what were the chances that she and Dan would simply give them to me? More than for the items themselves, my emotion was in response to their generosity, and for Tobey and Dan's understanding of the priceless value certain things might hold for another. Linda and I spent the rest of the day with

Tobey and Dan, not so much getting to know one another but "catching up" as you do with friends you haven't seen in a long time. I'm embarrassed to admit that I allowed Dan, at his insistence, to pay for lunch, even after he and Tobey had already been so profoundly generous. He's done it again since, always with a smile on his face. There has been a magical connection from the start: long lost friends from a different time and a different place. Tobey and Dan have shared in the experience of my learning about my birth mother, and both of them have remained vested in the journey to this day, offering their own occasional discoveries and celebrating as I share my progress and my own "pickings" with them.

CHAPTER SIX
The Other Side of the World

The Pantages Theater

Vancouver, British Columbia, Canada

As she hurriedly tried to keep up with Mack, Genevieve's heels clicked on the marble floor of the cavernous, ornately decorated Pacific Central Station. After almost three days of train travel that had taken her more than three thousand miles across the United States and into Canada, she emerged from the station and stepped into a new world. In front of the terminal, one side of the street was lined with taxis. On the other, she saw a park with elegant ornamental plantings, still green and lush even though it would soon be November. A light rain was falling as the sun peeked in and out through an overcast sky. The air was heavy with the smell of salt. When the sun appeared, it warmed the air, and the rain that fell was a welcoming mist, but when the sun was blocked by the clouds, the atmosphere turned inhospitable, the rain quickly becoming harsh and cold.

    The taxi taking Genevieve and Mack to the boarding house where the company was staying pulled away from the terminal on Station Street. Making a quick right turn, it traveled several blocks down Main Street before turning left on Hastings Street, one of the city's busiest thoroughfares. The driver steered around delivery trucks parked in the street. Blowing his horn, he dodged in and out between streetcars traveling in the opposite direction. Their tracks buried in the cobblestones caused their car to shudder and rattle. Both sides of the street were lined with storefronts, and the sidewalks were busy with merchants and shoppers.

As the jitney traveled west down Hastings Street, theaters with oversized neon-lit marquees advertising all-night movies and live entertainment appeared one after the other. Along the boulevard and down side streets, names like the Pantages, Palace, Rex, Orpheum, Avenue, Columbia, Princess, and Lyric appeared above the theaters' entrances. The area was the city's entertainment district, Mack explained. Many still referred to it as Vancouver's Great White Way, but Genevieve could see that the area had started to decline. Between the once flourishing theaters there were signs for beer parlors, and bedraggled men with no apparent place to go loitered in doorways and on the street.

During the Depression, thousands of men had traveled to Vancouver from across Canada to work in the railroad yards or on the docks or at the canneries. When times improved, the younger men returned home. Those who remained were older, sick, or injured, or they were the men who never were "right." They had no reason to think that things would be any better where they had come from, so they stayed and lived in hotels on the side streets. Once neat, clean, and catering to tourists, by the 1940s the hotels off Hastings Street had fallen into disrepair. Among the men were women in their twenties and thirties, some in their forties, and some who were just young girls. They approached tourists or locals who had come from other parts of the city looking for their services. There were those who had stopped calling this part of Hastings Street the Great White Way and had begun to refer to it as Skid Row.

The boarding house where they were staying was on a quiet street in a neighborhood of neatly kept homes several blocks from the theaters. Many of the older two and three-story homes that had been built in more prosperous times had Room to Rent signs in their front yards. On most street corners were small businesses—butchers, vegetable markets, fishmongers—but a number of them were dark and closed. Around them, there were houses that had been boarded shut. The taxi driver casually mentioned that when the war expanded to the Pacific, the Canadian government chose to isolate all of the country's Japanese residents—about eight thousand of them—in internment camps. Families had been removed from their homes, and their businesses were forced to close. Many of them came from the neighborhood surrounding the rooming house.

The house the troupe was occupying reminded Genevieve of her family's home in Flushing. This one must have been grand in its time, but now the floors were scuffed, the paint was faded, and the carpets were threadbare. The cast completely occupied the three-story home, filling each of its eight bedrooms. There were three bedrooms on each of the upper two floors, as well as two makeshift bedrooms that had been created on the main floor. Each floor had a bathroom with a toilet, sink, and tub. Everyone gathered in the main floor dining room for meals. Genevieve shared a second-floor bedroom with two other girls, only slightly older than her.

The Revue performed that November at a theater constructed during the First World War by Alexander Pantages, a Greek immigrant. Though he could neither read nor write, he eventually built a chain of fifteen vaudeville houses valued in excess of five million dollars. This was the second and the bigger of two he had built in Vancouver, and the illuminated sign on the elaborate front of the building identified it as the Beacon. With over 1,800 seats, it was one of the larger theaters in the entertainment district. As its ownership and its name changed from the Pantages to the Beacon, it had shown both first-run movies and featured live acts, operating twelve hours a day, seven days a week. A large canopy hung over the sidewalk and extended across the width of the building. On its façade, large electrified letters that could be easily rearranged and illuminated at night read McGowan and Mack Ice Revue.

While his wife readied costumes, Mack erected the portable skating rink on the large stage. Putting the ice in place was a laborious two-day process. Mack erected the wood frame for the twenty foot square of ice, and then inserted a liner before he laid down a serpentine of tubing through which brine, forced through a refrigeration unit, would be pumped. He spread sand and sawdust to cover the tubes, and once this base was cold enough, multiple applications of water would quickly turn to ice. Unlike the more convenient "muck" and "artificial ice" that other shows often used, this real ice would glisten beneath the colored lights suspended overhead and across the front of the stage. The lights reflected off the ice, flashing against the performers' sequined outfits, and left the performers in a private world, aware of the audience but unable to discern their faces.

It was in Vancouver, far from home, living in the rooming house with people she did not know, that Genevieve began her career. For seven days, with an assortment of comedians, dancers, magicians, clowns, and ventriloquists preceding their appearance, the Revue performed their show three times daily to music played by a house organist. Genevieve was part of the line that, in addition to its own routine, supported Mack, Ruth, and Joann. While other girls in the line mechanically went through the motions and seemed uninterested in their role, Genevieve seized the opportunity that being on stage presented.

Both Mack and Ruth were delighted by how easily Genevieve inserted herself into the Revue. She had visited often when they returned to skate at the Boulevard Tavern in October, studying the routines, memorizing every turn, spin, and glide. Now, finally on the lit stage herself, she recalled the April afternoon she skated at Rockefeller Center while the people in the restaurants along the ice watched her as they dined. She wished she could see the people in the audience, to make eye contact with them, but she was sure their eyes were on her. She smiled through the lights at them; she skated with a palpable joy.

After they had completed their second show on the first night at the Beacon, Genevieve walked out the stage door to the front of the theater. The glow of the marquees up and down the street brightened the sky. She studied the big letters that advertised the McGowan and Mack Ice Revue on the Beacon's marquee, each letter lit by electric light bulbs. When she had driven by it with Mack the day she arrived, it had not been illuminated. Now, though it glowed brightly in the dark, she saw that some of the letters burned brilliantly, some were dim, and others had burned out entirely. She thought of her grandfather. She was certain that if he were there, Aleksander would have told her, "Burn bright, Genevieve. Burn bright and they will notice."

Attendance at the Beacon steadily increased as word about the show spread. The Revue frequently performed before sold-out houses and extended their tour for an additional week. At the end of the second week, the group's slope-backed bus, sleek and aerodynamic for its day with its maroon painted, corrugated aluminum sides, was packed. The costumes and smaller props were placed in the baggage compartment in its belly, and the rink structure, the compressor, and the larger props were secured to the rack on its roof. Genevieve and the rest of the girls were excited to board the bus. Ahead of them was a three day, 1,100-mile drive that would take them along the coastlines of Washington, Oregon, and California. None of them minded. They were on the way to the sun and glamour of Los Angeles.

THE OTHER SIDE OF THE WORLD. Pantages Theater, Vancouver, British Columbia. Photo courtesy of the Vancouver Public Library.

THE OTHER SIDE OF THE WORLD. McGowan and Mack Ice Revue girls. Genevieve at far right.

Madame Zucca's Hollywood Casino

Hollywood, California

The trip was a long one, and the members of the cast slept, read, and chatted as they tried their best to contain their nervous energy. Genevieve thought of her three-day train ride and decided that it had been a luxurious experience compared to driving for days at a time on the bus. At least she'd had the opportunity to be out of her seat and moving around. On the bus she was confined to her seat, save for the occasional opportunities to get off to use the crude restrooms behind the gas stations when Mack stopped for fuel. Ruth came to sit with her on the second day. She asked Genevieve how she was feeling now that she was experiencing life as a professional. If anyone understood that being part of a touring company was not always a glamorous life, Ruth did.

Genevieve's enthusiasm was apparent though, and Ruth smiled as she leaned toward the young skater. "Mack thinks you can do more," she said in a voice so subdued that no one else could hear her.

Surprised, Genevieve nodded modestly and waited for Ruth to continue.

"You'll still skate in the line, but we plan to choreograph one of the numbers so the other girls will skate around you. Nothing too complicated to start with. Are you ready for that?"

"Oh, gosh, yes!" Genevieve responded. She was conscious to keep her voice down as Ruth did. "If you think I'm good enough," she added. Inside, she believed that she definitely was.

"You are certainly good enough," said Ruth. "Mack will be happy that you want to do it. We won't say anything to the others until we begin rehearsals in Hollywood. Mack will make changes to the routine then."

Genevieve felt as if she was ready to burst. She wished she could tell someone, but she knew the other girls might question why she had been selected. How she would love to share this with Aleksander. He believed in her, but he was so far away. This would have to wait until she called home on Sunday, when Genevieve knew that her family would all be waiting for the telephone to ring.

None of them truly knew what to expect from Los Angeles, but it was what all the cast members had imagined. The bus radio was on, and the announcer said that the temperature was sixty-eight degrees. With the skies clear and blue and the sun shining brightly, it seemed even warmer. The girls watched out the windows as they drove down a wide avenue lined with palm trees on both sides. Stately mansions with red-tiled roofs sat far back from the street behind high walls or fences. Luxury cars, many with the tops down, a few driven by uniformed chauffeurs, passed them. The girls were certain that the people in those cars must be movie stars. It didn't appear that the war was impacting this part of the country much, Genevieve thought.

Mack cleverly and purposely—to the delight of everyone on the bus—had taken a route through Beverly Hills and then down Santa Monica Boulevard through Hollywood. He smiled with satisfaction as one of the girls on the left side of the bus suddenly shrieked, "Oh my God, we're in Hollywood!" as she saw the famous Hollywood sign out her window. Mack continued to drive before turning on N Western Avenue and finally onto a side street of stucco homes. "Same boarding house, different city," one of the girls said. There was laughter all around as everyone gratefully climbed down from the bus. Genevieve ate her first Thanksgiving dinner away from home here.

The Revue was booked to perform for the opening week of Madame Zucca's Hollywood Casino on Sunset Strip. The club was named for the eccentric and flamboyant mother of Joe Zucca, its owner, and was a sister club to his other locations: Casa Manana and The Hollywood Club. Housed in the converted Cash is King Grocery Market that had opened on Sunset Boulevard ten years before, the night club's main room featured a dance floor, a live orchestra, and a stage for performers. Madame Zucca was known to frequently skirt the law with her activities, and behind carefully tended closed doors, an adjacent room offered customers, mostly military men on leave, the opportunity to play illegal poker, craps, and roulette.

Mack walked the girls, none of whom exhibited any apparent jealousy, through the changes in choreography that would bring Genevieve out of the line for the few brief moments. He found himself frustrated, however, as the refrigeration unit threatened to fail. It operated erratically and had difficulty freezing the ice once the rink was in place. With so many men enlisted in the armed forces, he had some difficulty finding a plumber to resolve the issue, forcing Mack to cancel the Revue's first two days of performances, much to the owner's consternation. He explained that performing on such poor, slushy ice would be dangerous to his performers and compromise the quality of the show. On the third day of their seven day engagement, the ice surface improved, but was still questionable. Mack decided to revert to the original routines. Sensing Genevieve's disappointment, he assured her that their next stop in Las Vegas would provide her with even greater opportunities.

THE GIFT BEST GIVEN

El Rancho Vegas

Las Vegas, Nevada

Compared to the trek from Vancouver, the drive to Las Vegas was a thankfully short trip—measured in hours rather than in days. The bus traveled through the canyons between the steep mountains east of Los Angeles before emerging in the desert. While the sun was bright and all the girls equated the word "desert" with heat, they were disappointed as the temperature began to fall. By the time the bus arrived at its destination that evening, the thermometer indicated that it was fifty-five degrees.

As they stepped off the bus, the members of the cast looked around. There was little in sight. They were booked to perform at the El Rancho Vegas resort for the next six weeks. Built just outside the city limits of Las Vegas only a year prior, this was the first of the properties that would be built on what would come to be known as The Strip. By the time the Revue arrived, Las Vegas, a city with no other purpose than to provide entertainment, had begun to blossom in the desert. Illuminated by the limitless electricity generated by the recently completed Boulder Dam, it offered visitors entertainment as well as easy access to gambling, liquor, and prostitution under the stewardship of organized crime,.

In the midst of the barren desert, El Rancho Vegas was an oasis. The cast members entered a low, sprawling building with a Spanish-style exterior and a cowboy frontier themed interior. Atop the structure were a tower and a large windmill that could be seen at a distance from every direction. Combined, the main building and the bungalows behind it held over a hundred rooms. With its riding stables and large swimming pool surrounded by elaborate landscaping, it had quickly become popular with both vacationers and overnight visitors. Its close driving distance from Los Angeles, its casino, and a large theater that booked major acts had quickly made it a celebrity destination as well. The six girls from the line were assigned to one of the resort's two-bedroom cottages on one of the manicured lanes crisscrossing the property.

There was a day of walk-through rehearsals before the Revue opened, and Mack announced that the choreography for the line's second appearance would vary slightly from what they had done in Vancouver and in Hollywood. The difference was more than Genevieve had anticipated. Mack drew her from the center of the line, spun her, lifted her, and then spun her again before returning her to her original place. As she had been in Los Angeles, Genevieve had been concerned there would be jealousy among the other girls. They were surprised, and there were questioning glances, but after the first walk-through, the girls clapped. With each practice, they seemed to increase their focus on making her exit from the line and her return flawless.

The Revue performed in the Opera House, the resort's theater, the last two weeks of December and resumed again immediately after celebrating the New Year. Genevieve called home on Christmas and on New Year's Day. While she could not deny missing her family, she was lost in the excitement of performing.

Instead of following a string of variety performers as they had in the burlesque houses, their appearances were preceded by the El Rancho Starlets, a precisely choreographed line of provocatively clad dancers. A full house orchestra provided music for the Starlets as well as for the Revue.

By their third week, others on the line quietly began to complain about being tired of the tedium. But Genevieve, with all the polished support, the luxurious accommodations, the sophisticated, sometimes star-studded audiences, and her increased role in the three times daily show, looked forward to each performance

After their second week, Mack had approached Genevieve. "I want to include you more in the show."

Though she was pleased and excited, Genevieve said nothing and waited for Mack to continue.

"We've been doing the one short lift between the couple of spins," he said. "I want to extend the lift; to take you out of the spin and into a lift where I circle the stage with you over my head."

Genevieve's mind raced as she pictured it. Mack was strong, and she felt safe when he lifted her. She nodded in agreement.

Mack waited for Genevieve to speak, but when she said nothing, he continued. "Where we do the second spin now, I'm going to insert a death spiral."

This time, apprehensively, Genevieve spoke. "A death spiral?"

"Don't worry," he said, smiling as Genevieve's eyes widened when she heard the term death spiral. "I'll hold on; you'll be safe."

She trusted Mack and practiced without fear. With his hand around her wrist, she lay back, one skate on the ice, arching her back until her hair was brushing the frozen surface as he spun her around. The sound of his skates cutting into the ice was loud in her ears. It was as exciting as anything she had ever done on the ice, and she was eager to perform it in front of an audience. That night, before the audience in the crowded Opera House, Genevieve did perform it, and she was lost in the sound made by Mack's skates and the audience's applause.

It was before the Revue departed the El Rancho Vegas at the end of January that she celebrated her eighteenth birthday and adopted the stage name, Genevieve Norris, which would stay with her for the rest of her life.

The Palace Hotel

San Francisco, California

San Francisco presented itself as posh and utterly sophisticated. And, while El Rancho Vegas had offered a comfortable home for the time they were there, Genevieve felt she had entered the lap of luxury as the Revue checked into the Palace Hotel in the middle of the city's downtown. Built originally in the 1800s and then destroyed by fire in the 1906 earthquake that devastated the city, the Palace was quickly rebuilt to its current splendor. Its 775 rooms and luxurious common areas reopened at the corner of New Montgomery and Market Streets in 1909. The Revue was booked to perform in the hotel's Rose Room, a plush space designed for nightly dining and dancing. Big band radio broadcasts often originated from the venue, which was so popular that it was able to maintain a cover charge every night.

On their first day in the hotel, Genevieve took the ornate brass elevator down from the room she shared with one of the other girls in the line and walked through the grand lobby with its highly polished marble floors overlaid with luxurious woven carpets. Passing through the Garden Court, all marble and gold with an arched, leaded glass roof high overhead, she found the Rose Room. It was painted and carpeted in soft pastels to match its name. French tapestry wall hangings in muted shades of pink adorned the walls. She was in awe of the room's opulence and feared it would be hard to concentrate when it came time to skate.

By the time the Revue began its six-week engagement, Phil Hiser, the man who had discovered Genevieve at Iceland and recommended her to Carl Snyder, had joined the troupe. A onetime speed skater, he was now billed as the show's funny man. With virtually all able-bodied young men enlisting or being drafted into the military, there was a shortage of male skaters. Hiser was an older performer, not as old as her father, but old enough to have qualified to register in the Old Man's Draft. He complemented Mack, Ruth, and Joann. Tommy LaVonne, Jackie Reese, an acro-skater, whose abilities Genevieve studied carefully, and Charlie Hadlett, a barrel jumper and acro-skater, filled out the cast. The girls, billed now as the "Ice-Kaydets" weaved their way through the show.

The show was presented on a raised stage at their previous venues, but the Rose Room offered the opportunity to skate at floor level, eye to eye with the patrons, the same way the show had been performed when Genevieve first met the McGowans at the Boulevard Tavern all those months ago. She was excited to be so close to the audience, to see their faces and hear their appreciative responses. The reception to the Revue was uniformly positive, and the local press was effusive in its reviews. Mack continued to challenge Genevieve as he inserted new moves for her into each of the Ice-Kaydets' routines, bringing additional attention as he allowed her to shine.

The Orpheum Theater

Los Angeles, California

The Revue was booked to play for ten days at the Orpheum before moving on to San Pedro, just to the south of Los Angeles, and then it would return to San Francisco. Housed in the twelve-story Beaux Art building, the Orpheum was another once-grand theater that had fallen into a state of neglect. Its glass surfaces had become smoke-stained, its gold gilt ceilings were peeling, and the theater's arched, marble passageways, once snow white, had become gray with grime. As had been the case in Vancouver, the Orpheum sat in close proximity to numerous other movie and burlesque houses with names like the Palace, the Regent, the Novelty, the Belasco, and the Hippodrome along South Broadway. As in Vancouver, South Broadway and the adjacent avenues had started to be referred to as the Great White Way by the locals. Genevieve had grown accustomed to the routine of Mack erecting and freezing the ice surface as Ruth readied the costumes. For the first time, Ruth altered Genevieve's costumes so that she would stand out from the other girls in the line.

Following a variety of other acts, the Revue performed three times daily to the accompaniment of music provided by a house organist. The show that the cast performed was the same one they had performed in San Francisco. Genevieve's confidence grew with each performance, and she hoped for the opportunity to do even more.

Ruth and Mack performed the feature of each show, a routine that they called Café de Apache. Genevieve marveled as they raced around the perimeter of the small sheet of ice, Mack lifting Ruth effortlessly and then spinning her almost violently, her body horizontal above the rink's surface. As Genevieve looked on, one of the girls whispered to her, "You'd never catch me doing that." Genevieve nodded, though she was thinking that was precisely what she wanted to do.

THE GIFT BEST GIVEN

The Del Rio Theater

San Pedro, California

By the second week of April, the Ice Revue had moved on to San Pedro, a gritty town along the Pacific Coast just north of Long Beach. Its economy was fueled by its Portuguese and Italian fishing communities, the local Coast Guard, and numerous military installations. The Del Rio, another small movie theater turned burlesque house—later destined to become a boxing venue—was located at the corner of West Sixth and Palos Verdes Streets, near other similar theaters and only a block away from the main channel of Los Angeles Harbor. As with most of the other venues, the cast performed three shows a day for patrons who paid sixty-five cents for admission. For the first time since Genevieve joined the Revue, this theater offered a mid-afternoon children's matinee on Saturday and Sunday for a quarter. She enjoyed those shows particularly, smiling at the kids' "oohs," and "aahhs," and at their laughter. Daytime shows during the week were more lightly attended than the two later shows and provided the solo performers the opportunity to experiment with variations to their routines. Mack continued to make subtle changes to Genevieve's routine and continued to expect more and more of her.

The Alex Theater

Glendale, California

The Revue returned to San Francisco for another week at the Palace Hotel's Rose Room after its engagement in San Pedro. Then, retracing its steps, they immediately returned to Glendale, a city about eight miles north of downtown Los Angeles. The ensemble was booked to appear for a week at the Alex Theater, which, like so many of the other theaters in which they performed, had originally opened as a vaudeville house in the 1920s. Above its large angled marquee was an elaborate one-hundred-foot-tall Art Deco tower with colored lights and a sparkling sphere at its top that could be seen from all around the area when illuminated at night.

It was at the Alex that Mack unexpectedly increased the speed of his spin while Genevieve was in the death spiral. He grasped her other wrist and lifted her completely from the ice. She was shocked, but as the bright lights flashed above her, she realized that this was a key piece of Mack and Ruth's Café de Apache dance. She was pale and shaking as she returned to the line, but she was elated. The movement remained in every performance afterward.

THE GIFT BEST GIVEN

Arena Coliseo

Mexico City, Mexico

It was mid-morning when the cast members arrived at the Lockheed Air Terminal in Burbank. Mack had been there since daybreak, and he was drenched with sweat as he supervised the airport ground personnel who were responsible for loading all of the Revue's equipment and baggage into the belly of the Mexicana Airlines DC-3. The ice rink's frame, liner, and tubing, along with the compressor and refrigeration unit had to travel with them. To minimize weight, Mack had made arrangements for the sand and salt for the brine to be provided at their destination. It was the second week of May, and the California sun was beating on the tarmac. The pilot and co-pilot, already perspiring through their shirts, were circling the aircraft as they completed their pre-flight checks.

THE OTHER SIDE OF THE WORLD. El Rancho Vegas, Las Vegas, Nevada.

THE OTHER SIDE OF THE WORLD. Grand Central Airport, Glendale California from which the MckGowan and Mack Revue departed for Mexico City.

The cast members were buzzing excitedly as they presented their identification and tickets. They were now part of the McGowan and Mack *International* Ice Revue. For most, other than their foray into Canada, this was their first time leaving the country, and most, including Genevieve, had never flown. Despite the heat, everyone was dressed for the occasion, men in suits and ties, the women in dresses and heels. They would fly for more than ten hours, making a stop to refuel in Laredo, Texas before reaching Mexico City, almost two thousand miles away.

The cast and the other passengers climbed metal stairs that had been rolled to the airplane's door. The DC-3 rested on the two wheels of its front landing gear and one small wheel under its tail, an arrangement that pointed the aircraft's nose skyward when taking off but pitched the aisle steeply down toward its tail when the plane was at rest. Genevieve cautiously picked her way down the center aisle and found her seat. A very handsome man, perhaps in his forties, was seated across the aisle and smiled at her. He had a dark complexion, carefully combed-back hair already beginning to show signs of gray—silver she thought, not gray—and dark eyes. He was dressed in a carefully tailored pale-blue poplin suit with a starched white shirt and silk tie.

"You are with the ice show?" he asked. His English was perfect, though it was heavily accented.

Genevieve shyly smiled back and said, "Yes, we are going to be in Mexico City for more than a month." She blushed, realizing how she was exaggerating the length of her words. This man's English seemed to be just fine.

He smiled. "At the Coliseo," he answered. "It has just recently opened."

"Is that the coliseum?" she asked. She had understood that they were performing at a coliseum, and she had visions of the ancient one in Rome she had seen pictures of, or of the ones where the bullfights that Ernest Hemmingway had written about took place. She hadn't been able to imagine how they could perform outdoors on ice in a structure like that.

"The Arena Coliseo," he stated. "It is near the middle of Mexico City. It was built for Lucha Libre, but already there is boxing there as well—every Monday night. And everyone is talking about your ice skating show coming," he added.

The aircraft shuddered as its two engines came to life, and their conversation was drowned out by their roar. The man turned to look out the window on his side of the aircraft, and Genevieve watched out hers as the DC-3 began to slowly taxi past the terminal to the end of the airport's one runway before turning, positioned for takeoff. She focused on the propellers as they began to spin faster, moving the plane down the runway. Bouncing on the rough surface, the airplane continued to move faster and faster until suddenly the vibrations stopped, and they were lifted into the sky. The DC-3 headed north, gaining altitude, before banking to the east toward the mountains that separated Los Angeles from the desert beyond. Later, it turned southward toward Laredo and Mexico.

Genevieve realized that the man had been looking at her, and she was slightly embarrassed by how excited she must have appeared as she craned her neck to see what was below them. She tried to recall what he had said. In a few sentences, he had told her more about the Revue's destination than she had known before boarding. She turned back to him. Once they were airborne, the cabin was quieter and conversations resumed. He raised his eyebrows as if to ask, "You have a question?"

"I don't know what Lucha Libre is," she said. "I never heard of that before."

He smiled more broadly. "Mexico loves Lucha Libre!" he exclaimed. His voice was deep and mellow. "It is professional wrestling. Sometimes mano a mano, sometimes four or six or eight are in the ring. It is sport, but it is also theater. All the wrestlers, the luchadores, wear brightly colored masks. It is an embarrassment to lose yours—the ultimate disgrace."

Trying not to sound insincere, Genevieve responded, "That sounds interesting."

The man smiled, understanding. "You will have to see it. The crowd sits close to the ring. Very close. They already call the new arena the Lagunilla Funnel. The ring is the narrow end of the funnel, and the crowd sits closely around and above it. It lets them be very involved. The patrons shout from the time the first match begins until the time they leave." Laughing, he added, "Most of the time we do not shout very pleasant things. Go with your friends one night when you are not performing—and when El Santo is wrestling. You will understand."

"El Santo, that means the saint, doesn't it? Who is that?"

"El Santo is Mexico's greatest hero. He is always dressed in silver with a silver mask. He is part of the drama, part of the theater. But no one knows who he is, and that makes him a mystery. Si, the Saint."

Unconvinced, Genevieve smiled, saying nothing as she wondered how a performer, a costumed actor in a theatrical wrestling match, could be the country's biggest hero. The man turned to his newspaper as Genevieve, through breaks in the clouds below them, watched the passing terrain and eventually fell asleep.

She was jarred awake as the plane landed in Laredo, bumping down the crude runway regularly utilized by Mexicana Airlines on its cross-border service. The airport was primitive—its terminal was little more than a flat-roofed concrete block building—but Genevieve was surprised by the number of military aircraft that were on the ground and by the large metal hangar with its US Army insignias. As she left the aircraft to stretch her legs, she heard the pilot explaining to Mack that the airport was currently being used by the army as a training location for new aviators. The pilot said that many of the small airports in Texas were being used for that purpose because of the wide-open terrain and the favorable climate. As more and more aircraft rolled off the wartime assembly lines, there was an almost inexhaustible need for more fighter pilots. Genevieve wondered if anyone who trained here would ultimately fly one of the planes that the Rosie the Riveter girls would build. She smiled as she thought about them. That trip already seemed so long ago.

After the plane was back in the air and had crossed into Mexico, the handsome man across the aisle left his seat to step into the restroom in the rear of the DC-3's cabin. He had said little for most of the flight, but when he settled himself back in his seat, he turned to Genevieve and unexpectedly asked, "Are you Catholic?"

She was surprised by the question. She was Catholic, of course. She had been baptized and confirmed, and she took communion at church with her family on Sundays, and she had gone to school at St. Michael's through eighth grade. Yet, she stumbled over her words when she finally said, "Yes, why do you ask?"

He nodded, appearing comforted by her answer. "You will be safe then. When the Arena Coliseo opened last month, Archbishop Martinez—he is over the Catholic Church for all of Mexico—came to bless the building. You will be safe performing there. I am going to bring my wife and my children to see you. You will fly just like this airplane does."

Arena Coliseo was close to the small hotel where the troupe was staying, a small drab building on a narrow side street, its gray façade brightened by red geraniums. Like most businesses in Mexico City, the arena was closed on Sunday. The Revue was scheduled to perform there on Wednesday, Thursday, and Friday evenings, and on Saturday afternoon. Boxing was featured on Monday and Lucha Libre every Saturday.

The description of the arena the man had given Genevieve, that it was the Lagunilla Funnel, was accurate. Seats surrounded the performers, and from the center of the ice, the seats climbed steeply. He had not told her that the arena was so large—more than eight thousand seats. The chilled air of the building was a welcome respite from the warm temperature and strong sun outside. Looking upward at the rows of currently empty seats, Genevieve wasn't sure if it was the chill within the arena or the thought of so many people watching that made her shiver.

It took a week's time for the cast members to become acclimated to performing in the thin air of Mexico City—at 7,400 feet of elevation—but their stay there was a resounding success. Though the large venue only occasionally sold out, they played to large crowds for every show, in particular on Friday evenings and for the Saturday matinees when the arena was filled with families.

Even as the days became cooler and rain more frequent, Genevieve wandered the city as a tourist would between rehearsals and shows, sometimes with other girls from the line, other times alone, though she always heeded everyone's admonition to, "Be careful where you go, not every street is a safe one." She returned numerous times to the Zocalo, Mexico City's main square. It was enormous, with the Templo Mayor, the Aztec temple and museum, on one side, the National Palace on another, and the National Cathedral with its many chapels on the other. Genevieve especially loved the tranquility of the cathedral, and every time she visited the square, she entered it to offer thanks for all her good fortune.

Before the Saturday matinee during the last week the Revue was in Mexico City, Mack approached Genevieve. "You know all the pieces that are part of the Apache dance," he said. "Are you ready to put them all together?" He watched her reaction.

She was stunned by the question. "You want me to do the Apache dance?" she asked, making sure she had understood.

"It will be a good thing for you. I wouldn't ask you if I didn't think you were ready. This is a perfect time."

Genevieve closed her eyes, thinking through all the pieces of the complicated routine—Mack and Ruth's signature number. She had always watched in awe as they performed it. Taking a deep breath, she opened her eyes, looked at him, and said, "Yes, I think this is a good time too."

The Revue performed their usual numbers during the matinee, but when the time came for the finale, Mack returned to the ice from one corner of the arena, and it was Genevieve who returned from the other. Ruth had been there to squeeze her hand and tell her, "You're ready for this, dear. Trust Mack, and trust yourself," before gently nudging her on her way. The performance seemed a blur to Genevieve, though she executed every element and responded to every cue as if she had been performing the number forever. As she lay face down on the ice after he slid her across the rink, and before he lifted her over his shoulder, she was only aware of Mack, the music, and the sound of their skates cutting the ice. Lowered to her feet to the ovation of the crowd, Genevieve beamed, before turning to Mack, who gave her a subtle nod as if to say, "I knew you were ready."

Mack and Genevieve exited the ice together and then returned with the rest of the cast to the applause of the audience. As they took their bows, Mack extended his hand to Genevieve and drew her out of the line, and the volume of the ovation increased as she curtsied and then stepped back. Leaving the ice, she recognized the man from the flight they had taken. He was every bit as handsome as when she had first met him on the airplane. Beside him was a woman who appeared to be about the same age as him. She was elegant, Genevieve thought, tall and slender with dark skin and dark eyes. In front of them, peering through the railings that separated the seats closest to the ice from the runway out of the arena, were two small children, a boy and a girl, who obviously were twins. They were equally as handsome, as elegant, and as perfect as their parents. The man smiled broadly. "You were magnificent! Do you remember what I told you about the Archbishop blessing this place?"

She did remember what he had said, but before Genevieve could answer, he exclaimed, "I told you that you would fly just like our airplane did—and today you did!"

Back in Los Angeles

Los Angeles, California

The McGowan and Mack group returned to Los Angeles the Monday following the show's closing in Mexico City. The cast had enjoyed a celebratory dinner on Saturday evening, and there was much buzz about Genevieve's performance with Mack. Although she was elated that she had had the opportunity to successfully perform the Apache dance, her enthusiasm, like the spirits of the others, was dampened when Mack announced that there were no more performance dates scheduled for the immediate future. Everyone would be on their own until more engagements were confirmed. A consolation was that he had arranged work on a movie already in production for any of the girls in the line who were interested. Not surprisingly, all of them were.

In the late 1930s and 1940s, numerous ice skating movies were produced in Hollywood. Sonja Henie, a multiple Olympic and World Champion ice skating star from Norway had started the trend, riding the success of a New York City ice skating stage show that featured her. She starred in her first film in 1936's *One In a Million*. *Thin Ice* followed the next year, setting her on a career which, for several years, would make her one of the most highly paid actresses in Hollywood.

Maria Belita Jepson-Turner arrived in Hollywood from Great Britain early in the 1940s, hoping to capitalize on the popularity of these ice skating movies. Billed simply as Belita, she also was an Olympic ice skater as well as a classically trained ballerina. By the time Genevieve and the rest of the girls from the Revue reported to Monogram Pictures' studio on Sunset Boulevard, the first of Belita's films, *Silver Skates*, had been released, and her second film, *Lady, Let's Dance*, a big band musical, was in production. While regarded as a superior skater to Henie, who was on contract with 20th Century Fox, one of the largest and most powerful studios, Belita was committed to Monogram, derisively regarded by some as a member of "Poverty Row" for the many low-budget, second-tier films they produced. Nonetheless, she was their highest-paid actress, and *Silver Skates* had already been deemed a success.

After the excitement of her final performance in Mexico City, the week's work was pedestrian and tedious. The two scenes in which she appeared were repeated numerous times, with the skaters dressed in winter costumes under the studio's hot lights. Nonetheless, Genevieve was grateful for the work and would be excited to see herself in the film the following year. Over the next months, she found other opportunities to perform, lost in the background and uncredited on movies being filmed at the 20th Century and Republic Studios where, the next year, Ruth and Mack would perform the Café de Apache in the film *Lake Placid Serenade*.

BACK IN LOS ANGELES. Genevieve (far right) appeared in the 1943 film, Lady Let's Dance, starring Belita.

THE GIFT BEST GIVEN

BACK IN LOS ANGELES. The Maxwell House Coffee facility where she worked prior to returning to New York.

With no local ice shows hiring, and with only limited opportunities to work for the motion picture studios, Genevieve decided to return home. She had rent to pay, food to buy, and she had spoken by phone with Carl Snyder who had been responsible for her becoming part of the McGowan and Mack Ice Revue. He assured her that when she got back to New York, he would be able to find another opportunity for her—"good work," as he put it. He said he had heard glowing reports from the McGowans. Genevieve needed a job.

It was an unlikely job for an aspiring performer to accept, but Genevieve thought if hopeful actresses could wait on tables or tend the counter at drugstores while they waited for their "big break," then she could do this one. Besides, it was a means to an end. She needed to save enough money to travel back to New York. July 5, 1943 was technically a holiday, but Genevieve had been told to report for her first day of work anyway. She boarded the Yellow Cars Number

Three bus at the corner of Larchmont Boulevard and Melrose Avenue in Hollywood and began the slow ride to the Maxwell House Coffee packaging facility on Mateo Street in downtown Los Angeles.

Every morning for the next six weeks, she would take the same bus, making a stop in front of Paramount Studios then driving through MacArthur Park. Then, passing Good Samaritan Hospital, the driver would invariably let everyone nearby know, "That's where Jean Harlow died back in '37," and she couldn't help but smile. He reminded her of the bus driver who, only a year before, would pick her up on the street corner back in Flushing and deliver her to the subway on her way to school.

Genevieve would spend the day sitting at a long stainless steel topped counter, side-by-side with many others doing the same job. With a carton of empty one pound Maxwell House Coffee bags beside her and a hose hanging from a stainless steel vat filled with ground coffee above, she would open a bag, release the coffee to fill it, and on the scale beside her, ensure that it weighed sixteen ounces—no more, no less. She would fold over the top of the bag twice and secure it with its lead wire tabs, and then she would place it on the conveyor in front of her, open another bag, and start the process again. Genevieve was paid pennies per bag and filled hundreds of them per day. Though her fingers were sore and her neck would ache as she rode the bus back to Hollywood, she knew this was temporary, and that she would soon be back home.

CHAPTER SEVEN
Traveling Home

Union Station

Los Angeles, California

It was early afternoon on Monday, August 9, and Genevieve once again stood at the intersection of Santa Monica and Larchmont, this time waiting for the bus that would take her to Union Station. She tilted her face to the sun and felt its warmth. The temperature was already in the mid-eighties, the air was still and bone dry; it hadn't rained in weeks.

All during July and the first part of August, Genevieve had worked her scheduled forty-hour week, as well as any overtime that was offered to her at the coffee bagging facility. Over the past six weeks, she hadn't had much opportunity for leisure, but all the hours she had worked and the countless pounds of coffee she had bagged were allowing her to return to New York sooner than she had originally hoped. Having already shipped most of her things home, she carried with her only her small suitcase.

She watched out the window as the bus passed Paramount Studios and then wound its way through a Korean and Filipino neighborhood, congested and teeming with signs of ethnic culture. Entering the city, the bus turned on North Alameda before finally arriving at Union Station. Genevieve knew that she would miss Los Angeles in many ways, but she was anxious to return home to her family. It had been almost a year since she had seen them, and she was also anxious to see what Mr. Snyder might next have in store for her.

Genevieve arrived at the station well before her train was scheduled to depart. She stood in front of the building and admired it before she entered. Constructed only four years earlier, it was new compared to the other stations she had traveled through. She had heard and seen it referred to as "the last of the great railway stations." Constructed in a mixture of architectural styles, the predominant being Mission Revival—one that she had only learned since moving to California. In contrast to the concrete that surrounded it in the middle of the city, the station was bounded by tall palm trees, lush gardens, and a thick lawn. As Genevieve entered and walked across the terra cotta inlaid marble floors, she was conscious of the sound of her footsteps. Her heels echoed on the hard shining tiles then fell softly muffled on the ones made of red clay. Above her, the high ceilings were fashioned from steel made to look like wood.

She followed the signs to a waiting area flanked on its north and south sides by enclosed patio gardens. As she had already done multiple times that day, she sat waiting, examining her ticket again. She had a reserved seat—a reclining coach seat, the ticket stated—in one of the coaches on the Union Pacific's City of Los Angeles. It was the railroad's most prestigious train, a streamliner powered by two diesel engines, painted from one end to the other in yellow and gray. Its engines and cars had been built shortly before the wartime restrictions placed on the use of steel and aluminum for anything but military purposes. The train would carry Genevieve through Las Vegas, Salt Lake City, Cheyenne, and Omaha on the almost forty hour trip to Chicago, where she would connect with another train to continue on to New York.

A Chance Encounter

Union Pacific's City of Los Angeles

Genevieve patiently waited for the call to board the train and discretely watched other passengers to pass the time. She sat, wondering who they were, what they did, and where all of them were going. It wasn't until the call to board came that she noticed a young man. With his sharp, chiseled features, dark eyes, and brown hair carefully combed back, Genevieve thought he had movie star good looks. She estimated he was a bit older than her, though perhaps only by a year or two. He had a slender physique, and though he appeared to be well under six feet tall, the dark suit he wore made him appear taller. She tried not to stare, but he turned in Genevieve's direction for a moment, and when she realized that he saw that she was looking at him, she turned away and blushed. Neither of them knew the relationship that they would establish in that moment, but he briefly smiled then turned back to board the coach with several other passengers between them.

Shortly after the train had departed Union Station, Genevieve was surprised to look up and find the young man standing beside her seat.

"Hello," he said, shyly. "My name is Gerry Verden. I recognized you when you were standing on line. I saw you skate earlier this year at the Hollywood Casino."

Genevieve was both pleased and surprised that he had recognized her. She smiled and said "I didn't think anyone knew who I was. Do you want to sit down?" She motioned to the vacant seat opposite hers.

"I am an ice skater too. I am traveling to New York to audition at the Center Theater for Sonja Henie's show.

Genevieve knew that the Center Theatre had opened a few years before and that it had a huge permanent ice surface. She had been in the audience for the first of several Sonja Henie productions. "You must be a very good skater," she said.

The young man seemed to consider his answer. "I came to the United States when I was eleven years old. From Austria," he added. "My parents sent me here to live with my aunt before the civil war, the February Uprising, occurred. I came with her mother." He continued, "My aunt was a national figure skating champion in our country. She came to the United States years before to perform. Now she teaches. She is the one who taught me to skate. We've lived all over. First New York, then Miami, and now we live in Los Angeles.

As they talked, the train left Los Angeles behind and rolled toward the mountains west of the city. Genevieve recalled looking out the window of the DC-3 she had flown in with the McGowan and Mack Revue and seeing the same range of mountains that the train would soon traverse.

She agreed to have dinner with Gerry, and the two walked through their car and the next one beyond it to the dining car. The sun set behind them as they ate, and they sat undisturbed, talking until well after dark. The train stopped briefly in San Bernardino before it began to twist through the mountains. Gerry asked what seemed like a never ending stream of questions, but she was happy to answer them. She told him about the circumstances that led to her becoming part of the McGowan and Mack Revue, where they had performed, what her role had been, what she liked and what she had not, and what she hoped she would do next. For every answer that she provided, Gerry would ask still another question. Their conversation was easy, but she stopped, finally, embarrassed by how much the conversation had been about her.

Changing the subject, Genevieve said, "The trip from Austria to the United States must have been exciting. Once the war is over, I hope I'll have a chance to travel to Europe or someplace else far away."

"We traveled in first class," he said. "It was very luxurious. There were many passengers in steerage. Being so comfortable made my aunt's mother and me very self-conscious. The ship left from Germany and, after many days at sea, landed in Havana in Cuba."

"You must have been grateful to be back on land," Genevieve smiled.

"It wasn't easy. My aunt met us in Havana and then by seaplane we flew to the United States but they wouldn't let us in until she could prove that she was my aunt and her mother's daughter and that she would be responsible for us. We were grateful to be here but weren't made to feel welcome."

Genevieve was silent for a moment and then said, "My grandfather told me that when he came here they wouldn't let him enter the United States until he could show them that he had at least twenty-five dollars."

"Don't misunderstand me," Gerry said. "I'm very grateful to be here. Terrible things have happened–are still happening–where I come from. At times I feel selfish doing what I'm doing. Being an ice skater is not an important thing when there's a war going on." Afraid he might have offended Genevieve, he quickly added, "I don't mean for you. For someone like me. A man who could be fighting, especially when his native country has been overrun."

"I understand," Genevieve said quietly. "When I was on the train to join McGowan and Mack, I met girls going to work in the shipyards and aircraft manufacturing plants. I said the same thing. They told me I shouldn't worry about such things. At times like these, if you can bring a smile to people's faces, that's a contribution too."

Gerry shrugged and sighed. "Thank you. But I don't know." As she watched his reaction to what she said, it appeared to Genevieve that he found little comfort in her words.

They returned to their seats in the coach, agreeing to breakfast together in the morning. Genevieve smiled at the passenger beside her; the person across the aisle was already sleeping. Genevieve wanted to be awake to see the glow of the neon lights when the train passed through Las Vegas at midnight, but as the trained rolled eastward, she reclined her seat, closed her eyes and was soon soundly sleeping.

The two met again for breakfast. They were still chatting about each of their hopes and plans for the future as the train passed through Salt Lake City shortly after ten o'clock, continuing its eastward journey. Verden was confident in his abilities but still expressed that he was feeling trepidation about the audition, which was scheduled the following week. Genevieve, wondering what her next opportunity would be and when it would present itself, empathized with him and told him about Carl Snyder. If things didn't work out at the Center Theatre—though she was sure they would—perhaps he would be able to help Gerry.

They followed the same pattern for the next twenty-four hours, eating their meals together and talking, then returning to their seats. As the train passed through Cheyenne, Wyoming late that evening, the two exchanged telephone numbers, Genevieve offering her parents' number and Gerry providing the number of his aunt's friend who lived in Manhattan and who had offered him a place to stay. Perhaps, they agreed, they might even meet to skate together at Iceland, Genevieve's former haunt, just off Broadway.

At four-thirty the next morning, the passengers left the train in Omaha, Nebraska, to connect with an identically painted train operated by the Chicago and North Western Railroad that would take them into Chicago. The time was early and inconvenient, but this was the second day of their travels, and Genevieve welcomed the opportunity to leave the train for a few minutes to breathe fresh air. She and Gerry had an opportunity for one more breakfast together before parting ways. While both were going to New York City, his ticket from Chicago was on the New York Central, the same route Genevieve had taken before as she traveled west; hers was on the Pennsylvania Railroad. Genevieve was anxious to see her family and to be home with them for a while. She knew that she needed to continue practicing and honing her skills until another chance to perform came her way. Before they parted in Chicago, she reassured Gerry that she definitely wanted to meet with him in Manhattan to skate.

Genevieve's train departed Chicago's Union Station at three o'clock in the afternoon. She was excited, wondering who would be there to meet her when she arrived in New York the next morning. She dozed fitfully, though she was tired from the already long trip. As the train arrived in Pittsburgh just after midnight, she was awake. Finally, as it ground eastward over the mountains of western and central Pennsylvania, she fell asleep. When she awoke, Genevieve was pleased to realize that the train had arrived in Philadelphia. She walked to the dining car to purchase tea and an English muffin, more to pass the time than because she was hungry. She knew she was less than two hours from New York City.

Genevieve walked out into the main concourse of Pennsylvania Station. It was at least as magnificent, perhaps more so, than Grand Central Station across Manhattan. Rush hour was at its height, but she noticed neither the crowds nor the vast space sheathed in marble and bathed in the light pouring in through its soaring glass roof. Standing there was her father and her grandfather. She hurried to them and put down her suitcase, first relishing Aleksander's embrace and then turning to her father, whose eyes were wet with tears. She hugged him for a long time, and when Leonard asked, "So how were things on the other side of the world?" Genevieve cried too.

Return to New York

Flushing, New York

Squeezed into the front seat of the car between Aleksander and Leonard, who was driving, Genevieve inhaled the familiar cigar smell that had permeated the Buick. Leonard turned on West Thirty-Third Street and then made a right turn to head uptown on Eighth Avenue. They passed the New Yorker Hotel on their left, a place that would become part of Genevieve's future, and shortly after that, Madison Square Garden appeared between West Forty-Ninth and West Fiftieth Streets. Genevieve craned her neck looking for the sign for Iceland, the skating rink just down the side street to her left where she planned to meet Gerry Verden. She looked out one side window of the car and then the other as the three retraced the route that had brought her to the city to board the train for the west so many months ago. All the while, Aleksander peppered her with questions about where she had been, how she had traveled, who she had met, and then would interrupt himself, saying, "No, no, no don't tell us, save it for your mother and your grandmother." Genevieve smiled thinking that so little had changed while she had been away.

Flushing looked the same. In bold letters, the marquee on the RKO Keith's advertised *For Whom the Bell Tolls,* starring Gary Cooper and Ingrid Bergman. At the whitewashed gas station, the overhead doors of the bays were raised as the mechanics labored inside. Elm trees shaded the sidewalk around the perimeter of Flushing High School as Leonard made the turn from Northern Boulevard to Union Street, and then quickly turned down Thirty-Fifth Avenue.

As soon as the car entered the driveway, the crunching of gravel under its tires announcing their arrival, Josephine, with Wanda behind her, opened the side door to the house and descended the three concrete steps to the driveway. Aleksander did his best to quickly get out of the car. Genevieve slipped out behind him and hurried to hug and to kiss the two women.

Her mother held her at arm's length, looking her up and down. "You're home. You look so grown up. Not a little girl."

Wanda reached out and took Genevieve from Josphine's arms. "Kochanie," she said as she beamed.

"Babciu," Genevieve responded, returning the endearment in Polish, wrapping her arms around her grand-mother's shoulders and holding her close.

Noticing Genevieve looking past her, and into the house, Josephine said, "Lucille, is working today. She wanted to be here but they couldn't give her the day off. She spent hours getting your room ready for you. She will be back before dinner."

Aleksander, now that everyone was together, began to repeat his questions from the car. Leonard, a smile on his face and carrying Genevieve's suitcase, followed the four into the house. It was a Thursday, a workday, but his daughter's return was important, and he had left his plumbing business in the hands of his foreman.

By bedtime, Genevieve was exhausted. She had traveled for three days, answered what seemed like a thousand questions from her parents and grandparents and sister, and she was sure that she must have gained ten pounds eating the special meal that Wanda and Josephine had prepared. She was delighted to be home, and as she lay there in her bed, it seemed as if the ten preceding months and all she had experienced during that time had been like some fairy tale. She smiled in the dark and let her mind drift, imagining all that the future might hold. Tomorrow she would call Mr. Snyder to let him know that she had returned and that she was anxious for that dream to continue.

Genevieve left a message for Snyder first thing the following morning. When he called back late in the afternoon, they spoke at length, and when she mentioned Gerry Verden, he was interested. The war was continuing to limit the number of available male skaters, and he knew of Gerry's aunt. He recalled that she had performed at the Ice Casino at Rye Playland, an amusement park just to the north of New York City. He wondered if her nephew had inherited her abilities. When Genevieve told Snyder that she and Gerry planned to meet at Iceland, he suggested that she let him know when they would be there, and perhaps, if his schedule permitted, he would stop by. He was eager to have a look at a new male skater but did not want to build any expectations.

She immediately called the number that Verden had provided her and was grateful when the woman who answered put him on the phone. Genevieve felt awkward about calling him so soon after they had parted in Chicago, but he seemed nice, and if there was a possibility she could help him with his own dreams, she wanted to do that. Gerry was excited to hear of Snyder's interest. His Center Theatre audition was Wednesday of the next week, and he planned on skating each of the days prior. He wondered if Snyder might be available to see him skate on Monday or Tuesday afternoon. Genevieve told him that she would let Mr. Snyder know, and the two agreed upon the time they would meet at the rink.

Northern Boulevard eventually changed to North County Road as Leonard, Josephine, Genevieve, and Lucille drove east on Saturday to visit Josephine's parents, Mary and Joseph. The girls' grandparents, along with their uncle, Adam, farmed on twenty-two acres of land in St. James. Though still a rural community, the extension of the Long Island Railroad had made St. James a popular summer destination for New York City's theater set. Long Island's sandy soil provided the perfect conditions for Joseph and Adam to grow bountiful crops of cabbage and potatoes and beans, which they would transport and sell at the Washington Market in downtown Manhattan each week. While farming demanded the family's constant attention, Mary had telephoned her daughter every Sunday afternoon after the time when Genevieve was to have called home, for an update on her granddaughter's travels and career. As early as she could remember, Genevieve had loved visiting the farm.

Her grandparents were stern and hardworking. Their lives were driven by the seasons and by the weather, with little time remaining for leisure. Joseph was tall and lean with weathered skin, knotted hands, and a bent back. His stooped shoulders were a testimony to a life lived constantly outdoors doing manual labor. Mary had given birth to ten children, only six of whom were now alive.

Beneath the babushka that covered her dark hair, Mary's usually stoic face was softened by a smile at seeing her granddaughters. Genevieve listened as Joseph spoke of the challenges the war had brought—of rationing of gasoline and replacement tires for the farm vehicles, and how difficult it was to find farm labor to harvest crops. More and more, it was local women who worked for the $3.50 per day that he paid. For the first time, Genevieve realized that Joseph and Mary were getting old. They were both now in their eighties. They were about the same age as Aleksander and Wanda, her other grandparents, but had lived much harder lives.

Genevieve's visit was a special event. Like Leonard with his plumbing company, Joseph rarely took time away from the farm. On this day, however, he left it in Adam's hands and traveled with the family to nearby Long Beach, a spit of land on Long Island Sound, to take advantage of the perfect August day. When they returned to the farm several hours later, there was another festive dinner, with fried chicken—from chickens that had been scratching in the barnyard that morning—farm-grown mashed potatoes, and coleslaw made from cabbages that Joseph had brought in from the field before the family arrived. It had been a wonderful day, Genevieve thought. As they left, she hugged her grandparents goodbye and wondered how much longer they could continue to live as they did.

CHAPTER EIGHT
Gerry Verden

Iceland

Iceland Skating Rink, West 50th Street, New York City

Late Monday morning, Genevieve left home, and as she had done countless times while in school, she walked past the large homes on Thirty-Fifth Avenue to Union Street to catch the bus to the subway. As the train emerged from the Roosevelt Avenue station, she looked out its windows, seeing Flushing Bay on one side and the World's Fair site on the other, and then all the familiar rooftops as the train made its way toward the city. She exited at Queensboro Plaza, went down the stairs to the street below before descending another flight of stairs that would bring her to the E Train. The need to pay a second fare to make the transfer had always annoyed her and she frowned as she dropped a small brass token into the turnstile. Still, she knew that it would take her directly to Eighth Avenue and West Forty-Ninth Street, where she'd emerge from the subway in front of Madison Square Garden's entrance doors. She anticipated the air being filled with the smell of grilling hotdogs escaping from the Nedick's adjacent to the subway stairs, and that Iceland would be just around the corner.

The chilled air was heavy with the pungent scent of skaters' sweat and the inescapable odor of their well-worn skates. Gerry was already on the ice when she arrived, and she watched through the glass partition before stepping out to join him. He was an accomplished skater, and the extra height added by the blades of his skates gave him an imposing presence on the ice. They greeted one another and chatted as they skated around and across the rink forward and then backward. Genevieve listened as Gerry talked about his upcoming audition. Although they had never been on the ice together, their movements seemed effortless, and Genevieve wondered if Gerry sensed the same unexpected synchronicity in their skating.

They had been skating for about thirty minutes when Genevieve noticed Carl Snyder watching through the window of the viewing area. She stopped in front of him, waiting to see if he wanted her to come off the ice, but he motioned and nodded toward Gerry as if to ask, "Is that him?" When Genevieve nodded, Snyder made a circular gesture with his hand telling her to keep skating.

"Mr. Snyder is here," she said, as she skated past Gerry. "Look good," she teased. She wondered if he was suddenly as self-conscious as she had just become. Genevieve could only speculate what Mr. Snyder might be thinking.

A short while later, Mr. Snyder came into the rink and beckoned Genevieve over. "You're looking very good on the ice. You've come a long way," he told her. "Every bit as good as Mack told me," he added.

Pleased, Genevieve said, "Thank you. I learned so much from being with them."

"Is that Marguerite Verden's nephew you've been skating with?" he inquired, confident that he already knew that it was. "Why don't you call him over and introduce us? Once you and I have talked, I'd like to speak with him as well. What do you make of him?"

Genevieve thought for a moment, wanting to give a useful answer, pleased that he'd asked her opinion. "He's strong and very comfortable on his skates. It all seems so natural to him. And he's very serious about his skating. The audition at Center Theatre is important to him. He wants to do well."

"Well, let's see about that," Snyder said, confusing Genevieve with his tone. "Call him over. I want to make sure he can stay around and talk a bit."

Genevieve made the requested introductions. She had told Gerry about Mr. Snyder and the influence he seemed to have. Verden appeared a bit nervous, but he eagerly agreed to talk in more depth with him later. He watched as Genevieve followed Snyder off the ice and into the adjacent viewing area.

When they were alone, Snyder asked Genevieve about her experiences on the West Coast and what it was like being away from home as long as she had been. She told him that she felt she had become a better skater, that her skills had grown, and though she had missed her family, she had quickly overcome any feelings of homesickness. Snyder, serious, said, "I have another opportunity for you if you're ready to be away again. You'll be part of a featured act. Everett said that you're ready for that. If you truly want a career, this is the next step to take."

Genevieve took a deep breath, attempting to slow her pounding heart, not wanting to appear too excited. "Yes," she said, "I'm ready to be away if that's what's necessary. I do want a career. I'll do what I need to do."

Snyder went on to explain that many of the major hotels that were not already doing so were beginning to book ice shows for their dining rooms and investing in their own ice rinks. Tank shows, he called them. He was currently locating and providing the talent for ice shows in some of the most prestigious hotels in the Midwest and in New York. He had recently booked Adele Inge, a woman a year younger than Genevieve, known for her acrobatics on skates, as the featured performer in an upcoming show, and he was now looking for another act—a pair of ice dancers—to support her. "I will have to find you a partner," Snyder said. "It's become a bit more difficult with all the young men being drafted. There aren't many good male skaters left around, but it can be accomplished. There's a partner out there for you. Think about it," he said. "You'll have to join the union, but you'll get union wages. It will pay well." Genevieve's mind was racing, and she nodded as he said, "Why don't you go back and skate a bit more? Send Mr. Verden in. I'd like to talk to him about this audition he's come to New York for."

It seemed like Snyder and Gerry were talking forever. Finally, Gerry reappeared at the barrier surrounding the rink and beckoned her over. Gerry was excited. "He wants to talk to us both," he said. Genevieve was curious as she followed him back to the warmer area where Mr. Snyder was waiting.

"Let me make you both a proposal," he began. "Genevieve, you've said you're ready for the opportunity that we discussed a while ago."

Both he and Verden watched her as she immediately nodded her head and whispered, "Yes." Embarrassed, realizing that she had just whispered, she repeated herself, this time in a more confident and affirmative tone.

Snyder turned to Gerry. "You've come to New York to audition for a job that you may or may not get, and you've told me that you would consider another job if it presented itself."

"Yes, I would. Absolutely, sir," Verden responded.

Mr. Snyder looked at Gerry and then to Genevieve. "What do you two think about skating together?" The two looked at one another, but before either could respond, Snyder continued, "Practice now through September in New York, do a couple of short bookings in Detroit early in October to get your feet wet, and then work through the end of the year at the Netherland Plaza, the most luxurious hotel in Cincinnati, perhaps in the east. This is their third year of ice shows, and they have ice permanently installed in their ballroom. You'll have the best costumes and the best production and choreography. We call the show Carnival on Real Ice. Three shows a day, six days a week. Oh," he added matter-of-factly, "as I mentioned, you'll receive union wages, one hundred dollars a week for each of you, with your room included."

Snyder said no more. Genevieve and Gerry were quiet. Later, they confided in one another that they were both wondering if he had really said one hundred dollars per week. Finally, Gerry looked to Genevieve and asked hopefully, "Do you need time to think about this?"

Genevieve shook her head. "No. I want to do this. I think that we should do this." This time she didn't whisper.

The Book Cadillac Hotel

Detroit, Michigan

All through September and well into October, Genevieve traveled each day to Iceland to meet Gerry and to practice the routine that had been provided to them, using only one corner of the rink to replicate the smaller ice surface that would be available in the hotel. Serious about their craft and meticulous in their preparation, they repeated each element of their routine over and over. Gerry, not as physically strong as he was handsome, was concerned about his ability to lift and throw Genevieve. The choreographer of the planned Cincinnati show was already in New York, also responsible for the ice show running at the New Yorker Hotel. He quickly modified the pair's routine to better suit Gerry's abilities. Snyder would often come by the rink, sometimes hiding in the warm room, to watch their progress and to critique and to encourage. At the end of October, he told them that he thought they were more than ready. It was time for them to go to Detroit, and then move on to Cincinnati to meet with the rest of the Carnival cast and to coordinate their skating with the hotel orchestra.

No strangers to trains any longer, Gerry and Genevieve departed New York for Detroit on the New York Central's overnight Detroiter, which left Grand Central Station at seven in the evening and arrived shortly after eight o'clock in the morning the following day. They took a taxi from the Michigan Central Train Depot to the Book Cadillac Hotel less than two miles away. The Book Cadillac was built as a monument to Detroit's prosperity in the 1920s as the trajectory of the automobile industry pointed skyward. It was twenty-eight stories tall, had 1,200 rooms, and its ground floor was lined with twenty retail stores. But, along with Detroit, the Book had fallen on hard times during the Depression. Now, the city prospered. Known as the Arsenal of Democracy, its factories were working overtime to contribute more to the war effort than any other city in the country. The hotel was flourishing again.

Arriving in time for a morning rehearsal, they immediately were fit into the Fantasy on Ice program that evening and would perform in the show for the next two weeks. With each performance, they grew more confident in the ballroom environment that would be similar to what they would find in Cincinnati.

Genevieve was delighted when Mack, Ruth, and Joann, who were appearing at the nearby rink on Belle Isle, visited the hotel to see their afternoon performance and then invited her and Gerry to appear with the Revue if their schedule at the hotel permitted. Mack teased that if Carl Snyder hadn't so quickly snatched her up, Genevieve would be back skating with them, "But we only have room for just so many stars!" She and Verden did find an opportunity to appear with the Revue—a guest appearance—as they would again do the following spring when the McGowans performed in Kentucky at the same time Gerry and Genevieve appeared in Cincinnati.

The Netherland Plaza Hotel

Cincinnati, Ohio

In mid-November, Genevieve and Verden once again boarded a train, this time to Cincinnati via Cleveland. Both were in awe as they arrived at the Netherland Plaza Hotel, dubbed a "city within a city." The luxurious hotel was flanked by a massive office tower, an indoor driveway for the convenience of its guests, and stores of all types on the street and adjacent to the lobby. They were directed to the rooms they would occupy during their stay at the hotel, and though the accommodations were in the rear of the property, they were spacious and comfortable, with views overlooking the city. "You'll be there through the end of the year," Snyder had said. Genevieve smiled as she unpacked and made herself at home.

She and Gerry met in the lobby to explore the room where they would perform. Genevieve thought back to how walking through the lobby of the Palace Hotel in San Francisco had taken her breath away with its beauty. This hotel was far grander than the Palace. It was rich in marble, glass, silver, and brass. They climbed the wide marble staircase to the mezzanine above the lobby and located the Restaurant Continentale. The two of them gasped at the same time as they walked through the door.

They stood at one end, an elevated area inside the room's

entrance. Urns filled with colorful flowers were positioned at the top of the stairs leading down to the main area of the restaurant. An expanse of dining tables surrounded both the dance floor and the ice surface. At the other end of the room, a matching set of steps led to another tier for the orchestra. Everything was crafted of highly polished stone. Elegant draperies surrounded large windows, allowing sunlight to flood the room and to reflect off the silver and crystal chandeliers during the day. When the drapes were pulled shut at night, silver and glass sconces would provide light for the diners. At each of the room's four corners was a mural depicting one of the seasons, reminding Genevieve of the large paintings on the walls in the main lobby at Washington Irving High School. She thought about how long ago it seemed since she had been in school, about how she had dreamed and planned, and about all in her life that had changed since then.

The next day, the two of them, along with Adele Inge and the six "De Icers," the line of girls who would skate in support of the featured acts, met with Donn Arden. It was Arden who was producing the Netherland Plaza show, as well as similar ones in other hotels, who had met with Genevieve and Gerry to modify their routine during their rehearsals at Iceland. He had already established himself as the preeminent choreographer and producer of ice shows and would ultimately go on to define the image of the Las Vegas showgirl as his career progressed. The six De Icers were outgoing and friendly, eager to meet the needs of everyone involved in the program. Edi Scholdan, a skating juggler, was a seasoned professional who was being carried over from the hotel's previous show. Absent from rehearsals, he would join the show when it opened.

GERRY VERDEN and GENEVIEVE NORRIS

GERRY VERDEN: Genevieve met Gerry Verden as she returned to New York City from Los Angeles. By November of 1943, they were performing at the Netherland Plaza Hotel in Cincinnati, Ohio.

Adele Inge was extremely reserved. Gerry later commented to Genevieve that Adele was quiet, almost to the point of being unfriendly. Nonetheless, as the producer rehearsed and fine-tuned each element of the thirty-minute show that would begin in the coming days, Genevieve admired Adele's acrobatic abilities and respected her intense focus. She learned later that Inge's father, recognizing his young daughter's potential, had built an ice rink in the basement of their Missouri home and coached her until he felt that she was ready to perform. For all the distance that Adele maintained between herself and the other skaters, concerned only with Arden's approval it seemed, Genevieve was surprised to see the starlet's smile ever-present while performing. Out of the audience's eye, her lips returned to a tight horizontal line, but Inge's prowess—and her smile apparently—resonated with the audience. After the first week of performances, a writer for *Billboard* wrote:

> Adele Inge, easily the most talented ice principal ever to show here. She uncorks a set of ice-skate surprises that had the first-show clientele applauding almost continuously. Her wizardry on the ice is punctuated with a vast assortment of daring spins, whirls and leaps across that made for thrills, and she wraps it all up in a package that spells confidence, showmanship, and polish.

The same reporter's evaluation of Genevieve's and Gerry's performance, while not unkind, was less enthusiastic:

> Also new in the current offering are Genevieve Norris and Gerry Verden, a nice-appearing youthful pair, who fared okay with their adagio nifties and standard skate bits. Need a little more work together to stack up with some of the teams seen here in the past.

Subsequent reviews in Billboard and in the city's daily papers, *The Cincinnati Enquirer* and *The Cincinnati Times Star*, were positive, stating that "Genevieve Norris and Gerry Verden now stack up as a smart ice team, having acquired considerable polish and show savvy since their opening here." The three times daily show routinely played to large audiences who paid $1.00 for complete lunches and $1.50 for dinner.

With revisions to the production numbers, it was held over through the end of the year and into 1944. Genevieve relished the comfort of her room at the hotel, and every morning she would find her way into the deserted restaurant to play the grand piano on the orchestra stage before meeting Gerry to practice their routines or working with a ballet coach she had enlisted to help her refine and build on her existing skills.

Gerry was comfortable with the day to day routine, but Genevieve realized that he didn't find the same joy in performing as she did. He stayed in his room most mornings listening to the radio and reading about the war in Europe in the daily newspapers. Thoughts of his former homeland and of his family and friends troubled him deeply.

With increasing frequency, when he would come down before their lunchtime performance, Gerry would tell Genevieve, "Things are going badly in Europe. It is probably worse than the reports tell. I feel helpless being here."

He and Genevieve would discuss it, and she attempted to show understanding for his concerns. "My family has relatives in Poland," she would tell him.

"It is not the same. You don't understand," he'd respond. "It is my country. I was born there. It is my close family." Genevieve would listen silently, thinking it fruitless to answer.

While she had hoped against it, she was not surprised when, early in March, Gerry told her he was going to call Mr. Snyder to tell him he was leaving the show to enlist in the army. Gerry continued to perform with Genevieve until the end of May, when Snyder found a replacement for him. Though there was no good time to lose a principal in the show, there were only two months left in their engagement.

Billy Peterson, a handsome young man who had previously skated at the Netherland Plaza before a lengthy stint at the Hotel New Yorker in Manhattan, was brought in to support Genevieve. She assumed the roles of such varying fairy tale characters like Little Red Riding Hood and Little Bo Peep, and the two of them performed as Jack and Jill in the then-current *A Midsummer Night's Phantasy on Ice* production. The two worked well together, though their partnership was temporary.

By the early part of July, Genevieve was back in New York waiting for Carl Snyder to insert her, at the producer's request, into another Donn Arden production. It was around the same time that she received an unexpected telephone call from Gerry. He told her that he had completed paratrooper training and that he promised to return to skate with her again when the war was over. He added with great pride that he was now one of the more than 100,000 non-citizens serving in the military and that he had been naturalized as a result of his enlistment.

CHAPTER NINE
Teddy Roman

HOTEL ICE SHOWS. Ice show at the New Yorker Hotel where Genevieve appeared in 1946.

HOTEL ICE SHOWS. Table-topper for Ice Capers at the Biltmore Hotel's Bowman Room, New York City.

A New Partner

New York City

Upon her return to New York, Carl Snyder almost immediately slotted Genevieve into another Donn Arden produced show, *Circus Daze*, which was already running at the Hotel New Yorker in Manhattan. Arden had recognized Genevieve's talents, respected the serious way in which she approached performing, and had told Snyder he wanted her to be part of the cast. The New Yorker had been featuring ice shows on a permanent ice surface installed in its Ice Terrace dining room for the past eight years. Genevieve skated twice in each of the three, thirty minute performances daily, paired with a new partner, Bob Ballard. Snyder told her that this would be a temporary arrangement, but that he would keep her working until he found a suitable permanent partner for her.

He was true to his word in both respects. Once the New Yorker engagement was completed, she found herself as one of the four "De Icers" in the Hotel Biltmore's *Ice Capers* show late in 1944 and early in 1945. She supported Joan Hyldoft, who had been a Miss America contestant three years earlier. Although this was a brief step down from her recent roles, Genevieve was happy to be so close to home and to be among friends—the other "De Icers" were girls she had worked with while at the Netherland Plaza. Early in the year, as she was once more stepping out of the line to double as a solo performer, Snyder introduced Genevieve to Teddy Roman.

Teddy Roman was the youngest of ten siblings, and like Genevieve, whose parents were Polish, he too was the son of Polish immigrants. Three years younger than her, he was stout and muscular and seemingly always smiling. Snyder told Genevieve that Teddy was, "Basically a good skater; a little bit raw." He had grown up skating on the ponds around Buffalo, New York before moving to Astoria where, coincidentally, Genevieve had lived as a child. He assured her that Roman's skills would continue to grow and that what he truly felt was important was Teddy's strength, which meant that he would have the ability to spin and lift and toss Genevieve in acro-adagio routines. She liked Teddy from the start, affectionately nicknaming him Strong Man.

Genevieve continued to perform at the Biltmore in the evenings as she and Roman began to practice together each morning on the same corner of the Iceland rink where she and Gerry Verden had rehearsed two years before. As in the past, Snyder would occasionally drop by the rink to see their progress. He knew that he had been right in his assessment of Roman. The young man's skills improved dramatically as he skated daily, and his strength allowed him to lift and carry and spin Genevieve as she had not experienced since she had skated with Everett McGowan. Teddy was a perfect match for Genevieve's fearlessness on skates. On one of these visits, Snyder announced that he planned to return Genevieve and her new partner to the Netherland Plaza. Hearing about her previous experiences there, Teddy was as eager to go as Genevieve was delighted to be going back.

Their arrival at the Netherland Plaza was like a homecoming for Genevieve. Her cheerful good nature had helped her make friends with the hotel staff during her previous stay, and they were pleased to see her again. The desk staff assigned her the same room she had enjoyed the year prior. During the duo's first week in Cincinnati, Germany surrendered, and the war in Europe was declared over.

Victory over Japan was declared in August. For each evening's performance of *Carnival on Real Ice*, the atmosphere in the hotel's Restaurant Continentale was jubilant, and Genevieve skated joyfully, knowing that Ed, Lucille's husband, who had been in a Coast Guard unit that had supported the Allies' landing on D-Day would return safely home. Her brother, Al, older than Genevieve by eight years and who she felt she barely knew, would arrive back in New York Harbor on a Victory ship, physically unharmed after having been among the troops to liberate Nazi concentration camps.

Reviews of a new show, *Summer Fantasy*, were excellent, with Teddy and Genevieve clicking from the start. One local paper said, "Teddy Roman and Genevieve Norris are receiving compliments from connoisseurs on their team stints ... patrons say their technique is original and their lifts a sensation." Still another reporter confirmed Snyder's early prediction, saying, "top skating honors go to the stocky and muscular Teddy Roman. Packs entertainment and showmanship into his solo spots, and on the doubles handles Miss Norris like a pound of feathers." This began an extended engagement for the two, and their popularity continued to grow.

Genevieve fell into a comfortable daily routine, and as she had before, she returned to her ballet lessons, this time accompanied by Ginny Walters who had stepped out of the line with her partner, Jerry Mapes, to become one of the featured performers in a new show, *An Evening at the Opera*. Genevieve also discovered that Teddy was an accomplished pianist with a taste for Chopin, similar to hers. The two would often play the ballroom's grand piano in the morning. With the shows periodically changing, they remained featured performers at the Netherland Plaza until May of the following year, when Snyder moved them to the New Yorker to perform in another elaborate Donn Arden production for three months.

Gerry Verden Returns

New York City

In May of 1946, at the same time that Genevieve and Teddy had started performing at the New Yorker, Gerry Verden was discharged from the military. He returned to California, where he stayed with his aunt who coached him and helped him recapture the skating skills he had not used for the prior two years. In late July, he made the transcontinental train trip to New York City. His arrival coincided with the end of Genevieve's and Teddy Roman's engagement at the New Yorker.

Genevieve was presented with a conundrum. When he had departed for the military, Gerry had told her that he would come back and return to skating, and she had told him she would be waiting for his return and looked forward to resuming their partnership. Now, however, she had a new partner, one with whom she enjoyed performing and who she felt was better able to help her display her ever-increasing abilities.

She talked with Carl Snyder, who left the decision in her hands. Sympathizing with her dilemma, he told her that if she chose to honor her commitment to Gerry, he would work hard to find opportunities for Teddy. It was a difficult decision, and she would be sacrificing what was beneficial to her to honor a promise she had made two years before. With Teddy's understanding, she resumed her former partnership.

Genevieve and Verden skated together in Donn Arden's latest New Yorker production during the month of August and then into September. Gerry had returned to his previous skating form—if anything, it had improved and he had become stronger—but he was more serious and introspective than ever, and he often seemed distracted. Snyder booked the two of them as solo performers for an engagement late in the month at The Cabana in Providence, Rhode Island. It was during the train ride to Boston and subsequent bus trip to their destination that Gerry confided in Genevieve that his passion for skating was no longer as strong as it had been. He felt guilty that his return had caused her to part ways with Teddy Roman and said that he had decided to call Carl Snyder and tell him that he planned to quit performing after their present engagement. By late in the year, Gerry had returned to California and had reenlisted in the military.

CHAPTER TEN
Ice Follies

Iceland Restaurant

Broadway, New York City

Genevieve emerged from the subway each day to the familiar smells wafting from the Nedick's outside Madison Square Garden. Once more, she was on her way to practice in the corner of the Iceland rink with Teddy Roman. They soon moved from their Iceland practices to perform at a new smorgasbord themed restaurant, coincidentally also called Iceland, located on Broadway at West Fifty-Third Street, only a few blocks away. Through early January of 1947, they were scheduled six days a week to perform dinner and late-night shows for its patrons.

At the same time that Genevieve and Teddy were beginning their engagement at the Iceland Restaurant, the Shipstads and Johnson Ice Follies was completing its two-week booking at Madison Square Garden. Founded in 1936 by Eddie and Roy Shipstad and their friend, Oscar Johnson, the Follies had been touring the country, performing in arenas in major cities, as well as at state fairs and other smaller venues. Madison Square Garden was the third stop in the Follies' eighteen-city tour that had begun in Los Angeles in September and would end in San Francisco in June.

Genevieve and Teddy were surprised as they came off the ice one night to find Eddie Shipstad and Oscar Johnson waiting to talk with them. The men introduced themselves and explained that they had been using their free time in New York to visit the various skating shows in search of new talent for the Follies. They had been impressed by their performance and said they thought the two would be a good addition to their show. They asked if Genevieve and Teddy would care to discuss the possibility further.

A NEW PARTNER. Promotional photos of Teddy and Genevieve most likely taken prior to their engagement at the Iceland Restaurant on Broadway in New York City late in 1946.

Both of the skaters were cautious but interested, and asked what role they would play in the show. Eddie Shipstad suggested that, if they joined the tour, they would skate in the line for several performances to get a feel for the production. While they did that, the production staff would develop an adagio routine for the two of them in the season's remaining shows. As opposed to performing for hundreds in restaurants and ballrooms, the thought of skating in front of thousands in large arenas excited the two of them. Trying not to appear overly eager, they said that they would be interested, but that they had an obligation to Carl Snyder and a commitment to fulfill at the restaurant. They needed some time to think about it. Oscar asked how much longer they were scheduled to perform at Iceland. When Genevieve replied that they were scheduled to perform through the first part of January, he said that waiting for them to join the Follies would not be an issue.

The Shipstad brothers and Johnson were staying at a local hotel, and Eddie gave them a slip of paper with their room and telephone number. He asked them to give his proposal their consideration and to call within the next three days with their decision. "Leave a message about how to reach you, and I'll call you back." Then, as if the question had just occurred to him, he asked, "Oh, by the way, how much are you being paid for your shows here?" Shipstad, an astute businessman who probably already knew the answer, smiled when Genevieve said they were being paid at the American Guild of Variety Artists' standard rate. "Well, we can pay you twice that. You know how to reach us, just let us know what you decide."

Genevieve and Teddy, their decision already all but made, watched the two men walk away through the crowded restaurant. Teddy adored and respected Genevieve. Since they had begun skating together, she had taken the lead role in their relationship. Genevieve was older than Teddy and had more professional experience. While he sometimes seemed infatuated with her, Genevieve kindly treated Teddy like a younger brother. He turned to her and asked hopefully, "We're going to do this, aren't we?"

Excited, she responded, "Yes, we'll call him before the first show tomorrow. But first we need to let Mr. Snyder know, and I want to talk to my sister's husband to make sure he thinks we're doing the right thing. I'll call both of them tomorrow morning."

Genevieve made the calls the next morning. Charles was concerned about receiving a call from her so early, but he quickly relaxed when she explained why she was calling. He thought they should pursue the opportunity. "Go where the money is," he said, but cautioned her to make sure that everything was clearly spelled out in the contract with the Follies.

She was nervous when she called Carl Snyder. He had been instrumental in her career success, and she was concerned he would see this as a betrayal of some sort. Snyder was understanding, however, and expressed his appreciation for Genevieve and Teddy being committed to completing their engagement at the restaurant. They chatted a bit longer, and then Snyder told her, "I'll see the two of you before you're done at Iceland. I have a feeling this won't be the last time our paths will cross, Genevieve. Let me know if there's anything I can do to help you."

Teddy was waiting when Genevieve arrived at the Iceland Restaurant the next afternoon. "Did you speak with them? What did they say?"

Genevieve understood Teddy's eagerness to know what her brother-in-law and Carl Snyder had said. She smiled. "Both of them agreed that we should go ahead. We need to make a telephone call. I think we're going to be joining Ice Follies."

Using the coin telephone that hung on the wall outside the

dressing rooms, Genevieve dialed the hotel's number and asked for the Shipstads' room. She expected to have to leave a message so she was surprised when Eddie Shipstad answered.

"Hello, this is Genevieve Norris," she said nervously.

"Of course, Genevieve. I'm glad to hear back from you so quickly," Shipstad responded. "I'm hoping that you're calling with good news for us?"

Teddy stood by and smiled as he heard his partner say, "Yes, we've thought about what you told us last night. We want to accept your offer to join Ice Follies."

"My brother and Oscar will be delighted to hear that." Shipstad sounded pleased. Then, in a businesslike tone, he continued. "So that everything is clearly understood, let me just go over what we talked about last night."

As he quickly reviewed what had been discussed the previous night, and, as he moved from one point to the next, Genevieve answered, "Yes, that's what we understood," "Yes, that's right," "Yes, Teddy is right here, he agrees with that also."

"When will the two you be available to join the show?" Eddie inquired.

"We were thinking we could come to Philadelphia in the middle of the month, if that's okay." Genevieve waited for his response.

"Just a second. Hold on, please." There was a brief, murmured conversation in the background on Shipstad's end of the line. She heard other male voices. When Shipstad returned, Genevieve imagined she could see him smiling as he said, "Philadelphia will be fine. It looks like Ice Follies has two new skaters; we're very pleased."

Joining the Show

The Arena, Philadelphia, Pennsylvania

January 15 was a Wednesday, and no family members were at Pennsylvania Station late that cold morning to see Genevieve and Teddy off. Traveling had become a regular occurrence for them, although joining Ice Follies would mean that they would travel even more and be away for extended periods of time. At eleven o'clock, they boarded a train destined for Chicago, and two hours later, they left it as they stepped off at Philadelphia's Thirtieth Street Station.

After checking in to the accommodations that had been arranged for them at the Penn-Sheraton Hotel, they took a taxi to the Arena, known years before as the Philadelphia Auditorium and Ice Palace, where the show's cast was preparing for that night's performance. As they entered through the performers' entrance, they were met with the smell of twenty-five years of beer, popcorn, and cigar smoke hanging from the rafters. Walking to the edge of the rink, both were quietly struck as they looked up and contemplated performing in front of an audience of 5,500. Neither realized that in Cleveland, at the tour's next stop, they would play to audiences almost twice that number.

Eddie Shipstad, a man who they learned was always hands-on with the show, had been expecting them. He walked them through the facility to familiarize them with it, introducing them to other cast members as he did. Genevieve was surprised when they encountered Jo-Ann Axtell. As Shipstad began to introduce them, Genevieve, recalling the For Victory Ice Revue where Carl Snyder had first approached her, explained that she and Jo-Ann had skated together almost five years prior. She still had that broad smile, and Genevieve thought to herself, "Does she ever not smile?" Jo-Ann asked if Genevieve had come to join the line. Eddie stepped in to explain that the two new skaters would skate in the line in Cleveland, and then perhaps as soon as the Memorial Stadium performances in Buffalo, they would be performing as a featured pair. Watching her old acquaintance's face, Genevieve thought she saw Jo-Ann's smile fade for just a moment. The rest of the afternoon was spent with the wardrobe staff, and then on the ice carefully observing the cast rehearse. As Shipstad suggested, they practiced with the cast each afternoon while watching each of the remaining Philadelphia shows from seats near the edge of the ice, intently studying each routine.

During the week of the Follies' Cleveland performances, Genevieve and Teddy, the Shipstads, and the show's choreographer and musical director consulted each day to design a production number for the two skaters. It would feature the daring moves that had attracted the Shipstads to the young skaters to begin with. Alone, under the spotlight, there would be no margin for error. To provide ample time for rehearsals, they decided to insert the number into the program just after the show's lavish opening, when the Follies reached the second of its Canadian destinations in Montreal during the second week of February.

By the time the show arrived in Buffalo the next week, Genevieve had replaced one of the five female skaters who had been supporting Harris Legg, a cast member from the Follies' inception and now one of the show's stars. Having recently returned from his military enlistment, Legg performed each night as "Modern Mercury," making daring leaps through flaming hoops.

The Shipstads had the show's printed program modified to call attention to the new pair joining the show, citing them as "the most promising adagio and 'ice-crobatic' team to appear on the figure skating horizon in a long time." As planned, Teddy and Genevieve's featured adagio performance was introduced as the Follies opened its stay in Montreal. Other touring ice shows, both large and small, also featured adagio acts. However, with Teddy's strength and Genevieve's ballet training and confidence in her partner, the duo's refinement and technical prowess took their craft to new heights. Audiences were left gasping during the pair's minutes on the ice and applauded thunderously as the two bowed.

The show moved from Montreal to Boston and then to Providence, Pittsburgh, and Minneapolis before breaking for a one month vacation. Genevieve was grateful for the opportunity to return home to her family, but as she and Teddy traveled from Minneapolis to Chicago and back to New York, they were already looking forward to the remainder of the season, and to the following year's tour.

After regrouping in Minneapolis, the Follies traveled west on its own private sixteen-car train. Despite the management's best paternal efforts, travel on the train could be raucous. Many of the young men and women of the cast were out of the reach of their parents for the first time, exploring their newfound freedom. Over meals in the dining cars, and in the six sleeping cars, relationships were established, some lasting only for a night. Certainly, Genevieve had her share of admirers within the troupe, but she chose to keep her private life and her life with Ice Follies separate, and she counseled Teddy to do the same. Even at their young ages—Genevieve was just twenty-two and her partner nineteen—both tended to keep company with the more senior members of the cast.

Watching the changing scenery, Genevieve realized that the train was retracing the same route that first took her west from New York to join the McGowan and Mack Ice Revue. It was hard to believe that it had been almost five years since she had spent all those hours on the train with the Rosie the Riveter girls as the war raged on. She smiled every time she saw a picture of Rosie the Riveter, having known the real faces behind the visage. She often wondered which of the women had returned home once victory had been declared and which had stayed in their new locations. Even more frequently, she thought of the lady she talked with on the train when she first left New York—the one who had assured Genevieve that she would one day be a star before sadly confiding that there'd been no word from her son who was in the army somewhere in Europe. Genevieve wondered if he had returned home.

Winterland

San Francisco, California

Once in Seattle, the Follies performed its show nightly with matinees on Saturdays for three weeks. It then moved on to Portland for its two-week engagement. Afterward, the cast traveled to San Francisco, which had become the summer home of Ice Follies, arriving there early in June. The Winterland Ballroom had hosted the show since its inception in 1936. In the empty arena each morning, the cast would rehearse the coming season's program and perform the current show in the evening before enthusiastic audiences.

Given the length of their stay in San Francisco, cast members were responsible for their own housing, and they dispersed over the area. Accommodations ranged from houses shared by numerous members of the line to luxury hotels in the case of the more significant, more highly paid performers. Genevieve shared a small apartment within walking distance of the arena with another girl from the show, and the two had an easy and convenient relationship, sometimes socializing together, sometimes not.

Winterland Ballroom was located at the corner of Post and Steiner Streets, and had been called the New Dreamland Auditorium when it first opened in 1928. A skating rink meant to be convertible to a venue for seated events, it managed to survive the Depression, emerging in the 1930s with its new name. The arena was as she remembered it from her visit to San Francisco in 1943, though the surrounding area had changed.

When she voiced this observation to Werner Groebli, one of the long-term cast members, the "Mr. Frick" of the Frick and Frack ice skating team, he explained to her that the neighborhood had been largely populated by members of San Francisco's Japanese community and had been known as Little Tokyo. The residents had been meticulous in the care of their homes, apartments, and businesses. He went on to tell her that in 1942, in the months after Pearl Harbor had been bombed, virtually every United States resident with Japanese heritage was forced to leave everything they had established behind. Selling what they could, often for pennies on the dollar, they were placed in government concentration camps. The majority of them were United States citizens, he added, and over one hundred thousand of those people came from the West Coast. When the war was over and the "inmates" of the camps were released, each was given twenty-five dollars and a train ticket back to the place they had been taken from. By then, however, most had nothing to return to. In his posthumously published autobiography, *Swiss Movements*, Groebli explained further:

> At the time, with war material plants desperate for workers, thousands of people migrated to San Francisco from the south and took over the area where the Japanese-Americans had been living ... the next time our show came

to San Francisco as that transition was taking place, we hardly recognized the area. The neat, clean and safe section had been transformed virtually overnight into one that was sloppy, dirty and exceedingly dangerous.

Though it could hold thousands of patrons around the perimeter of the ice rink and in the mezzanine above, Genevieve found Winterland to be an intimate venue, and she enjoyed both rehearsing and performing there. Each show, she and Teddy would enthusiastically perform their adagio routine with its many spins and lifts and throws before sold-out audiences. In rehearsals, they worked hard to perfect the Persian Festival, an elaborately choreographed and costumed feature designed specifically for the two of them and supported by a large cast. It would open the second half of each performance in the coming season.

Summer Romance

San Francisco, California

Summer in San Francisco offered opportunities for relaxation and sightseeing, and, for a young and attractive woman like Genevieve, for romantic relationships. There were cast members within the show who remained persistent, though Genevieve maintained her distance. There were admirers who would approach her after the show, and she would occasionally accept an invitation to dinner and to dance, if her roommate would come along.

She noticed a man who began to appear more and more often during rehearsals. He was impeccably groomed and well dressed, always wearing a white shirt and never wearing the same stylish suit or tie twice. He would stand by the partition that separated the seats from the ice and watch with apparent interest. It seemed to Genevieve that every time she looked in his direction, he was staring at her, though he showed no recognition when their eyes would make brief contact. Trying not to show particular interest, Genevieve asked several people if they knew who the man was. She was told that he was someone who had connections to Winterland and that he knew people with the show.

As she was leaving the arena after rehearsal one morning, the man drove up the ramp from the small underground parking area that she understood was reserved for special visitors. He was in a shining Alfa Romeo sports car, just imported from Italy, a burgundy convertible with cream-colored, leather upholstery and black-spoked, wire wheels, its top down to take advantage of the warm, sunny San Francisco weather. She wasn't sure if she should, but when he offered her a ride, Genevieve got in the car.

The man introduced himself as Dick Wales. Several years older than her, he seemed charming, and, over the weeks to follow, the first ride home turned to invitations to lunch, to dinner, and then drives to see the sights in and around the city. For the first time, Genevieve found herself involved in a more than casual relationship. She enjoyed his company and his spontaneous nature, and she admitted to herself that she enjoyed the envious glances of the other girls in the show when she would leave with him after rehearsal. She was flattered by his attraction to her and his desire to spend time alone with her.

Still, there was something a bit unsettling about his always insisting on choosing where they would go or what they would do when they were together.

"Can we go to the Palace Hotel?" she asked one evening.

"It's a stuffy, snobby place," he had replied dismissively. "Why would you want to go there?"

"I thought I had told you. I skated there when I was in San Francisco before. It would be fun to see it again. I thought it was beautiful."

"You did tell me that," he replied coolly. "That's in your past. I'll pick someplace better."

Similar suggestions or requests she made were repeatedly ignored by Dick, or he would reposition them as being his idea.

Although he would go on at length about his own business and what interested him, Dick paid little attention when Genevieve spoke about Teddy, the Follies, or of her family at home.

In September, when the Follies departed San Francisco to begin the 1948 season, Genevieve was sad when they parted but felt that somehow it was for the best.

The Show Heads East

Los Angeles, California

The debut performance of the Ice Follies of 1948 tour took place at the Pan-Pacific Auditorium in Los Angeles on September 18, 1947 and was broadcast via national radio. Pan-Pacific, a sprawling wooden structure, was the city's premiere venue for indoor performances, and the opening night of Ice Follies' annual tour was a highly anticipated event. With the show's program recalling "their routine of gravity-defying and breathless lifts and spins at mid-season a year ago," Genevieve and Teddy premiered Persian Market, to rave reviews.

While in Los Angeles, they were delighted not only to skate before the nightly sold-out audiences of six thousand, but were in awe of the numbers of celebrities who filled the rows of seats closest to the ice every night. As skaters came off the ice, they would report seeing George Montgomery, Ronald Reagan, Dinah Shore, Dorothy Lamour, Ceasar Romero, Peter Lawford, and William Powell. Teddy glowed when he met comedians Bud Abbott and Lou Costello backstage after the first night's show.

ICE FOLLIES. Genevieve nicknamed Teddy Roman "Strongman." Promotional photos of Teddy and Genevieve taken for their Persian Market adagio performance for Ice Follies 1948.

Genevieve celebrated with the rest of the cast after the successful opening night, but then went back to her room feeling more tired than usual. She was puzzled by her fatigue but did not mention it to anyone. She thought perhaps it was simply five years of performing almost nightly that was catching up with her. Trying to increase her stamina, she became increasingly guarded of her free time and put more focus on her diet. Though her fatigue made it challenging, she rehearsed and performed as she always had, putting all her effort into each night's show.

When the Follies ended its Los Angeles engagement, the days off and the rest they provided were welcomed. The show moved on via its private Sante Fe Railroad train across the southwest, and then north to Chicago, where they were booked from late October until the middle of the following month. Genevieve woke the first morning on the train feeling nauseous and puzzled over it. Over the past five years, she had spent endless days on trains, and their motion had never before made her queasy. She ate lightly and it passed, but the same feeling returned the next day and the next after they had reached Chicago.

Other than to change trains, Genevieve had never been to Chicago, and she did her best to do things that would take her mind off her early morning nausea and late-night fatigue. Together with friends from the show, she attended the Chicago Bears game against the Detroit Lions at Wrigley Field. The crowd was raucous, and in the sunlit afternoon, the air was cold as it blew from the north across Lake Michigan. As the sun warmed her face, she smiled as she thought about how excited her father and grandfather would be when she called home and told them about her outing.

A Concerned Call Home

Chicago, Illinois

For a while, Genevieve was distracted from her concerns. But they didn't go away; in fact, they became more troubling. Since she had started skating, she had not had regular periods. When she had mentioned this to her doctor two years prior—somewhat embarrassingly—she was told that it was not uncommon for women like her who exercised strenuously. Genevieve had paid little attention when she missed it in September. When her period failed to arrive in

October, however, Genevieve felt a sense of alarm. She had never missed two periods in a row, and this, along with her fatigue and the sickness she experienced every morning, made her believe she might be pregnant.

She was frightened, and even with more than one hundred skaters around her, she felt alone. How could she have allowed this to happen? She had never been in a serious relationship before and had only had teenage boyfriends. Dick had been so charming, so persuasive, and when she had expressed reluctance—she had never been with a man before—he had been so persistent. In the end, she had consented. She was so furious with herself that she never thought to be angry at him. All she had needed to do was say no.

Genevieve gathered herself, praying that this was a false alarm or some sort of odd coincidence. She said nothing to anyone, practicing and performing harder and more focused than ever; Teddy said it felt like she was attacking the ice. She bided her time until the Follies was preparing to leave Chicago to travel to New York City's Madison Square Garden for its Thanksgiving holiday engagement. All her family was in New York, and though she had been looking forward to this return home for months, Genevieve was now dreading the reunion. She needed to speak with her sister, Eleanore, eleven years older and a wife and a mother. Eleanore would know what to do. She could confide in her.

Eleanore, Charles, and their two young children were living with Leonard and Josephine and Aleksander and Wanda in the house opposite the high school in Flushing. It was a large, three-story house, with a broad front porch, a wide stairway, and numerous bedrooms. Now, however, accommodating four generations of the family, it offered little privacy. After her mother had handed her the telephone handset, Eleanore had to clench her jaw in order to keep from letting out a gasp when Genevieve, now suddenly crying, blurted, "Please, you can't say anything. I think I'm pregnant."

Eleanore turned to face the floral paper on the kitchen wall. She didn't want her mother to see the look of shock she was certain was on her face. With Josephine nearby, all she could say in response to her sister was, "Oh, really, that must have come as a surprise. We'll have to talk more about it when you get to New York."

"Can you find me a doctor?" Genevieve implored. "I can't go to anyone who knows Daddy and Mommy. I need to find out for sure."

"Well, you know Charles," Eleanore answered, now more composed and attempting to sound matter-of-fact. "He's in and out of the studio in Astoria. He knows lots of people through there."

"I have to know," whispered Genevieve. "Please. As soon as I get to New York."

"Well, you have a safe trip. Don't worry. Charles will look into that for you. Of course, I'll send Grandpa and Grandma your love. See you soon."

Taking a deep breath and hoping the color that she was sure had drained from her face had returned, Eleanore placed the handset back in the telephone's cradle. As she turned back to the kitchen, Josephine asked her, "What was that about? What does Gennie need?"

"Oh, some talk about making films of the skaters when they come to New York," Eleanore lied. "Gennie doesn't even know how anyone knew that Charles has connections. I told her I'd ask."

She had only been on the telephone for ten minutes, but the call had been exhausting for Genevieve. She had been forced to make small talk with her mother, who was alarmed at first that she was calling during the middle of the week, and then she had to tell Eleanore what was troubling her. As difficult as the call was, she had taken the first step. Having confided in Eleanore, her burden seemed lighter.

In bed that night, their children asleep, Eleanore told Charles about the phone call with Genevieve. "She thinks she *might* be pregnant?" he repeated in a hushed but alarmed voice. "Who's the guy?"

Eleanore, her eyes closed in the dark, said, "She didn't tell me who he was. She did tell me why she thinks she's pregnant. I don't think there's any question that she is."

"No one else knows?" Charles asked. "Is she okay?"

"She needs to know for sure. We need to find her a doctor. And she's sick thinking about how she'll tell Mommy and Daddy."

"There are people who deal with these things and keep them quiet, places you can go. There are a couple of people at the studio who will know. I'll talk to them tomorrow."

"I told her you would take care of it," Eleanore said as she moved close to him. "She knows that she can trust and count on you."

Lying in the darkened bedroom, staring for a long time at the ceiling, Charles asked again, "Are you sure you don't know who the guy is? I'd like to have a word with him."

CHAPTER ELEVEN
Difficult Decision

Ice Follies Return to New York

New York City

The Follies cast boarded their private train with its sleepers, coaches, diner, and freight cars around lunchtime on Monday, November 17. All the night before and into the morning, staff had packed and loaded the show's costumes and props. Ice Follies was scheduled to open two days later, on Wednesday evening, at Madison Square Garden in New York. The arena's ice, which was usually striped and marked for the New York Rangers, the building's resident hockey team, had already been replaced by a surface that was gleaming and white.

Genevieve sat alone, looking out the window, barely aware as the couplers pulled taut between the cars and the wheels began to turn. By the next morning, the train would cross Michigan and Ohio after leaving Illinois. It would then traverse Pennsylvania and New Jersey before finally arriving in Manhattan. Genevieve had traveled over the route often enough that she recognized certain landmarks and could anticipate stops at the major stations along the way. She was impatient to be back in New York.

When Teddy came and sat by her, she was too distracted to make conversation. He had been concerned about Genevieve for the past two months; she hadn't seemed like herself, but he knew she didn't want to discuss whatever was going on. He respected her privacy, so he sat there saying nothing, and as the train pushed on, the rocking of the coach lulled him to sleep. Genevieve smiled. She found his nearness comforting.

Genevieve and Teddy shared a table at dinner that evening with Werner Groebli and Hansruedi Mauch, the two Swiss skaters who performed as Frick and Frack, delighting audiences at every show with their slapstick routines. As silly as they often looked on the ice, Genevieve recognized what strong skating skills they needed to possess to do what they did. Groebli had a wonderful sense of humor, and Genevieve enjoyed talking with him. For a while, as he joked and teased, she was distracted from her other thoughts.

After dinner, Genevieve returned alone to her seat in the coach and listened to the engine's whistle as the train approached road crossings. She watched for lights in scattered houses and the occasional small town as the train passed them by. At ten o'clock, she went to her sleeper compartment. As frustrated as she had recently been with the fatigue that would wash over her every evening, this was a time when she welcomed it. Tonight she wanted to sleep, to blot the concerns from her mind. She dreaded what a doctor might tell her, but she needed an answer.

The train arrived at the West Side Yards adjacent to Pennsylvania Station in Manhattan early on Tuesday morning. As the cast disembarked and went to their hotel, the crates containing the costumes and props so carefully loaded in Chicago the day before were removed and taken by truck up Tenth Avenue and then across West Fiftieth Street to Madison Square Garden. The cast's hotel was on Eighth Avenue, near Times Square.

Genevieve went to her room to wash her face and unpack her suitcase before returning to the restaurant connected to the hotel's lobby. She tried to separate the aroma of brewed coffee from the smell of frying bacon. The aroma of the coffee was comforting; it reminded her of summer, of California, and of her job filling bags with coffee for Maxwell House. Life was so much less complicated then. The smell and the sizzle of bacon on heavy china plates being delivered to nearby tables made her queasy. She ordered tea and toast, and after she ate, she returned to her room to bathe.

As the elevator operator pulled the door aside to open it, Genevieve stepped out of the car and found Charles waiting. The two walked toward one another, and Genevieve bit her lip to keep from crying, feeling safe and protected as he wrapped his arms around her. He stepped back, hands on her shoulders, and looked at her. "It's going to be okay," he said calmly. "Whatever it is, we'll take care of it. Eleanore and I will take care of you." Genevieve's eyes filled with tears as she pressed her face to his chest. Charles handed her his white handkerchief, freshly laundered, starched, and ironed. Its smell reminded her of things taken in off the clothesline in her parents' backyard. She dried her eyes and breathed in the familiar scent of laundry soap and fresh air.

The hotel's doorman offered to hail them a taxi, but Genevieve told Charles that she would rather walk. The sun had just risen above the tall buildings to the east, and the swirling wind blowing off the Hudson River swept across the city's crosstown streets, pushing them along to their destination. With the collar of his overcoat turned up and holding onto his homburg to make sure it didn't blow off his head, Charles explained to Genevieve that they were going to meet with a doctor who ran a private hospital. In addition to excellent care, he had been told that it ensured a high degree of discretion. The sound of the traffic, the cars, and the yellow-painted taxis coming toward them almost drowned out her words as Genevieve said, "I hope I won't need it." Then, after a brief pause, "But I'm afraid I—" and said nothing more.

They turned off Lexington Avenue and stood at the corner building's entrance on East Fifty-Fifth Street. Barely noticeable beside the building's glass and wrought iron double doors, was a small, brightly polished brass plaque that read, Lexington Hospital. Genevieve was surprised. She stepped back to the curb and looked up. The first two floors of the façade were covered in narrow horizontal bands of light stone. Above them were four additional stories, sheathed in an elaborate weave of dark brick with ornate stone trim around the windows. She would learn that a rooftop level, which she couldn't see from the street, housed additional rooms and a solarium. An unaware passerby would not realize that the building housed a hospital.

Charles glanced at his watch then turned to Genevieve. "We should go in. He'll be waiting for us." Climbing the two steps from the sidewalk to the building's entrance, Charles held one of the heavy doors open for Genevieve and followed her into the lobby. A woman, older than Charles but not as old as her parents, was seated at a large desk. Conservatively dressed in a dark, fitted suit, her blonde, almost white, hair was pulled back and twisted into a bun. Her pale complexion accentuated piercing blue eyes. Behind her, on a credenza that matched her desk, was a large floral arrangement. It filled the reception area with an aroma that Genevieve found heavy and overpowering.

Greeting them with a slight smile, the woman looked inquiringly to Charles, then to Genevieve, and then back to Charles. Genevieve felt self-conscious, as if the woman's eyes had looked through her. It was the same look that her mother had always given her when she thought that Genevieve might be trying to pull something over on her. It made her feel like she was shrinking. She heard Charles calmly say, "I'm Charles Hans, and this is my sister-in-law, Mrs. Knorowski. We're here for an appointment with Dr. Soresi. He's expecting us."

Standing, the woman once again looked from Charles and then to Genevieve before returning her attention to Charles. "Yes, surely, the doctor is expecting you." Her words were clipped and businesslike, and Genevieve thought she might have a trace of a German accent.

The woman walked to the front doors and abruptly twisted a polished brass nob to lock them. In the marble entranceway, the sound was unexpected and sudden, like a gunshot, and it made Genevieve flinch. "We are not expecting any visitors," the woman said by way of explanation. "The hospital is very concerned for our patients' privacy." With a touch of a button, the doors of a small elevator opened, and she motioned for them to enter ahead of her.

Dr. Soresi's office was large. His desk was positioned in front of three windows that overlooked Lexington Avenue. The sound of traffic wafted up from below. He came from behind his desk to greet them as the woman wordlessly left the room, closing his office door behind her. Genevieve was surprised. She had expected someone younger, maybe her father's age. And she had pictured someone in a white coat with a stethoscope around his neck. But the man before them was in his sixties, she was sure. His gray hair was carefully combed back, and his complexion was ruddy, like someone who spent great amounts of time outdoors. He was shorter than Charles, but he looked physically powerful. Looking more like a business executive than a doctor, he was wearing a carefully tailored suit of chalk-striped gray wool. Genevieve was sure it must be expensive.

"Mr. Hans, Mrs. Knorowski," he said, extending a hand to Charles and smiling at Genevieve. His smile was understanding and seemed to acknowledge the secret that had brought them to his office. "I am Angelo Soresi. It is my pleasure to meet you. Please, sit down so we can discuss what brings you here today." His voice was mellow, his tone suggesting a concern for her situation. His speech was formal and tinged sufficiently to suggest his arrival from Italy years before.

There was a very large table at one end of the room, the top highly polished and the legs ornately carved, but he guided them instead in the opposite direction. A couch upholstered in deep brown, tufted leather was against the wall with a coffee table in front of it. Matching club chairs were positioned at the end of each table. He gestured toward the couch, and Charles and Genevieve sat. Dr. Soresi took one of the chairs.

"Mrs. Knorowski," the doctor began, "I understand you have been experiencing some physical issues that concern you. How long has this been going on? And please," he said, looking into her eyes, "be as factual as you can. We at the hospital are not here to judge you. We're here to help."

Genevieve knew these questions would arise, and she had tried to prepare. The answers, especially in front of Charles, came with difficulty. She took a deep breath, and in a whisper, she said, "In August. I was with a man in August. Only once. One time." She had been looking down at her hands folded in her lap, and as she looked up, she noticed the scar on the doctor's forehead between his eyes. She tried not to stare at it.

Dr. Soresi, softly, in a voice only a bit louder than Genevieve's, asked, "What did you notice afterward? When did you notice?"

"I just got so tired," she said. "So tired at night I could barely stay awake."

"When did that begin?" Soresi made notes on a small lined pad.

Genevieve swallowed, thought for a moment, and said, "It was the middle of September. I would get so tired; it's still that way." Then, thinking a moment and adding before she was asked, "I didn't get my period in September, but that wasn't unusual. But then not in October either, and now it's due again and nothing. Nothing," she repeated as she held her eyes closed.

"I know this is very difficult for you," Soresi said reassuringly. "But we will not jump to any conclusions. I have been told that you are quite a physically active woman, Mrs. Knorowski. That sometimes brings its own complications. I am a surgeon. We will have one of our doctors who specializes in these issues examine you, and we will do some blood tests. Then we will know how to proceed. In the meantime, your brother-in-law and I will talk."

Dr. Soresi went to his desk, picked up the telephone and dialed the operator. Genevieve listened to the purring sound of the rotary dial, and then, from where she and Charles were sitting, she could hear the phone ring and then the indistinguishable voice of a woman. "Thank you, yes. Mrs. Knorowski is ready now. Is this a good time?" There was a momentary pause and then a respectful, "Thank you," as he returned the phone to its cradle.

Genevieve had never minded going to the doctor when she was a girl, but as her body changed, so had the nature of the exams, and she dreaded them. Perhaps it was because she had learned to perform in front of crowds, perhaps it was how dire her situation presently seemed, but she had steeled herself for this examination. She knew it was necessary. Only a few moments later, a nurse in all white knocked and opened the door to Dr. Soresi's office. Charles squeezed Genevieve's hand as she stood to leave. Dr. Soresi calmly said, "We will be waiting for you here. You will not be gone long, Mrs. Knorowski."

The nurse accompanied Genevieve to the elevator, and the two took it to one of the upper floors. "You're nervous," the nurse observed. "It's natural, but you'll be back down there soon. The exam won't take long, and I'll be in the room with you all the time."

Genevieve felt only mildly comforted by this reassurance. "Thank—" she started in a whisper again, but this time she stopped herself, cleared her throat, and said again in her normal voice, "Thank you." Pausing for a moment, trying to find the courage to smile, she admitted, "I'm very scared."

The nurse reached out gently and touched Genevieve's arm for just a moment. "Being scared is natural, but we're here to watch over you."

When the nurse returned Genevieve to Dr. Soresi's office, he and Charles were sitting as they had been when she left them forty-five minutes before. The doctor immediately rose to his feet and said, "I trust you have been treated well, Mrs. Knorowski?"

"Yes, thank you. Everyone has been very kind to me," Genevieve responded, smiling wanly. It had been easier than she had anticipated, but she was exhausted; she knew she must appear pale. Without being directed, Genevieve again took her seat on the couch next to Charles.

"Your brother-in-law and I have been talking, Mrs. Knorowski. First things first: we will know by the end of the day tomorrow if your concerns are founded."

"So quickly?" Genevieve interrupted. "I expected that it would take longer." She was relieved at this bit of good news, though she feared what she might learn.

Dr. Soresi smiled. "Science moves on, Mrs. Knorowski. These days, we can determine your situation in twenty-four hours. And save the lives of some rabbits along the way." He chuckled as Genevieve did her best to smile in response.

Charles reached out and took Genevieve's hand. "Dr. Soresi has told me that no matter—" he stopped to choose his words, "no matter what we find out, he and his staff can handle it." Pausing again, needing to communicate something he didn't want to say, he continued, "They can address it however you choose."

Dr. Soresi interjected, "You have time to make decisions, Mrs. Knorowski. Perhaps you know already exactly what you want to do, but do not be afraid to take some time. Mr. Hans has my business card. You or he can call me here tomorrow at five o'clock. I will be expecting your call, and I will let you know what your blood test has told us. If you have no further questions, we will talk then." Without waiting for questions, Dr. Soresi stood up, signaling an end to their meeting.

Other than the woman at the desk, the lobby was empty as they stepped off the elevator. The air was as heavy with the smell of the flowers as it had been when she and Charles had arrived. Genevieve couldn't wait to get back outside to breathe fresh air. The woman stood, her eyes once again moving from Charles, to Genevieve, and then back to Charles. She smiled the same slight, piercing smile that she had when they arrived and followed them across the lobby to the door. "Mr. Hans, Mrs. Knorowski, good day," she said, nodding curtly as she twisted the lock to allow them out. The metallic clacking sound of the lock being closed behind them was drowned out by the din of midday traffic.

St. Patrick's Cathedral

Fifth Avenue, New York City

As he had earlier, Charles offered Genevieve a taxi back to her hotel, but she refused, saying she wanted to walk, that she needed the fresh air. The sun was at its height, and though the air was cold, the streets were now flooded with light. They walked across East Fifty-Fifth Street, and then when they reached Madison Avenue they turned downtown. Lost in thought, Genevieve was quiet as Charles walked beside her. Waiting for the traffic light where East Fifty-First Street crossed Madison Avenue, Genevieve looked to her right, and as soon as they were across the street she began to walk toward Fifth Avenue.

St. Patrick's Cathedral loomed over them. Charles waited as Genevieve stopped at the foot of the stairway leading up to the cathedral's north entrance. Anticipating her thoughts, he asked, "Do you want to go in?" Genevieve smiled gratefully, and without saying anything, they climbed the eight granite steps to the walkway around the building. Four more steps took them to the heavy wooden double doors bordered by richly sculpted brass panels.

St. Patrick's was cavernous, with space for three thousand worshipers in pews facing the towering marble main altar. Five smaller chapels were located on each side of the cathedral. Genevieve walked in, pausing a moment to let her eyes adjust to the light, and then stood before the main altar. She looked upward before genuflecting and making the sign of the cross. Charles did the same, following several steps behind as his sister-in-law slowly walked and then stopped before the altar to the right of the sanctuary. Charles was aware of the soft hum of conversations between tourists and the sound of visitors' footsteps on the cathedral's marble floors. He noted that Genevieve, though she was wearing heels, moved silently.

A bank of candles was situated to the right of where they had stopped. Genevieve turned to Charles and spoke for the first time since they had agreed to walk back to the hotel. "Do you have ten cents?" she asked. Pushing his overcoat back, Charles reached into his left pants pocket and took out some change. He had dimes, but instead pressed a quarter into her hand. He walked to the first row of nearby pews and sat, watching Genevieve deposit the coin in the offering box, light a candle, and then kneel to pray.

As they left the cathedral, walking down the main aisle with its many rows of pews on either side, it was as if a cloud had been lifted from Genevieve. She walked beside Charles and pointed out the various altars of the side chapels, the stained glass windows that had been imported from all over the world, and the intricately detailed rose window that let in light over the cathedral's massive entrance. She told him how her art class at Washington Irving High School had come here for a tour. Charles and Genevieve exited St. Patrick's, stopping briefly on the steps to look across Fifth Avenue. It was jammed with cars and taxis, and the exhaust fumes of double-decker busses tainted the city's air. In front of one of the buildings of the Rockefeller Center complex was a statue of Atlas holding the world on his shoulders. Genevieve smiled wryly and thought to herself, "I understand."

They crossed the avenue, and turned to walk down Rockefeller Center's crowded promenade toward the skating rink. Opposite where they stood, the now world-famous Christmas tree had been erected, although its decorations had not yet been completed. It would not be until the first days of December that the tree would be illuminated. It had so quickly become a tradition. Workers building Rockefeller Center in 1931, during the height of the Depression, had erected the first, which was twenty feet tall. They decorated it with homemade garlands and with shiny tin cans hung from its boughs. The tree lighting celebration was made official in 1933, and the tree placed there each subsequent year was taller and its decorations more ornate than the one the year before. Genevieve's parents had brought her here with Lucille for the annual event when they were younger, and it seemed that all of New York City turned out. In 1944 and 1945, due to wartime restrictions, the trees were erected and decorated, but their lights were left dark. Genevieve wished that she could be here for this year's lighting.

As she and Charles leaned on the granite wall overlooking the skating rink, Genevieve recalled how she had skated by the statue of Prometheus five years before. Looking at the restaurants at either end of the rink, with their floor-to-ceiling windows looking out on the ice, Genevieve wistfully smiled. Charles noticed and asked what she was thinking. She responded in a soft voice, her eyes returning to the Prometheus statue, "This is where I was sure I could become a professional," she said. "I was so sure of everything then. I'm not sure of anything right now."

Genevieve napped once she was back at the hotel, and then Charles returned at five o'clock, driving Leonard's Buick, to take her to her parent's home in Flushing. Months before, Josephine had decided there would be a special dinner to celebrate her daughter being back in New York. Genevieve understood that her performance at dinner would have to be as good as her performance on the ice the next night, since she had arranged for her family to have front-row seats for Ice Follies' opening night at Madison Square Garden. She hated that she needed to hide anything from her parents, but until she knew something concrete, she had no choice. Even then she wasn't sure what she would choose to do if what she feared was true. It was already dark as Charles navigated through traffic, the streets illuminated by traffic lights and storefront neon signs. Genevieve looked out the car's passenger side window and saw that not much had changed since she had last made this trip.

When they arrived, her family was waiting. Leonard and Josephine eagerly hugged her as her grandparents waited for their turn. Eleanore, her infant son in her arms and six-year-old daughter at her side, embraced her. Eleanore was aware, understanding, and accepting, and Genevieve was comforted as she felt her sister's arms around her. Lucille and Ed were there. Genevieve had been the maid of honor at their wedding two years before. Everyone had a seemingly never ending stream of questions for her about where she had traveled, how long she would be in New York, what her next destination was, how she enjoyed skating with her partner, and what was it like to be a star.

THE GIFT BEST GIVEN

For a while, the flood of questions distracted her, though knowing what she was withholding from them was never out of her mind. Each answer brought more questions, and the evening was filled with animated conversation and the festive meal that Josephine, Wanda, and Eleanore had spent the afternoon preparing. Genevieve was exhausted by the end of the evening, but in these familiar surroundings, her weariness was welcomed, and it enveloped her like a goose down comforter—comfortable, weighty, and safe. She was disappointed when the time came to leave. Still, it was a relief to end her pretending.

Eleanore slid into the Buick's front seat next to Charles, and Genevieve sat beside her, finding comfort in their closeness as they pulled out of the driveway to return to Manhattan. They commented briefly that, even on a work night, lines were forming in front of the RKO Keith's. The brightly lit marquee advertised *Gentleman's Agreement,* starring Gregory Peck and Dorothy McGuire, which had premiered only the week prior. With reviewers across the country suggesting that it would win the Oscar for the year's best movie, the public was thronging to see it. There was a brief pause in their conversation, and then Eleanore said, "Tell me about your visit with the doctor."

Genevieve took a moment to consider her answer. Eleanore had been the first to know that she was concerned that she was pregnant and had made the arrangements for her to see a doctor without anyone but Charles knowing. She deserved a complete answer, but Genevieve knew that Eleanore was someone who wanted facts; all the details could come later. "The doctor we met with seemed to be in charge of things, and he sent me to be examined by another doctor who deals with women's issues."

Genevieve paused briefly, but before she could continue, Eleanore asked impatiently, "What did he say, Gennie? What does he think it is?"

Genevieve's audible sigh filled the sedan as Charles continued to steer down Northern Boulevard toward the city. "He said I could have anemia. That could make me tired and even have caused me to miss my periods." Genevieve blushed in the dark of the car having this conversation with Charles so close by. Knowing that Eleanore was about to probe for more, she continued, "But he's pretty sure that's not it. He's pretty sure I'm pregnant."

In the dark, Eleanore took Genevieve's hand in hers. "When will he be able to tell you?" Eleanore had been frustrated all night, wanting the details that Genevieve and Charles already possessed, although she knew these things could not be discussed at home where they could be overheard.

"I'm supposed to call Doctor Soresi tomorrow at five o'clock. He's the one in charge of the hospital. They'll know then."

Charles, realizing his wife had turned to him as if to ask for more information, added "The hospital seems to be a good place—a discrete place. It's very small and very private, and Dr. Soresi said if Gennie's pregnant..." He had trouble completing his thought. "They can help her in whatever way she chooses."

"God," Eleanore whispered. "Are you okay, Gennie? You know we'll take care of you no matter what, don't you?"

"I do know, and I'm okay. You won't say anything to Mommy or Daddy?"

"They don't need to know anything right now," Eleanore responded. "They might react better than we expect, but it's probably best they don't know until you're certain and you decide they should know."

Charles added, "If you don't want them to, they don't have to know. Ever."

"I can't believe I've done this," Genevieve blurted out. "To you, to them ... I'm so angry with myself for letting this happen."

There was a silence as the car turned on to the bridge that spanned the East River. "Do you want to tell us about him?" Eleanor eventually asked. "Should he be part of this discussion?"

Genevieve's response was immediate and emphatic. "No. It was a mistake. My mistake. He was a mistake. That's why I'm angry at myself. He's not someone I would turn to. I don't think he would even take responsibility. So no, he's not important. He's not important at all."

Charles pulled the car up to the curb in front of the hotel and asked if Genevieve would call the doctor the next afternoon or if she would like him to. Genevieve said that she would make the call. She took a deep breath, knowing that her sister and her brother-in-law would soon be pulling away and that she would be alone again. As she exited the car, she said, "I'll see all of you at Madison Square Garden tomorrow night. I'm sure you'll be able to tell what the news is."

Genevieve's family arrived at Madison Square Garden the next evening, and their tickets for seats in the first row at the center of the ice surface awaited them at the Will Call window. The show began promptly at 7:30 p.m. When Genevieve and Teddy emerged from the Ninth Avenue end of the arena, both were dressed in elaborate costumes that shone under the lights. They glided confidently to the center of the ice, turned and paused, facing her family who watched eagerly. Only someone looking for some signal, some indication, would have noticed Genevieve's smile momentarily vanish, her eyes close, and the very slight movement of her head side to side in a sign of resignation. As quickly as Genevieve had delivered her unspoken message to Eleanore and Charles, it was as if she suddenly ignited, radiating a presence that filled the arena as she and Teddy launched into their routine, dazzling the capacity audience with their performance.

As the crowd applauded each daring spin and lift, Eleanore leaned to Charles. "She's going to be all right, isn't she? This will turn out okay?"

Their performance completed, Genevieve stood in the center of the ice, again looking toward them, silently affirming her news. Charles felt a sense of responsibility for Genevieve being in the situation that she was. Though he wasn't sure at all how this would turn out, he whispered confidently to Eleanore, "Gennie's going to be fine. Everything will be fine. I promise."

A Solution Offered – A Decision Made

The Office of Dr. Angelo Soresi

On Monday of Thanksgiving week, Genevieve returned to the hospital to meet with Dr. Soresi, this time accompanied by both Charles and Eleanore. Josephine had agreed to watch their children, believing that Eleanore and Charles were having lunch with Genevieve. It had been confirmed that she was pregnant, and now there were more questions to be answered and important decisions to be made. Genevieve wanted as much support as she could gather.

Dr. Soresi, wearing dark-blue pleated trousers, a wing-collared white shirt, and a burgundy tie, was sitting at the coffee table as they entered. The double-breasted jacket of his suit was draped over the back of his desk chair. Charles introduced his wife, and the doctor directed Eleanore and Genevieve to the couch as Charles took one of the armchairs. In a calm voice, Soresi stated, "You are now approximately three months pregnant, Mrs. Knorowski. You are strong and healthy, and your pregnancy appears to be quite normal. If you take good care of yourself, there is no reason you should not have a healthy child. We can help you with all of this."

Genevieve asked in a quiet voice, "How much longer can I continue to skate, to perform?"

The doctor smiled. "I took my wife to the Ice Follies this past Saturday evening, Mrs. Knorowski. We had the pleasure of seeing you perform. You do some rather daring things on the ice." Then, looking directly into Genevieve's eyes, he cautioned, "But let me put it this way. The things you do, if you make no mistakes, will do no harm to you. They will not do any harm to your baby either. Should you do something, make some mistake that might injure you, you risk injury to your baby as well. You are both one."

"You are both one." Genevieve considered the doctor's words, turning them over in her mind. She thought for a moment as she considered the risks. She was a confident skater who seldom made the kind of mistakes the doctor was talking about, but they did occur on occasion. "When will I begin to show? When will people be able to see I'm pregnant?"

"You are a very petite woman," Soresi said. "You will begin to show earlier than some women, and I caution you to not restrict eating hoping to delay looking pregnant. A healthy child needs a mother who is well nourished." Genevieve, saying nothing, continued to look at the doctor. He smiled. "You want specifics. Let us say by the end of January."

As he spoke, Genevieve thought about Ice Follies' schedule. Their next stop was in New Haven and then Hershey before the short Christmas break. Philadelphia would follow in the first half of January, and then Cleveland. "So quickly," Genevieve said to Eleanore. "They won't let me skate if I'm pregnant. I can't let anyone know in any case."

Charles stood and walked to look out one of the windows over Lexington Avenue as Dr. Soresi spoke again. "If you need a place to stay until you give birth, we can accommodate you as early as you like. Our arrangements are very safe, quite comfortable, and extremely private. As early as you like," he repeated, "and for as long as you require."

"Mommy and Daddy can't know," Genevieve said. Her eyes were closed, and then she opened them as she turned to Eleanore. "They would be sick and angry and hurt. I can't do that to them. God, imagine what Grandpa and Grandma would think." Eleanore said nothing, but she placed her hand on her sister's.

The doctor rose and walked toward his desk. Genevieve's and Eleanore's eyes were on him as he paused, turned, and took a deep breath. "Miss Norr—I'm sorry—Mrs. Knorowski. I am neither soliciting nor recommending, but I feel a responsibility to inform in cases like this. You find yourself in difficult circumstances. You are young, and you have a successful career. It is early enough that the option exists to safely terminate your pregnancy. Barring any unusual circumstances, you would be away from your skating for only a matter of days."

Genevieve looked at Dr. Soresi without responding and then looked to Charles, who was still standing at the window, his back to her. His jaw appeared to be clenched, and she heard him exhale heavily. She turned to her older sister, who was now staring at an oil painting hanging on the wall at the end of the couch. The office was silent, and it seemed that even the traffic on the street below had gone quiet. Genevieve turned back to the doctor. "That sounds like a very convenient option," she said, her voice barely more than a whisper. Charles turned back from the window, and she sensed that Eleanore was no longer looking at the painting but was again looking at her. "But none of this is convenient, Dr. Soresi. There are no convenient answers," she said, as she looked from her sister to her brother-in-law before again addressing the doctor. "Thank you for informing me. I'm responsible for where I find myself, and I'll see it through. Terminating," she paused, "an abortion," she swallowed as she forced herself to say the word out loud, "is not a consideration."

As Genevieve stepped off the elevator into the lobby with Eleanore and Charles, the woman at the desk stood to escort them to the front door. For the first time, Genevieve saw what she thought was a glimmer of warmth in the woman's smile. The air in the foyer seemed to have lightened since they had arrived. On the credenza, a large, wilting, floral arrangement had been replaced by a delicate arrangement of budding pink roses, deep green ferns, and baby's breath. The woman, as she unlocked the door, nodded politely to Eleanore and to Charles before turning to Genevieve and said, "I will look forward to seeing you again, Mrs. Knorowski." It was the way her mother's eyes, in a moment's time, could go from piercing and inquiring to understanding and sympathetic. Unlike the first time she had encountered the woman, Genevieve didn't feel she was being judged. And, this time, as the door closed behind them, there was no sharp clack of the lock. Instead, the sound was safe and reassuring, the sound of pieces finally fitting together.

Genevieve was the first to speak as the three stood on the sidewalk outside the hospital's doors. Having made one decision, even if it was a decision about what she would not do, had made her feel better. "I'm starved. Can we get something to eat? There's so much I have to figure out."

"Take us to lunch, Charles," Eleanore smiled. "My little sister is eating for two these days. Let's see if we can help her sort all this out."

Charles nodded in response, ushering them in the direction of Third Avenue, a block to the east, where they entered P. J. Clarke's, a saloon that first opened in 1884, according to a sign inside the door, and which was a New York landmark by 1947. The establishment was filled with the lunchtime sounds of clanking dishes, boisterous patrons at the bar calling to the bartender for another drink, and the hum of hushed conversations as business deals were negotiated in the dining room over plates of shepherd's pie, steak, and broiled fish. As they were guided to a table in the back of the saloon, Genevieve glanced from side to side, looking at what everyone was eating. She had not eaten since morning, and this was the time of day when her appetite peaked.

Craning her neck to see the table beside theirs, Genevieve, with a smile, asked, "Will you buy me a steak, Charles?"

"A steak?" Charles responded in surprise. "Really?"

"All right then, a hamburger. Everything looks so good. It even smells good. I haven't said that much lately."

They placed their order, and as they waited for their meal, the three of them talked. Eleanore and Charles were surprised by Genevieve's deliberation and focus as she spoke in rapid-fire bursts about how much longer she would perform, who she needed to talk with, and what she would tell them. There would be time to decide what to do next once she stopped skating. There was both regret and conviction in her voice when she announced that her mother and father could never know. She would somehow have to lead them to believe that her career would keep her away from home until after she had given birth.

Eleanore and Charles would have to help with that, and Genevieve enlisted them in her deception. Looking to one another as they considered the implications of keeping and facilitating such a secret, they then turned back and nodded in silent agreement. As rapidly as she had been speaking, Genevieve abruptly stopped. "I'm going to have a baby," she said in a tone that suggested it was the first time she had confronted that fact. As if hoping that they would have the answer, she continued to look across the table to her sister and her brother-in-law. "What am I going to do with a baby?"

CHAPTER TWELVE
An Unexpected Discovery

Isabel
Churton Grove, Hillsborough, North Carolina

April 27, 2017

By the time we traveled to Atlanta to meet Dan and Tobey, I had confirmed that Genevieve, my birth mother, was no longer alive. But, as we drove, I hoped that the "auction box" that they would bring to the hotel the next day would harbor clues that might provide me with the ability to better see Genevieve as she was in life.

That Saturday morning, as the four of us sifted through the pieces of Genevieve's memorabilia, what most captured my attention was the series of professional publicity photographs of other skaters, each inscribed to Genevieve. Among them, "to my beloved partner," "one of the nicest girls in the show," "to Miss Personality Plus," and still another simply signed "Dottie O'Brien, Big Blonde." My birth mother was no longer alive, but I wondered if one of these people might be. Certainly, I could paint my own picture and create my own story of her life as I imagined it to have been. I already had begun to do so, but someone who had known her could confirm or alter or add to my script and make that picture more real.

After we had taken home all the items that Dan and Tobey had brought, one picture, one name at a time, I tried to determine if any of these women who were so young and vibrant and beautiful in the 1940s were still alive. I had immediately dismissed the photograph of Teddy Roman, the only male in the group, who had offered Genevieve, his "beloved partner," all his love. Only nineteen when they performed together in Ice Follies, I already knew that he had died fifteen years before.

One by one, I worked through the photographs of the women: Dottie O'Brien, the "Big Blonde," had died a year earlier; Ginnie Walters, Jeannie McKellen, a Mary without a last name, each either untraceable or deceased. And there was a picture of Freda Consigli. I encountered a clerk in the grocery store recently whose name tag said Consigli, and when I told her I was writing a book and that I knew of another Consigli who I planned to include in it, her stare was blank and uninterested. She might as well have said, "Whatever," as she handed me my $2.71 change and thanked me for shopping at Food Lion. Sadly, in the end, I found that Freda Mae Consigli, a resident of San Rafael, California, wife of William Kothgassner, was also no longer alive.

Finally, I got to Isabel Smith, four of whose pictures, one calling Genevieve "a swell roommate" and signed "Izzie." Who would have known my birth mother better than a roommate? As I did with the others, I checked the Ancestry database, but found nothing. I googled. After all, Google is there to provide inquisitive minds with answers, isn't it? An obituary appeared, but not an obituary for Isabel. It was an obituary for Marvin A. Holt of Plymouth, Minnesota, an attorney who had crossed the English Channel as a captain in the Normandy Invasion in 1944, worked in the Judge Advocates Office in Naples, Italy after the war, and then returned to active duty during the Korean Conflict in 1951. He had passed away in 2007 at the age of ninety-four, leaving behind two sons, five grandchildren, and his wife of fifty-seven years, Isabel, a skater with Shipstads and Johnson Ice Follies.

I searched unsuccessfully to find contact information for Isabel. Then, searching for one of the two sons, I found an address close to where his father and his mother had lived. I labored over an awkward,

"Hello, you don't know me but our mothers were friends in 1947, and my mother is no longer alive, but I was hoping yours is so I can talk with her, so please give me a call" letter. This communication took a bit of work to make it seem like something other than an inquiry from a deranged man or a scam artist, and I included copies of a couple of his mother's photographs and one of Genevieve to add to the authenticity of my claim. I sent it off and waited with the most guarded of expectations.

Looking back through my notes, I saw it was nine days after I mailed my letter that I received a call from Isabel's son. His voice was animated and enthusiastic, and he seemed delighted to have heard from me. Yes, his mom was alive and in good physical health. He had shown his mother the pictures, and she recalled them; she would be delighted to talk with me. "Just one thing," he cautioned. "Mom is in a memory care facility." He must have read the disappointment in my momentary silence and offered, "The good news is that she may not be able to remember what she had for breakfast this morning, but she can tell you everything that happened in 1947. She's got all her picture albums from those days in her room." Isabel's son—Brad—provided me with directions on how to reach his mother and encouraged me to call, wishing me well. "Call the main number and ask for Memory Care. Tell the nurse that you're calling for Isabel Holt, and they'll put her on the phone. She's looking forward to hearing from you."

I tried to prepare as best I could for the call I would make a couple of days later, knowing that, "Tell me about my mother," might be too vague a request to draw the kind of information I was hoping to find. Yet, it was that—or something like it—that I asked Isabel once we spoke. As her son had promised, she did seem happy to be speaking with me. She was bright and alert as I told her my story, and her voice was strong. I stopped to explain that I didn't want to burden her with too many questions, and that I knew to ask someone who was ninety-two to recall events that happened seventy years prior was unfair. There was a momentary pause. "I'm not ninety-two," Isabel said, sounding a bit offended. "I'm eighty-eight. As a matter of fact, I'm eighty-five." I calculated quickly. If she truly was eighty-five as she said, then she would have been fifteen when she was skating with Ice Follies. I realized that the vanity of one who had been in the spotlight was at play here. I smiled and thought it best not to question further.

We talked at length, and Isabel asked questions of me as she responded to my queries. Yes, she remembered Genevieve very well. They had kept in touch intermittently after my mother left Ice Follies. Isabel recalled her as "very quiet, very sweet, well-spoken; she got along with everybody." Whenever she could, she would spend time with Genevieve because of those qualities, whether stationing herself beside her in front of the dressing room mirror or going on dates together. She reminisced about being two young attractive women living on a shoestring. "Oh, we laughed and we danced. What we really wanted from our dates was a good dinner!"

Isabel rued the tight control the Shipstad brothers and Oscar Johnson, the show's owners, kept over the skaters when they were not practicing or performing. "I loved to have a good time," she said, adding that she understood management's concerns. The cast was comprised largely of wholesome, well-scrubbed young people, most of whom had never been away from home before, and promises were made to concerned parents that their sons and daughters would be looked after. She nonchalantly mentioned though that management "looked the other way when I dated Ronald Reagan."

"You dated Ronald Reagan?" I asked. By way of explanation, Ice Follies spent July and August in San Francisco every year, rehearsing in the morning for the coming season and continuing to perform the current show every evening. The show would then move to Los Angeles to premiere its new season in early September. In its day, this grand opening was a major event, and celebrities turned out in force for it.

ISABEL SMITH HOLT. Promotional photograph from Ice Follies 1948. Inscription reads "to Gen – a swell roommate. I have enjoyed living with you. You flaky redhead!"

ISABEL SMITH HOLT. Author with Isabel in Wayzata, Minnesota, September of 2018.

"There were all sorts of celebrities around. I guess I caught his attention," Izzie said. "I would go to his house for lunch, and we'd swim. He was a perfect gentleman."

As our conversation began to wind down, Isabel said almost wistfully, "Your mother was a star," and then added, almost apologetically, "I don't know who your father is. I don't know who she dated. I didn't know she was pregnant when she left."

I thanked her for her time and said how much I had enjoyed speaking with her. I told her perhaps at some point if I could gather up the hotel points and airline miles we would come to visit her.

There was a brief silence, and I can now imagine her leaning back with a coquettish smile as she recalled earlier times, a hint of gardenia scented perfume surrounding her and brushing a stray hair from her forehead as she asked flirtatiously, "So, how old did you say you are?" And, when I answered that I would soon be seventy, Isabel replied, "I'm sixty-five, you know."

THE GIFT BEST GIVEN

An Unexpected Discovery
Churton Grove, Hillsborough, North Carolina

May 12, 2017

While the conscious decision to explore my adoption traces its way to the cold Wednesday in February in a New Jersey cemetery, it was preceded by another event—a random decision. The December prior, faced as I am every year with what to give Linda for Christmas, I had ordered each of us a DNA kit. For some time, she had been suggesting that even if I wasn't interested in researching my parentage, that I submit a DNA sample to determine my ethnicity. I must admit that I had a certain level of curiosity about what parts of the world I could trace my ancestry to. From the time I was young, based on my adoptive parents, I presented myself to be of Italian descent on my father's side, Ukrainian on my mother's. How accurate was that description? Was it accurate at all? The kits offered the opportunity to address this question and held still an additional benefit: Linda would be relieved of her sad yearly duty of informing me that, "This is beautiful, but it doesn't fit" as she opened her presents.

The kits were ordered, and when they arrived, I wrapped and placed them under the tree to be opened on Christmas morning. Linda was delighted that I had followed up on her suggestion, and I think she was relieved that this was a gift that would not need to be returned in the days to follow. I read to her all about how to produce a useful sample of saliva, how to insert the toy-sized funnels into the provided tubes, and how to then seal and return them. Little did I know, however, that Linda would soon declare herself "too busy to spit." Too busy to spit? She was busy—very busy, I'll admit—so, in a display of patience and understanding not always characteristic of me, I didn't press her on this and told her that I would wait until she was ready. Who knows how accurate the results returned would be if the sample submitted was impatiently and only grudgingly provided!

Weeks went by, and it became apparent that Linda's kit would remain unopened on a shelf of the bookcase in our living room. I bided my time, until our cemetery visit in February prompted me to delve unaccompanied into my ancestry. Expecting that the test would reveal my ethnicity and nothing more, I opened my box and carefully followed the directions provided. Making sure to not eat, drink, smoke, or chew gum in the preceding thirty minutes, I filled the tiny test tube to the prescribed line with my saliva. Removing the equally diminutive funnel, I replaced it with the cap provided which, as I twisted it into place, released its stabilizing solution. After shaking the tube vigorously for the prescribed five seconds, I placed it in the provided mailer and sent my sample off, confident I would soon have a better understanding of where on the earth's surface I had originated.

Early in April, I was delighted to see an email from Ancestry, and I opened it eagerly. "Thank you for your patience," it offered. "Due to high volumes of samples received over the holidays, processing will take longer than usual." The Christmas holiday was four months past, but it was understandable they would be busy, and I thought it commendable that the company would set expectations from the start.

A couple of weeks later, another email dropped, telling me, "Your sample has been registered. We'll be analyzing it soon." I remained patient; I was occupied with learning about my birth mother's family and her career as I waited. "Your sample is in the lab. Results will be available soon," read the next email that arrived early in May. By then, I had learned of my maternal family's Eastern European heritage, Austria-Hungary, Russia, or Poland depending upon the day of the particular year in which such information was gathered.

Working backward from my birth in May of 1948, I calculated that I had been conceived in August of the year prior. Whoever he was, my biological father and my mother had at least a passing relationship, and I was curious to know where it occurred. I researched newspapers and found that Genevieve Knorowski, by this time performing as Genevieve Norris, and her skating partner had joined Shipstads and Johnson Ice Follies early in 1947. To confirm this, I purchased a copy of an Ice Follies program from that period (25 cents when new in 1947; $12.95 plus shipping on eBay for the used copy of the same program in 2017), and in it I found them with a photograph and text welcoming them to the show. So where was the Follies when I was conceived? Another eBay purchase, this one an advertisement listing the show's schedule, placed them in San Francisco at the Winterland Ballroom for the entirety of the summer of 1947. Without knowing who my father was, where I was conceived really made little difference, but I was satisfied to have discovered this bit of trivia.

I received an early birthday gift when, on May 12, a fourth and final email arrived announcing, "Here are your results." I was excited to open the attached link and immediately went to the pie chart that would show me my ethnic origins. The roughly 50% Eastern European slice of the pie was of little surprise, but I grinned when I learned that I was 25% Ashkenazi Jew. I wondered if that would have made a difference to the mother of my high school girlfriend, who would tell me, "You're such a nice boy; it's too bad you're not Jewish." Interesting, I thought, that the remainder of my DNA was divided between Scandinavian and English-Irish ancestry. Confident that my birth mother came from families of practicing Catholics in Eastern Europe on both her mother's and her father's side, the disparate doses of Jewish, British, and Scandinavian DNA would have to be attributed to my unknown father's family.

I read further and found out that I had 967 cousins. I was quite impressed with the number, although I now know there are those whose DNA cousins number in the thousands. These were mostly third, fourth, and more distant cousins, but one name, the name at the top of the list, stood out. Under a label of "Close Family" and identified with a confidence factor of "Extremely High" was an individual—a male—suggested to be a first cousin. Again, this was unexpected, though I had not really thought to expect anything. I pondered this for a moment. A first cousin would be the son of a sibling of either my mother or my father. Based on the research I had previously done and what it had revealed about my mother's family, I was confident that this person was not the child of either of Genevieve's sisters or her brother, so he had to be on my birth father's side of my emerging family tree. If this individual was truly my first cousin, then his uncle, a brother of either his mother or his father, would be my father. This suddenly brought me far closer to knowing who my father was than I had ever thought to dream.

Miraculously, I saw that this predicted cousin had an extensive family tree publicly posted online in conjunction with his DNA data. I examined it closely, looking for male siblings of his parents. It appeared that his father was an only child, so I moved on to his mother's side of the family. I discovered she was the youngest of six children, five sisters and one brother: one brother. Could he be my father? Could discovering my father truly be this easy?

Harris Lofthus, born in 1911 in Corson, South Dakota, subsequently moved to attend law school at the University of Texas in Austin. Online records showed that he died in 1999 in Dallas, and there was nothing I could find that indicated he had ever left Texas after arriving there. Nor could I find anything that suggested my mother had ever been to Texas, an event that might have provided the opportunity for her and Harris to have known one another. Still, trusting in the integrity of this new cousin's family tree, and confident that the testing company was accurate in predicting our relationship, Harris Lofthus seemed to be the only possibility. I reached out to my new first cousin using Ancestry's messaging functionality. Sending out another in my series of "Hello, you don't know me but I'm exploring a possible family relationship" messages and hopeful I would hear back, I prepared to wait.

I was unprepared for how quickly I did hear back. Fifteen minutes, twenty at the most? My suggested first cousin responded via email, expressing excitement over this discovery and offering to help in any way possible. He told me that he was a technology professional living on the West Coast, working for one of the country's most prestigious universities. He acknowledged that Harris Lofthus was his only uncle. Before Linda and I could finish discussing his reply, I received another email from my cousin saying that he had noticed the slice of my pie chart that indicated Jewish heritage. He asked if this was attributable to my mother's family. I answered that I didn't believe so. A third email from him followed shortly—the proverbial game-changer. Harris Lofthus had no Jewish ancestry. So someone else must have provided the 25% of my DNA that was Ashkenazi. Harris Lofthus could not be my father.

AN UNEXPECTED DISCOVERY. With my paternal half-brother, Rich Wales, in Menlo Park, California, February, 2019.

AN UNEXPECTED DISCOVERY. My father, Dick Wales, with his then wife, Mary, who he married in 1949.

Ultimately, we determined that this person who the testing company suggested was my first cousin was not my cousin at all. On his father's paternal side, my supposed cousin was descended mostly from English immigrant coal miners, and on his father's maternal side, from German and Polish Jews. The genetic distribution was a perfect fit. This person with whom I had been exchanging emails for the past hour was my half-brother. We share the same father. His father—our father—accounted for the 25% Ashkenazi Jewish DNA and 25% British Isles DNA found in my pie chart. (Ancestry, along with 23andMe, now correctly identifies our relationship). I've come to be very grateful to my new brother, Rich, for many things, not the least of which was his willingness from the start to refer to his father as our father and his ability to quickly sort out which parts of this puzzle fit and which parts did not, which kept me from going down a blind alley.

My father's name was Richard B. "Dick" Wales. He was born in 1919 in San Francisco, and like Harris Lofthus who never left Texas, Dick never left California. He worked as an insurance adjuster, and later in life as a private investigator. He died in Gridley, 140 miles northeast of his birthplace, in 1999. Rich provided me with a photograph of Dick and his wife, Rich's mother, who he married after I was born (the third of his five wives, this marriage lasting ten years), taken in 1949. Even in the black and white photograph, his complexion, which Rich called "olive," was apparent. All my life, others had told me that I had an olive complexion.

My brother was candid about our father, describing him as impetuous, impulsive, financially irresponsible, and given to unpredictable mood swings. Rich's honesty and candor is another thing I'm grateful for. Perhaps it was the fact that his father left him and his mother in 1959 that allowed Rich to write, "You most likely had a far more stable and supportive life growing up with your adoptive parents than you would have had with your biological father."

Eighteen months later, Linda, James, and I traveled to San Francisco to meet Rich and his family. Linda is one who quickly sees resemblances and who is likely to say, "Wow, you both have the same nose." In these situations, I tend to nod as I think to myself that I'm not seeing the resemblance. On this trip though, I did see the resemblance. Certainly we're not carbon copies of one another, but we're close enough to be brothers.

Rich later took us to visit his mother, Mary, who lives a half-hour away. When he and I first discovered our relationship, he was concerned about what her reaction would be. He soon reported back that the news that her former husband had fathered a child had not come as a surprise to her. She even offered to Rich that she knew Dick had been friends with some "big wigs" at Ice Follies in those days and had a girlfriend from the show, but that was before he and Mary met. Happily, it was apparent that she was as interested in meeting us as we were in meeting her.

Mary lives in the quintessential 1960s era home on a street of modest houses with a neatly landscaped and maintained yard. The house's one-car garage points to a time when a second car was a luxury not considered by most. With a carefully decorated, impeccably clean interior, the house is a time capsule of the era. Rich's mother was ninety-seven. Recovering from a recent fall, she was sitting in an upholstered chair in her bedroom, wearing a blue quilted robe with an afghan over her lap. We were amazed by her appearance. With lively blue eyes, a fair complexion, and hair still more blonde than gray, she's a vibrant and attractive woman who looks much younger than her years. Mary was wearing makeup and lipstick, and while these may have been applied in anticipation of our visit, I wouldn't be surprised if it was part of her everyday routine. She was warm as she greeted us with a strong voice. Then, making it clear she wanted me to remain, she told Rich to show Linda and James the rest of the house and the artwork created by the man she married in 1964 and with whom she lived for 35 years after her divorce from Dick Wales.

"I want to tell you about your father," Mary said after the others had left. I was both interested to hear what she had to say and appreciative that she felt this was something she wanted to share with me. While she said that Rich was sensitive to the things that she would say about Dick, much of what followed closely mirrored what he had told me previously. One fact I had not recalled Rich telling me was that Mary attributed Dick's undesirable characteristics to his mother.

"She was a mean woman," Mary said, "and very small," holding her hand parallel to the floor to indicate height, not character, though perhaps she was suggesting both. "She sent him to boarding school. His parents lived in a luxury apartment building in downtown San Francisco and didn't even have a bedroom for him. Much of the time he lived with his grandparents in Russian River." Mary seemed to suggest that Dick's mother, Selma, played the dominant role in his parent's relationship.

"He could be charming," she continued, referring to her former husband. "He was married twice before me and twice after," she added. "He mentioned Ice Follies to me but never said anything about a relationship."

Though I didn't question it, I wondered about Mary's last statement. Rich had previously told me that she was aware of a girlfriend with the Ice Follies before their marriage and had said, "He talked a lot. If he knew your mother was pregnant he would have said something, if not to me, then to someone else who would have told me."

Mary went on to talk about Dick's need for control. "After we married, he insisted on making the rules. If we went to a movie he would decide which one we would go to see. And he told me that Saturday was his day. He would be away all day, and I knew he was probably up to no good."

Dick was impulsive. Mary referenced his compulsion for purchasing luxurious cars. "Once he bought a car—a Jaguar—on Friday and sold it again on Monday so he could buy another."

Finally, as their relationship deteriorated, she told me, Dick moved out of their home on three separate occasions. It was the third time that he announced he was going to file for a divorce. Mary told him he needed to deed their house to her—which he did—and they would be done. I sensed sadness and still lingering disbelief when she told me, "He never even said goodbye to Rich when he left."

CHAPTER THIRTEEN
Parting Ways

Teddy and the Shipstads

The Lincoln Hotel and Madison Square Garden, New York City

When they left P. J. Clarke's, Genevieve this time accepted Charles' suggestion of a taxi. She wanted to get back to the hotel. She needed to rest before going to Madison Square Garden for the evening's show. Charles and Eleanore agreed that she should tell people that she had become very fatigued over the five years that she had been performing, and that her doctor was concerned. Genevieve would say that he had recommended she fulfill her current obligations as best she could and then take a six-month hiatus to regain her energy. Others had witnessed her fatigue and expressed concern over her not feeling well during the day; it would be a plausible explanation.

She would ask the Shipstads for some time to meet with them the next day. She wanted to tell them that she would depart the Follies after their engagement in Philadelphia in mid-January. But she needed to tell Teddy first. She was more concerned about telling him than about informing anyone else. They performed as a pair and, on the ice, they performed as one, each dependent on the other. She wondered if he would believe her explanation. He knew her; he knew her well. Charles, always thinking like a businessman, advised Genevieve that she should also make contact with Carl Snyder to let him know what was going on. "Keep all your avenues open. Make sure he has a way to contact you that won't alarm Leonard and Josephine," Charles said. Then he added, "If you want to return to skating afterward, you might need his help." She cringed as he said that. She had never considered that she would not return to performing.

That evening, after completing their Persian Market performance, Teddy and Genevieve hugged as they did every night once they were off the ice. The embrace was a sharing of their appreciation for each other's skill, the crowd's adulation of them, and most importantly, their reliance on one another—their partnership.

"I need to talk to you, Teddy," Genevieve said. "Can you come down to breakfast tomorrow morning?"

"Talk about what?" Teddy looked at her with concern.

Genevieve paused for a moment before she said, "Really, it's not anything, but we need to talk. I'd rather we talk tomorrow."

"Does this have something to do with San Francisco? Something hasn't been right since then." Teddy looked into his partner's eyes.

Genevieve took a deep breath, trying to maintain her composure. Finally, she smiled and reached out to take Teddy's hand. "Please, let's talk tomorrow."

Leaving the dressing room after the show, she found Eddie Shipstad in the hallway under Madison Square Garden's lower tier of seats. She told him that she had something important to discuss and wondered if she might be able to talk with him and his brother the next day. Always affable, and elated at the reception the Follies had received in New York these past nights, he quipped, "Are we not paying you enough?" Then, seeing the serious look on Genevieve's face, he said, "Of course, we can meet tomorrow before rehearsal."

Genevieve slept restlessly. Her eyes would close, and she would doze, only to wake up, finding herself in the midst of rehearsing what she would tell Teddy and the Shipstads. She was anxious for this all to be over with, but she dreaded the morning light that would come through her window.

Teddy was waiting in the hotel's dining room when Genevieve arrived. She could feel his eyes on her, already questioning her as she walked toward his table. "Is everything okay?" he asked. "Are you all right?" Genevieve hated that his concern was so sincere. He deserved more than the explanation she was about to offer.

"I've been so tired, and I haven't been feeling well. I went to the doctor when we first got here. He said that I'm exhausted and that I need to take six months off." What she said was not unreasonable.

Teddy said nothing as he looked at her. To Genevieve, it seemed like an impossibly long silence. Finally, he asked, "Are you sure? Is that really what it is?" There was no reason he should not accept her explanation, but he knew her so well.

Genevieve took a deep breath. "I'm going to tell the Shipstads later. They don't know."

Teddy looked at her sadly. The look was not accusing, but Genevieve thought it implied, "You can trust me. You can trust me, but you're not telling me what's going on."

"I'm sorry, Teddy. I didn't expect it. It's the last thing I wanted to happen to us."

Teddy smiled for just a moment; his eyes were kind if not believing. "When? When are you going to leave the show?"

"After Philadelphia," Genevieve said. "I'm so tired, but I have to give the Shipstads time. I have to give you time, Teddy." She whispered, "I'm so sorry. Really." Genevieve turned away.

When she turned back, Teddy was looking at her. "Don't worry about me. Everything will work out. I just want to know that you're going to be okay." Then, with a brief, slight smile, he asked, "Are we going to have some breakfast?"

"I don't have much of an appetite right now. I don't think so. I'll see you this afternoon," she said as she rose and walked from the dining room, her back to him, her eyes filled with tears that Teddy could not see.

Heeding Charles's suggestion for her to have a way for people to contact her, Genevieve stopped to establish an account with one of the many theater-district answering services before continuing to the Garden to meet with the Shipstads. Walking up Eighth Avenue, she rehearsed what she would say to the brothers. She would tell them how grateful she was for the opportunity they had given her, how she had been terribly tired and not feeling well for weeks, how her physician had recommended time away, and how disappointed she was to feel that she was letting them down.

Genevieve didn't have to wait long. Both of the Shipstads and Oscar Johnson were waiting when she arrived, and they ushered Genevieve into the arena where they sat in the first rows beside the ice. Nearby, a man sweeping the floor, wiping down and folding seats, stepped on a peanut shell, and the sound crackled in the empty arena.

The three men listened as Genevieve told them about her need to leave the show. It was a relief to be unburdened of the task, but it was made more difficult by the way they responded to her. Agreeing that her well-being was more important than an act in the show, they asked if it would be better for her to leave sooner than January. They accepted her explanation and seemed grateful that she had given them time to prepare for her departure. Their concern for her made her wish that she could tell them the truth, but Genevieve knew she couldn't afford to. Even if she was forthright, they wouldn't have allowed her to continue with the show, and her situation would be revealed to everyone. She found it disquieting when, as they parted, there was mention of deciding how they would need to address Teddy's continued role in the show.

Genevieve called Carl Snyder's office. It was lunchtime, and he was out. It took her two more attempts to reach him and to explain to him that she needed to take a hiatus.

"I'm sorry to hear that, Genevieve. I've never heard of another situation like this," Snyder said, "but it's good that you're taking care of it."

"My doctor said if I rest, I should be able to be performing again before the end of the year." Genevieve held the phone, her eyes closed, hoping that she sounded truthful.

"Have you spoken to the Shipstads? They're very influential people. What have they said?"

"I spoke to them this morning. They were very understanding and said I should do whatever was best for my health." She paused. "They're such nice people."

"Did they say anything about Teddy? What are their plans for him once you leave?"

Once again, Genevieve was reminded of how badly she felt about how Teddy might be impacted by her departure. "They don't seem to be sure, yet."

Snyder was silent for a moment. "Tell him to call me. If they don't have a plan for him, then I might have an opportunity he'd be interested in. Tell him to call me tomorrow."

She was relieved that there might be another option for Teddy if one did not remain at the Follies. At the same time, it felt as if someone was taking him from her. She scolded herself—she hadn't even told Teddy the truth—she had no right to feel that way.

During rehearsal later that afternoon, Genevieve told Teddy, "I spoke with Mr. Snyder yesterday, to let him know I have to leave the show."

"What did he say?" Teddy asked.

"I just told him why and he said that he understood. He asked about you; what you would do after I leave. He asked me to tell you to call him. He said if the Shipstads don't keep you in a role like the one you're in, he might have something you would be interested in."

Teddy's expression brightened. "I'm worried the Shipstads won't have any use for me once you leave. I'll call him tomorrow morning. If Mr. Snyder has something interesting he can offer me, I want to hear about it."

His trust in her, seemingly bruised the day before, appeared to be restored, and Genevieve abruptly decided she needed to confide in Teddy. "Tonight, after the show, I need to talk to you. Back at the hotel."

In the hotel's mostly empty dining room that evening, as waiters and busboys cleared tables and swept the carpeted floors around them, Genevieve told Teddy everything.

"Teddy, I'm not leaving the show because I'm tired," Genevieve began. She paused, trying to find the right words. Turning to avoid his eyes, she blurted out, "I'm pregnant." After a moment, she felt his hand on hers, and she turned back to face him.

"That's what I thought. You've been tired and not feeling well for months, and when you said you had to take time away, I knew." Teddy spoke in little more than a whisper, and his voice was calm and reassuring. Genevieve's fear that he would judge her was unfounded.

She hurried to explain. "It was in San Francisco. It was my only time with him. My first time." Genevieve's jaw stiffened. "I'm so angry with myself. So ashamed. It's not just about me. Look at what I'm doing to you and to the Shipstads. And I can't possibly tell my parents."

"The guy in San Francisco with the fancy car, was it him? I knew I never liked him."

Genevieve covered her face with her hands, drew a deep breath, and then exhaled. "Yes, it was him," she hissed. "But this isn't about him. It's my fault. I did what I knew I shouldn't. So now everyone else is suffering: you, the Shipstads, and I'm asking my sister and her husband to lie to my parents and keep this from them."

They sat quietly for what seemed like a long time. At first, the only response that Teddy could offer was to gently squeeze Genevieve's hand. Finally, he asked, "How can I help you?"

Genevieve sat for a moment with her eyes closed. It felt, by telling Teddy, like a great weight had been removed from her shoulders. She smiled at him and said, "The day after tomorrow is Thanksgiving. Would you come to my family's house for dinner before the show? I could use the support."

His hand remained on hers, and Teddy smiled. "Have you ever seen me turn down a meal?"

Parting Ways

Penn-Sheraton Hotel, Philadelphia, Pennsylvania

When Ice Follies departed San Francisco and began to travel east three months before, Genevieve had looked forward to returning to New York and to be close to her family. By November, as the show ended its engagement at Madison Square Garden, she was relieved to be departing the city.

She was relieved also that Carl Snyder had suggested another opportunity to Teddy in the event that the Shipstads could not employ him in a featured role. But the Shipstads did want him to remain with the show, only in a supporting role as one of the Follies Boys. Regrettably, there currently was no need for a solo adagio skater, nor was there a suitable partner available to replace Genevieve. Teddy was not surprised at the news, and he informed the Shipstads that he would depart the show when Genevieve did. By the end of January, Snyder would have him paired with Jeanne Sook, a young woman from California who had been performing at the New Yorker Hotel that fall. Together, she and Teddy would go on to have a successful pairs skating career in hotels and with major ice shows. They would eventually marry.

As the show moved to New Haven for the first half of December and then to Hershey for two weeks before taking a brief Christmas break, Genevieve and Teddy found themselves skating with a newfound sense of reliance on one another. She was happy that she had decided to confide in him. He had deserved to know, and there was no one else with whom she could confide. Off the ice, both listened patiently to one another, Teddy conjecturing over performing with his new partner and Genevieve concerned about how her family would react if they should ever find out she had hidden her pregnancy from them.

"I don't know if they would be angry or not," she said, referring to her parents. "But they would be so hurt knowing that I hid this from them."

"You must think about it every day; about what you're going to do," Teddy said. He knew that she did. Almost every day, he listened patiently while Genevieve pondered her situation.

"There's no way that I can have the baby and keep him or her without them knowing. I just can't imagine what they would think."

"Maybe they would help with the baby, so you can continue to skate," Teddy suggested.

"No, I won't tell them." Genevieve's response was emphatic. It was the same way she replied each time she and Teddy discussed her situation. "I need to find an answer, Teddy," she said, although she had no expectations that he could provide one.

The Follies arrived in Philadelphia on Christmas Eve, and Genevieve checked into her room at the Penn-Sheraton Hotel. It was the same place that she and Teddy had stayed when they first joined the show a year before. In her bra and half-slip, she stood in front of the mirror in the bathroom, looking at herself as she stood barefoot on the cold tile floor. The light over the framed oval mirror was harsh, unkind, and revealing. Genevieve wondered if others recognized the changes that she could feel but not yet see. Looking at her reflection in the mirror, she thought about how quickly the year had passed and how her life had abruptly changed. She wished that she could see the future. "Mirror, mirror, on the wall," she thought, shaking her head as she turned off the light and prepared to dress and join others for an early dinner.

The three weeks in Philadelphia passed quickly, and there was a string of farewell celebrations for Genevieve and for Teddy. Even their most casual acquaintances in the show came to wish them well. Genevieve treasured all the photos she received, inscribed with their personal messages and best wishes and kept them pressed flat between two sheets of cardboard in one of the hotel room's dresser drawers. When it came time to leave Philadelphia, she carefully wrapped the folio in one of the hotel's heavy towels and placed it in the bottom of her suitcase.

As the Follies cast hurriedly left the hotel to travel to Cleveland, Genevieve and Teddy took a taxi to the station on Thirtieth Street to board a train back to Manhattan. Though their paths on the ice would cross in the future, it would be their last journey as partners. Teddy was returning to stay with relatives in Astoria and to rehearse with Jeanne Sook before they would travel to Chicago for a prolonged engagement as featured performers at the Stevens Hotel.

Several weeks before, in a stroke of good luck, Gerry Verden, had written from California to tell her that he was reenlisting in the military. Though it had been more than a year since they had spoken, Genevieve decided to call and to wish him well. In the course of the conversation, she mentioned that she was departing the Follies and was returning to New York. He asked about where she would be staying and offered that the same friend of his aunt, who had given him a place to stay when he first came to New York in 1943, was currently staying with Gerry and his aunt in California. If Genevieve had any interest, this woman would be happy to sublet her Manhattan apartment until she returned home in July. Genevieve had been more than eager. Calls were made, conversations took place, money was wired, and now she was returning to New York with a key to the apartment in hand. She would stay there, secreting herself from all her family, other than Charles and Eleanore, until her baby was born.

With tears, hugs, and promises to remain in touch, Teddy and Genevieve parted after arriving at Penn Station. Not looking back, Teddy walked away into one of the station's underground tunnels that would lead him to the subway to Astoria. Watching until she could no longer see him in the crowd of people, Genevieve crossed the marble floor with the domed glass ceiling high above and exited the station to find a taxi to deliver her to the apartment she had rented. Teddy was gone, and while Charles and Eleanore knew where she was and would be nearby and in close touch, this was the first time in over a year that Genevieve was totally alone. It was January in New York, but she wasn't sure if it was the cold of the morning or her situation that made her shiver as she slid into the yawning back seat of the Checker taxi that would take her uptown to Riverside Drive.

CHAPTER FOURTEEN
Alone in New York

A Place to Call Home

Riverside Drive, New York City

Genevieve was weary as she stepped off the elevator and unlocked the door to the third-floor apartment. She was pleased as she entered and looked around. The apartment was filled with natural light and was tastefully decorated. A comforting hiss escaped from the steam radiators under the windows. Closing the heavy door stirred dust that had accumulated during the time that the apartment had been unoccupied, and Genevieve watched as the floating particles reflected the sunlight.

The elegant building was on the corner of Riverside Drive and West Eighty-First Street. On one side, the apartment's large living room windows overlooked the side street. On the other, they afforded expansive views of Riverside Park, the Hudson River, and the wharves and industrial buildings on New Jersey's shore beyond. Genevieve explored, slowly turning corners and opening doors, moving with the caution and curiosity of a cat suddenly finding itself in new surroundings.

She found the large bedroom, also facing the river, and pulled back the large white sheet that had been spread over the sleigh bed to protect it. Beneath it, the bed was covered with a thick down-filled comforter, its swirled rose and orchid taffeta cover iridescent in the daylight. At the end of the hallway, adjacent to the bedroom, was a large, marble tiled bathroom with an enormous clawfoot bathtub. Touching the porcelain handles on its polished brass fixtures, she imagined the pleasure she would find enjoying long soaking baths in it. Quickly, she moved on to examine the rest of the apartment.

On the other side of the living room, she found the kitchen. A sink with a small window above it looked out over West Eighty-First Street. There was a stove on the wall to the sink's right, and on the wall opposite the stove was a refrigerator. The kitchen was spacious enough to hold a small, round oak table that was covered with a brightly colored floral cloth. Genevieve found a large pantry and a door on the other side of the refrigerator leading to a tiny bedroom with a correspondingly small bathroom. Gerry Verden had probably slept in it when he stayed there.

She returned to the living room. From one end of the apartment to the other, the thick plaster walls were painted a stark white. Where they met the high ceilings, they were crowned with wide, carved molding. The floors of the living room, the bedroom, and the hallway that connected them, were highly polished herringbone parquet, stained dark coffee brown. She sat for a long time on the couch overlooking the river before she rose to empty her suitcase. The place already felt like home.

Genevieve quickly settled into a routine and embraced the apartment as her home. Each morning, and then again later in the evening when she would watch the sun disappear over the bluffs above the Hudson River, she would choose a record and place it on the Victrola in the living room. Railway Express delivered her trunk of clothing and personal items. It was the same trunk that she'd sent ahead when she traveled to Vancouver more than five years before. It was new then, but now the dark green sides were scuffed and dented, the paint on the black steel bands that braced it scraped, and the once shiny, chrome hardware pitted. She placed her skates in the coat closet by the front door, planning to continue a regimen of skating as long as she was able.

From the apartment, she walked to West End Avenue, then to

Broadway. All she needed was right there. Groceries came from a Gristedes market, and a bakery was next door. Even in winter, a florist displayed colorful bouquets, and the drugstore beside it, smelling incongruously of perfume and penicillin, provided for her toiletry needs. On her first visit, Genevieve bought a package of bubble bath, thinking of the claw foot tub back in the apartment. At the Emigrant Savings Bank branch, she traded five one-dollar bills for a roll of dimes. She still had weekly calls home to make, even if she was pretending to call from distant locations.

Genevieve called the Lexington Hospital and made an appointment to return there. She was now five months pregnant, and the physician that Dr. Soresi had referred her to had emphasized that she would need regular checkups to ensure the health of both herself and her baby. As confused as she was, thinking about what she would do once her baby arrived, Genevieve was committed to bringing it into the world healthy and well cared for. She would go to her appointment alone.

Lilacs in January

Lexington Hospital

When she awoke that morning, the New Jersey shoreline could only be seen through breaks in the gray clouds hanging low over the river, and the sound of traffic on Riverside Drive was muted by several inches of snow that had fallen overnight. Genevieve boarded the bus at the stop opposite her building and looked out its windows, listening to the sloshing sounds of its tires rolling through already melting snow. The bus traveled down Riverside Drive, across West Seventy-Second Street and then down Broadway before it turned across Manhattan on Fifty-Seventh Street. Even in the falling snow, Manhattan's streets became busier and more congested, densely packed with both cars and pedestrians. She exited at Lexington Avenue and walked the two blocks to the hospital.

As Genevieve climbed the steps to the entrance, the woman with the hair pulled back tightly and the blue inquiring eyes rose to allow her in. The way the woman had looked at her on her first visit had made Genevieve feel uncomfortable. It was the same way her mother looked at her when she suspected she wasn't being truthful. The woman had emphasized her title when she addressed her as "Mrs. Knorowski" telling Genevieve that the woman knew she was hiding the truth. Of course, Genevieve was being dishonest as she attempted to guard her secret, but was it that apparent? However, as she, Eleanore and Charles had departed after the second visit with Dr. Soresi, there seemed to be a glimmer of warmth in the woman's eyes. As they had stepped from the elevator into the lobby, the woman seemed to have smiled sincerely; her countenance had softened.

Certainly it was a coincidence, but on this third visit the woman's makeup was more subdued. Her lipstick was of a softer color, and beneath the jacket of her suit, the woman wore a blouse of pale pink silk. As she entered the lobby alone, Genevieve no longer felt that the woman's eyes were piercing. "Mrs. Knorowski, it's nice to see you again."

Genevieve was startled to hear herself say, "Miss Knorowski. It's Miss Knorowski."

The eyes that had felt so disapproving the first time suddenly were warm. The woman smiled with understanding, appreciating Genevieve's unexpected admission. "Of course, Miss Knorowski. Rather a miserable winter day, isn't it?"

Genevieve looked past the woman. There were lilacs on the credenza. She wondered where lilacs had come from in the middle of winter, and she inhaled their sweet, subtle fragrance. "Yes, it wouldn't be so bad if the sun would only come out, but it's so dark and gray."

Stating the obvious as she picked up her phone to announce Genevieve's arrival to someone elsewhere in the hospital, the woman observed, "I see you are alone today."

As she unbuttoned and removed her coat, Genevieve decided to accept the woman's inquisitiveness as a sign of friendliness. Running her hand over her stomach, she replied, "Well, not totally alone."

The woman's face, which had already displayed warmth, brightened discernibly. "You two have each other," she said almost reverently. "It's a gift."

Genevieve wanted to say more. Other than to her sister and Charles and to Teddy Roman, she had spoken to no one about being pregnant, and even with them, their conversations had been guarded. Suddenly, this stranger who had once seemed to look at her so disapprovingly was someone she wanted to talk to. Before Genevieve could think of what to say, what to ask, how to continue the conversation, the nurse who had been present for her first visit stepped off the elevator to accompany her upstairs.

As she entered the elevator, Genevieve looked back to the woman, who called, "You are in good hands. They will take very good care of you. I will be here when you are done."

As if reading her thoughts, the nurse said to Genevieve, "Mrs. Blumenthal. She sometimes seems gruff at first, but she's a warm and caring woman. She treats our patients as if they are family."

Until almost its last moments, the visit with the doctor had seemed routine as he reviewed the notes he had previously taken and asked

Genevieve questions about how she felt and what she had been experiencing since her visit with him. Then he checked her weight, temperature, and blood pressure, all of which the nurse recorded. It seemed unnecessary that she had been asked to change into a gown, but just as she thought the visit was coming to an end, the doctor asked her to lie back on the examining table. She had anticipated it, knew it was unavoidable, but she detested feeling so vulnerable and exposed.

Genevieve closed her eyes then opened them as she felt a smooth, cool object being drawn over her abdomen. She looked down to see the doctor leaning over her with a curved wooden device in his hand. Only six or eight inches long, it was smooth and polished. Genevieve thought that it looked like a miniature horn of a cow. She could feel the warmth of the doctor's breath on her skin as he squinted, slowly moving the instrument over her flesh, the end with a wide bell against her skin and his ear to its narrower end. Finally, he stopped, and in a whisper said, "Yes." He smiled with apparent satisfaction. Genevieve watched as he lifted his other arm and shook back the sleeve of his white coat to expose his watch. She stared at its second hand as it moved across the Roman numerals on its white rectangular face. In the quiet of the room, she thought she could hear its ticking. Finally, without looking up, he said to the nurse, "One five two."

Genevieve turned her eyes to the doctor as he remained bent over her. Finally, after waiting what seemed an eternity for an explanation, she asked, "One five two, what does that mean?"

The doctor straightened, rolling his head from side to side, as if leaning over Genevieve had made his neck stiff. He smiled, pausing as he put down the wooden device. Finally, he explained, "I was listening for your baby's heartbeat. We use what we call a Pinard Horn. It is quite an old device, but it's the best we currently have. The one I use has found and listened to the hearts of many, many babies."

Genevieve waited for further clarification, but the doctor seemed to be enjoying the suspense. "You said one five two. Does that mean—"

The doctor interrupted. "Yes. Your baby's heartbeat. It is strong and regular. One hundred fifty-two beats per minute." Saying no more, he listened again, this time using his stethoscope, running its bell over her abdomen. He stopped and, holding it in place, looked up to Genevieve. "I imagine you would like to hear your baby's heartbeat too." Without waiting for an answer, he handed the stethoscope to the nurse, who positioned it in Genevieve's ears.

She closed her eyes and listened, her mouth open, but not breathing, fearing she wouldn't be able to hear if she did. She smiled. It was like the sound of a runaway alarm clock buried beneath a pile of pillows. She exhaled loudly, and when she opened her eyes they were wet. She looked at the doctor, seeking reassurance. "It beats so fast. Is that normal?"

"Totally normal," he replied, smiling. "As your pregnancy progresses, the heartbeat will slow down. But, for now, it is expected to be as rapid as it is."

The nurse patiently waited until Genevieve nodded and allowed her to remove the stethoscope from her ears. Hearing her baby's heartbeat had drained her. She wondered how the presence of something that was already so real, whose existence was already so perplexing, had become even more so? This had been anything but a routine visit to the doctor.

The lady at the desk in the lobby—Mrs. Blumenthal, the nurse had said—looked up as Genevieve stepped off the elevator and announced, unprompted, in the voice of someone trying to comprehend unexpected news, "I just heard my baby's heart beat."

Mrs. Blumenthal smiled and motioned her to the velvet

upholstered chair beside her desk. Making no assumptions as to what Genevieve's response might be, she asked, "A reassuring sound, I imagine, Miss Knorowski?"

"Genevieve. Please, my name is Genevieve." She felt a need to share, and she could not do that with someone who addressed her as Miss Knorowski. "I didn't expect it. I hadn't thought about it. I should have." Genevieve stared at the lilacs sitting on the credenza in their yellow Chinese porcelain vase. Hearing her baby's heartbeat had been as unexpected as seeing lilacs in January.

"Now you truly know you are not alone." Mrs. Blumenthal smiled. "Such a gift to be given on a day like this," she continued, studying Genevieve, who was lost in thought.

"I don't know." Genevieve sounded as if she was trying to decide whether or not this was truly the case. "My skating, my career, that was the gift I was given. And now this. I don't know that I can have them both. I don't know how to choose between them."

"Life is about choices, Genevieve. What you do with your life, what you do with your gifts." Mrs. Blumenthal spoke softly and slowly. Then she continued, "This is not always a world of convenient answers and simple solutions."

Genevieve listened. Then she stood to put on her coat. "That's what I told Dr. Soresi when he first told me that I was going to have a baby; that there were no easy answers."

The two walked toward the doors. The heat in the lobby had fogged the glass so only the silhouettes of passing cars and pedestrians on their other side were visible. When Mrs. Blumenthal opened the door to allow Genevieve out, both saw that the snow had stopped. She turned to Genevieve and placed a gentle hand on her shoulder. "You are strong and you are brave and you are not alone. The answer to what to do about your gifts will come to you."

Genevieve smiled an unconvinced smile as she said goodbye and stepped out onto the sidewalk. She had taken only a few steps when she heard Mrs. Blumenthal call after her. She turned and took a step back toward the hospital's entrance. Her new friend, this person in whom she had confided thoughts she had not shared with anyone else, said to her, "Sometimes, Genevieve, the best gift is the gift that you give to another."

Wiping the condensation on the glass door away with her fingers, Mrs. Blumenthal watched as Genevieve disappeared around the corner onto Lexington Avenue.

When she returned to the apartment, Genevieve filled the teapot and flipped through the shelf full of records as she waited for the water to boil. Finding the one she was looking for, she placed it on the Victrola. As she sipped her tea, her bare feet up on the couch, covered by a patchwork quilt assembled from squares of fabric of which no two pieces were the same, Genevieve watched tugboats pushing barges on the river as she listened to Basil Rathbone narrate the children's symphony, *Peter and the Wolf.* In the room's dim light, tenderly rubbing her stomach, she closed her eyes and spoke aloud to her baby for the first time. "You have a heartbeat—it's time for you to start listening to music."

Genevieve fell asleep as French horns announced the wolf's arrival in the meadow and the clarinet signaled the cat's escape up the tree. The sky was dark when she awoke, and the only sound she heard was the scratching of the phonograph's needle on the vacant soundless space at the end of the record as it rotated on its spindle.

EDWARD DI GANGI

Eleanore and Charles

Genevieve's Apartment, Riverside Drive

Genevieve did not leave the apartment the next morning. The overnight cold had frozen the melted snow, glazing the sidewalks with ice. By noon, however, the sun was high, the temperature had risen, and almost all the ice had melted. Bundled in a heavy woolen coat and with a knit cap pulled over her auburn hair, Genevieve ventured out and walked down West Eighty-First Street, where the pristine, white snow was transformed into gray slush as it was shoveled from the sidewalks into the street by the janitors of the buildings along the way. Her boots crunched on the rock salt that had been scattered afterward to melt the remaining obstinate patches. Charles and Eleanore were coming to the apartment for dinner, and she needed to prepare. Josephine had been accommodating of Eleanore's weekly lunches or dinners out with Charles, watching the children for her, not knowing the true purpose of those outings.

At the market, she bought a thick ham steak and three small potatoes. As she ran her thumb over their smooth brown skins, she wondered if they might have been grown on her grandparents' farm on Long Island earlier in the fall. Wanting the dinner to be special, Genevieve selected a can of asparagus. The bright steel can with its glossy label lettered in gold and red and emblazoned with a fleur-de-lis on a background of black looked as luxurious as its contents.

Three doors to the left as she exited the market, Genevieve stopped to look in the window of the bakery. The traffic on Broadway, behind her, reflected in the glass as she admired the display of cakes and pastries. Genevieve stepped inside, a bell over the door announcing her entry. She purchased a loaf of dense black bread from the shelves behind the counter, and as it was being sliced, she inhaled the warm and fragrant smell of the sweets and other loaves of bread baking in the ovens in the rear of the store. She surveyed the three glass-front display cases, which, like the trays in the outside window, were full of tempting treats.

The lady behind the counter, wearing a white apron and spider web hairnet, slid the sliced loaf of bread into a white paper bag and turned back to Genevieve to ask if there would be anything else. Walking to the window, Genevieve pointed to the tray of individual Charlotte Russes, arranged shoulder to shoulder, each with a swirled mountain of whipped cream overflowing its cardboard sleeve and topped with a bright red maraschino cherry. The woman placed the three that Genevieve selected into a small cardboard box lined with wax paper and tied it tightly with red-and-white twine.

Genevieve was delighted to see Eleanore and Charles. She had been back in New York for almost two weeks. This was the first opportunity to be together with them. They ate dinner at the oak table in the kitchen. Genevieve had exchanged the bright floral table cloth for another that she had found in a drawer. It was coarsely woven, the same shade of blue as she recalled the Pacific having been. Against it, the silverware and the delicate white china stood out boldly. A small bouquet of perfect, bright orange and yellow ranunculus blossoms with their countless layers of tissue-thin petals and sturdy straight stems stood in an eight-sided glass vase in the center of the table. She had seen them in the window of the florist on West End Avenue on her way home and had allowed herself the indulgence, thinking of Mrs. Blumenthal as she paid for them.

Charles told Genevieve about the business he and his brothers had formed to produce industrial and training films, but most of the conversation was about their family. Eleanore told her about their parents and about how their grandparents were still well, even though they were all approaching their nineties. She filled her in on Lucille's and Ed's marriage, and she said that her parents seemed to have accepted her feigned calls from the Ice Follies just as they had accepted all the calls that had preceded them.

As Genevieve took the pastries from the refrigerator, she told them that she had visited the doctor the day before.

Looking first to Charles, and then to Eleanore, she quietly stated, "I heard my baby's heartbeat." When neither responded, Genevieve continued. "I wasn't prepared to hear it. I didn't expect it. Everything suddenly became different."

Eleanore responded, "I remember what that was like."

"We came home from the hospital and listened to music," Genevieve said, then added, "My baby and me. We listened again today, and we're going to do it together every day."

The three sat in comfortable silence as each spooned whipped cream from their desert before reaching the layer of sponge cake at its bottom.

Finally, Eleanore asked, guarded, "Have you decided what you're going to do?"

Genevieve slowly twirled the cherry by its stem as she looked down at her plate. "No. All I can think of is that I have to choose. I can't have a baby and skate too. Skating is my life, but that sounds so selfish. No matter what I think, it all sounds selfish."

Charles, seated on the opposite side of the table, leaned forward and said, "You still have time to make your decision. You need to do what is right for you. Whatever you need, whatever your decision, you know that we will be here to help you."

GUARDIAN ANGELS. Eleanore, Genevieve's sister and her husband, Charles Hans. Photo courtesy of Paul Hans.

"The Date Picture," Genevieve in San Francisco with Ice Follies, August, 1947. Photo from collection of Ted Meza.

As she was about to respond, Genevieve touched her stomach. She smiled, and her eyes widened. "It moved. Until I heard its heartbeat, I didn't realize what I was feeling. The baby's moving."

Eleanore stood and leaned over Genevieve. Putting her hand on her younger sister's abdomen, she was quickly rewarded with a soft bump that brought a smile to her face. She hugged Genevieve and repeated Charles's words. "You know we'll be here to help you. We'll always be here to help you both."

Faith, Wisdom and Hope

Lexington Hospital

Each night before going to the bedroom, Genevieve would plan the next day. Alone in the quiet of the apartment, she would sit overlooking the river with music from the record player softly filling the room. Of all the music she played, she was certain that her baby best liked the flute of the bird and the clarinet of the cat in Peter and the Wolf. She would speak out loud and ask, "What shall we do tomorrow?"

There were the weekly lunches or dinners with Eleanore and Charles, and sometimes an extra daytime visit with Charles during the week. She skated at Iceland three times a week in February and the first week of March, but the fact that she was carrying a baby had become increasingly apparent. She would wear a loose-fitting jacket when she skated, but she encountered too many casual acquaintances at the rink and didn't want to take the chance of her situation becoming known.

Whenever New York's winter weather allowed, she walked wherever she could, and if no one was nearby she would speak and tell her baby what they were passing. Almost weekly she would visit the Museum of Natural History on Central Park West, a short walk from the apartment. Her favorite place within the museum was the fourth floor, with its cavernous, dimly lit exhibit halls filled with dinosaur skeletons and fossils. If she went there first thing in the morning or later in the afternoon, the rooms would be free of the crowds of excited school children and she would be there alone. During her midweek visits, she could stand in front of the ancient creatures, and read the descriptions to her baby in a whisper.

On other days, she would walk to the corner of Riverside Drive and Seventy-Ninth Street to board a bus that would take her across Central Park. As it reached Fifth Avenue, she would get off for the three-block walk to the Metropolitan Museum of Art's main entrance. Genevieve would wander through the museum, her hand on her abdomen, surreptitiously describing to her baby the polished coats of armor, Egyptian sarcophagi, Leonardo Da Vinci's drawings, and the richly colored oil paintings by Thomas Eakins. She knew that she was living a privileged life as she waited for her baby's arrival. She was grateful that she had the ability to be living as she was, but she realized that it was the money she had made from her skating career that made it possible and that she would eventually exhaust her funds. What would she do if she gave up her career? Where would the money come from? How would she take care of a baby? The thoughts were the last ones she had before falling asleep at night and the first she would consider in the morning when her baby would wake her with a gentle kick.

Genevieve's prenatal exam during the second week of March went quickly. The doctor was pleased with her vital signs, and her weight gain was precisely what he had hoped it would be. Using just his stethoscope on this visit, he listened for the baby's heartbeat and smiled as he looked at his watch before he again offered Genevieve the opportunity to listen. When she returned to the lobby and stepped off the elevator Mrs. Blumenthal was there.

A tall glass vase filled with the same kind of irises that grew wild, flourishing in the always damp earth of the ditch along the Long Island Railroad track that ran through her grandparents' farm, was on the credenza. Offset by their deep green leaves, the regal purple of the blossoms was the same color as the amethyst pendant around Mrs. Blumenthal's neck. She smiled as she saw Genevieve staring at the arrangement. "Irises. Some say they represent faith and wisdom and hope. How are you feeling, Genevieve?" she asked. "You look well. Is the doctor satisfied?"

"Thank you. I'm feeling good, and the doctor seems to be happy. He says I've gained just enough weight. I could never have imagined feeling so big." It still perplexed Genevieve that this woman was now someone she looked to for comfort. Her coat folded over her arm, and without being invited, she sat in the chair beside Mrs. Blumenthal's desk. She paused for a moment and then said, "May I ask you a question?"

Mrs. Blumenthal studied Genevieve's face and then raised her eyebrows as if to say, "Feel free to ask." Her eyes were very blue.

"Do you remember when I left after my last visit? I was out on the street and you called out to me."

Again, Mrs. Blumenthal didn't speak, but she smiled and nodded slightly, her eyebrows still raised.

"I keep thinking about what you said." When Mrs. Blumenthal said nothing, Genevieve continued. "You said, 'Sometimes the best gift is not the one you receive but the one you give to another.' What did you mean?"

"Have you ever received a gift, Genevieve, and it was precious but there wasn't a need for it or a place for it on your shelf or in your closet or in your life?"

Genevieve said nothing. She waited for the woman to continue.

Mrs. Blumenthal tilted her head toward her right shoulder, thinking, and then turned back to Genevieve, saying in a pensive, hushed voice, "That it does not fit into your life makes the gift no less precious. But it might change the life of someone else."

Genevieve closed her eyes and held them shut. She understood. She had understood since that day on the sidewalk a month ago, and she had thought every day about what the woman had said. Her hand returned to her stomach, as it did so often now, and when she opened her eyes, tears blurred the purple blossoms and green foliage of the irises in their glass vase. "There are no easy decisions," she said with resignation.

The older woman reached out, patting the back of Genevieve's hand with her own. "No, no easy decisions. There is just the hope," she paused before continuing, "and the faith that the decisions you make are wise ones."

Easter Sunday 1948

Holy Trinity Church, New York City

> Paraders Defy Raw Weather to Carry on Easter Tradition: Forenoon Worshipers and Fashion Heralds Brave Temperature of 35 (New York Times Headline, Monday, March 29, 1948)

Easter was the last Sunday in March. Genevieve's family would be celebrating the holiday together in Flushing. As she thought about them, she could almost smell the ham and the braided loaves of bread baking in the oven on Easter morning. The windows of the kitchen would be steamed over as Wanda, Josephine, and her sisters rolled the dough, cooked the potato and onion filling, and boiled pierogis. From Joseph and Mary's farm, there would be hard-boiled eggs dyed in rainbow colors, pickled beets, and horseradish so pungent it would make your eyes tear and take your breath away.

Genevieve would be celebrating the holiday alone and had planned to attend Easter mass at St. Patrick's Cathedral, then stroll down Fifth Avenue in the annual Easter Parade. She had hoped that being in the company of fellow churchgoers and the crowds on Fifth Avenue would make up for the feeling of loneliness she knew she would experience. In the days before Easter, however, the city was gripped by unexpectedly cold late winter weather that blew in from the northwest, bringing high winds and skies laden with thick gray clouds.

On Saturday morning, Genevieve stood looking out the window. The wind churned the river, and white caps stood out against the slate-gray water as it flowed downstream toward the Lower Bay and then to the Atlantic. Pigeons, their feathers ruffled, picked through windblown leaves, the granite wall separating Riverside Drive from the park beyond providing them shelter. Both her hands on her now prominent belly, smiling at the occasional flip or kick of her baby, she said aloud, "A change of plans, I'm afraid. I'm not keeping you out in all this. You and I will shop for Easter dinner, and tomorrow we'll stay close to home." Then, with a sigh, she said, "Plans change. Plans change all the time."

On Easter morning, Genevieve slipped into a loosely fitting dress purchased in anticipation of mass at St. Patrick's and the hopefully sunny stroll down Fifth Avenue. Morning temperatures were hovering at around twenty degrees as she dressed, and she buttoned a heavy cardigan sweater over the dress before buttoning her woolen coat around her. With the river and the cold gusting winds at her back, she walked two blocks to Broadway then turned left and walked one more block to West Eighty-Second Street, where Holy Trinity Church was halfway down the street. Going to church on Easter was important to her. Going to church when she was feeling as alone as she was would hopefully bring her some degree of comfort. She had passed this church before but had never been in it. On that cold Easter morning, it would provide a good alternative to traveling across the city to St. Patrick's.

Genevieve could hear organ music as she momentarily stood on the street studying the inscription in gold mosaic tiles over the church's three pairs of doors. *Gloria Patri et Filio et Spiritui Sancto.* Glory be to the Father, to the Son, and to the Holy Spirit, she recalled from her years of school at St. Michael's. She climbed the six steps from the sidewalk to the doors and entered the church. The sanctuary was bathed in soft light, organ music playing. The perfumed scent of at least one hundred potted Easter Lilies on the altar filled the air.

Genevieve sat on the aisle in a pew not far from the back of the already crowded church. She shyly returned a smile from the woman seated beside her. She reminded Genevieve of the lady she had met on the train the first day she had left home more than five years ago. Off and on since then, she had wondered if that woman's son had returned from the war in Europe. Genevieve was sure that this woman looked for a wedding band on her finger but then she unexpectedly leaned toward her, touching the back of her hand and whispering, "Happy Easter, dear. God bless you both." Genevieve felt warm, and safe, and comforted in the church. She felt as if she had been sent there, not to St. Patrick's, for a reason.

The priest read from the Gospel of John and then delivered his homily. Already thinking of God's precious gift of his only son,

Genevieve was mesmerized when she heard the priest read, "The weight has lifted from my heart, the doubt has disappeared from my mind." She stared at him standing on the altar, and it seemed as if he was looking across the church, speaking directly to her when he went on, "I no longer feel alone or afraid." Genevieve closed her eyes and swallowed hard. She was spiritual and she was religious, but she was not one to believe in miracles. Yet, at that moment, she no longer felt alone or afraid, and the questions about her baby's future—her future—were answered.

On the way back to the apartment, Genevieve stopped to call home as she did every Sunday, pretending to be calling from whatever city Ice Follies was in at the time. This charade always left her feeling guilty, but though it was Easter Sunday, as she stepped into the telephone booth at the corner of West End Avenue and West Eighty-First Street, she was distracted, and her regrets over lying to her family slipped into the background. She spoke first to Josephine and then to Leonard, who impatiently asked where she was and where she was going and wasn't there a quieter place she could have called from. Her grandmother and grandfather briefly spoke with her next, and then Lucille. Finally, Eleanore came to the phone. "At last," Genevieve thought.

"Where are you calling from? Is it cold there? It's very cold here at home."

Genevieve was impatient with the deception but knew it was necessary. "I need to see you and Charles. I've decided what to do."

"Yes, Charles is here too. He'll be happy to hear that things are going so well for you in the show. I know he's looking forward to seeing you come home."

"Please, tell Charles to leave a message with the answering service about where and when to meet. Any time is good; any place. Here at the apartment, anything you like. Ask him to call as soon as he can, Eleanore. It's important."

"Oh, I understand." Again, Eleanore stood facing the wall as she had when Genevieve had first called and told her that she feared she was pregnant. She hoped that no one listening to her end of the conversation would suspect anything. "We're looking forward to seeing you soon too. We have so much to talk about. I'll wish Charles a happy Easter for you. Goodbye, Gennie. I hope you have a wonderful day. We'll talk again soon."

Genevieve stood in the shelter of the phone booth listening to the silence at the other end of the line before she returned the handset to its cradle. Looking through the glass sides of the enclosure, she saw that few cars were on the street and that no one was on the sidewalk as the blustery winds blew the signs hanging over closed storefronts. "Let's go home," she said as she rubbed her belly through her heavy woolen coat and stepped out of the telephone booth. "Today is a special day. Let's go home and celebrate." The wind blowing from the river carried the steamy puffs of her breath away as she spoke the words.

The day before, thinking of what her family's Easter dinner would be like, Genevieve had shopped and was pleased when the butcher sliced her a lamb steak, cautioning her not to cook it too long lest it become tough. She had found a small jar of mint jelly and a can of tiny peas, and finally, a small, forlorn-looking sweet potato, guessing it was probably the last of the previous year's crop. She had stood thinking for a moment. She had eggs at home. Genevieve, walking down the three aisles of the small market had finally found what she was looking for—a small red-and-white box no larger than a deck of playing cards. The only one remaining, it had four teardrop shapes on its label, one yellow, one green, one blue, and the last one red. As she took it from the shelf, she smiled. There was a familiar sound as the four tiny glass bottles of vegetable coloring, each with a metal cap the color of its contents, clicked one against another. "We'll color Easter eggs," Genevieve had whispered.

Although the wind was still buffeting the windows when she returned from church, it seemed that the apartment had never felt so warm and safe. Genevieve turned on the lamps in the living room and then took *Peter and the Wolf* from the shelf and placed it on the Victrola. "Your favorite," she said as she slowly twirled, the sounds of the flute and the clarinet filling the spacious room. "Such a good story it is; a scary situation with a happy ending." She went to the kitchen and stood over a small ceramic bowl, blue on the outside, white on the inside, containing the four eggs she had boiled and colored the day before. One was deep green, another brilliant yellow; she had let them sit in the dye a long time to intensify their colors. The other two she had removed quickly from their color baths, yielding one egg that was pink, the other powder blue. A hand on either side of her belly as if expecting an answer, some sort of sign, she said, "What do you think? Which shall it be?" Laughing at her silliness, she took the blue one, tapped its large end on the table, and began to peel away the shell.

An Unexpected Opportunity

The Museum of Natural History

Genevieve was impatient, but she controlled herself. Hoping to have received a call from Charles, she waited until lunchtime then went out to call her answering service. She had received few messages other than ones from Charles or her sister to arrange for their weekly lunches or dinners and calls that came every other week or so from Teddy Roman telling her where he was skating, that he missed her and that he hoped she was well.

This time, the Monday after Easter, when Genevieve called she was given two messages. The first was from Charles saying that he and Eleanore would meet her for lunch two days later, on Wednesday at noon, at the Schrafft's on West Fifty-Seventh Street. She knew that this was only a few blocks from her brother-in-law's office. The other message was from Carl Snyder. Genevieve had assured him that she would contact him once she was available to return to skating. He had agreed that he would wait for that call and not bother her, but this message said, "Important to contact Mr. Snyder. He will be available all day Monday at his office."

Genevieve was curious about why he was calling, but she was apprehensive as well. She had not spoken to him since she left the Ice Follies tour. Would Mr. Snyder ask to meet with her about something? She could not possibly have him see her like this. She could not call him from the street corner telephone booth. She needed quiet and privacy. The wind and cold temperatures of the previous days had subsided. The sun was out so Genevieve decided to walk to the museum on Central Park West as she frequently did. There was a row of telephone booths there and during the week the museum often seemed eerily quiet. She hoped that Snyder would be at his desk.

Mr. Snyder was in his office when Genevieve called. When he picked up his phone he apologized for bothering her and asked how she was feeling. He inquired if the rest she had been prescribed was helping her to regain her strength. He had not wanted to disturb her, he said, but he had something important to discuss that he did not think could wait. Genevieve assured him she was feeling much better, but still needed more time and explained that she was not yet ready to skate or even to meet with anyone. She hoped that she sounded convincing.

Mr. Snyder had been responsible for her career, and she felt guilty about prolonging the story she had told him. Snyder told her that a meeting was not necessary, at least not at the moment. There was time, but he wanted to know if she was interested in something that would be coming up in the fall. Genevieve felt a surge of excitement. Yesterday she had reached a difficult decision based partly on the hope that there would be opportunities in the future to resume her career. Here, the next day, one was possibly being presented to her. Of course, she was interested.

"The management at Holiday on Ice is looking for an adagio team, and they inquired about you," Snyder told her. "Actually, what they want is a team that will begin performing with their Ice Vogues show. Do you know about the Vogues, Genevieve?" he asked.

Holiday on Ice and Ice Follies were competing shows. They competed for the same audiences, and they competed to employ the same performers. Genevieve knew that Holiday on Ice had formed the Ice Vogues to perform in smaller markets using the bigger counterpart's show from the previous year. It was not as glamorous as either of the big companies, but if it was a way to resume her career it would be hard to refuse.

"Yes, I know what the Ice Vogues is," Genevieve replied. "Do you think it's a good situation?" For at least the moment, her mind was on her career, not her baby.

Snyder smiled at his end of the line and leaned back in his leather desk chair. "It is if you like to travel. They want someone who would be willing to travel out of the country in addition to performing on their usual US circuit. If you think you would be interested, I can tell you more."

"Out of the country? Where? Yes, I'm interested. You remember I went to Mexico City with the McGowans."

"I thought this situation might intrigue you. It's why I thought I should call. As I said, touring the US, but at the end of the year, traveling to Havana and to Puerto Rico. How does that sound?"

Genevieve clenched her eyes shut. She couldn't believe that she was sitting single, alone and pregnant in a telephone booth at the Museum of Natural History talking about being on ice skates in those exotic places. Her hand on her abdomen, she took a deep breath and replied that she would be very interested.

"Would you like to hear more?" Snyder asked.

"Yes," she said in barely a whisper, biting her lip and wishing she didn't have to hold back her tears. Her baby was kicking.

Snyder went on, "The usual domestic dates the first half of next year and then South America: Rio and Sao Paulo and Buenas Aires, an extended stay. Sounds good?"

It sounded almost too good, Genevieve thought. Did she really deserve this if it were to happen? She cradled the phone between her shoulder and her ear and wrapped both arms around her baby. "Yes, it sounds very good."

CHAPTER FIFTEEN
A Decision Made

With Mrs. Blumenthal

Lexington Hospital

On Wednesday, Genevieve left the apartment early, choosing to slowly descend the stairs rather than take the building's small elevator. As she had in the past, she crossed Riverside Drive and waited at the stop to board the bus that would take her downtown. It was the last day of March. The gusting winds had subsided overnight. They were calm in the morning, and although the air was chilly, it was being rapidly warmed by the rising sun. She hoped it was a signal that springtime weather was on its way. The bus was filled with the last of the rush-hour commuters, and Genevieve self-consciously squeezed into a seat between two other passengers opposite the rear exit door.

As the bus turned and made its way across West Fifty-Seventh Street, it passed Carnegie Hall. Genevieve knew from the newspaper that Billie Holiday, the well-known jazz singer, had performed there four nights before, the evening prior to Easter Sunday. The posters for her performance had been replaced by ones announcing an appearance by Vladimir Horowitz in two days. She saw the opulent Russian Tea Room next to Carnegie Hall and then the Horn and Hardart Automat, when the bus stopped and the doors opened at the corner of Sixth Avenue. From her seat on the bus, she could look through the restaurant's tall glass windows, and suddenly she had a taste for one of the slices of coconut custard pie that waited behind a chrome-framed glass door for a patron to deposit three nickels to release it.

As the bus approached its next stop, she pulled the overhead cord to alert the driver that she wanted to get off. The crosstown street carried two lanes of automobile traffic in each direction, and its wide sidewalks were crowded with pedestrians. Genevieve stood for a moment feeling the sun warm her face, taking care not to be jostled.

Crossing Fifth Avenue, she turned downtown through one of Manhattan's grandest and most extravagant districts. She passed Tiffany & Co., with its precious jewelry and carved crystal displayed in the windows. To her right, the Fifth Avenue Presbyterian Church loomed over the avenue at the corner of West Fifty-Fifth Street opposite the Gotham Hotel on the other side of the street. She paused to admire the diamond creations in the window of Harry Winston Jewelry. Winston, the King of Diamonds, was renowned for his travels to remote places in pursuit of extraordinary stones, as well as for the diamond-laden jewelry that he loaned to those attending the Academy Awards.

It wasn't until she had reached the street corner, looking back to admire the jewelry one last time, that she noticed a young man beneath the store's windows. He was legless. Balanced on a crude wooden dolly padded with scraps of carpet, he wore a khaki field jacket to which a purple heart was pinned, and he held out a cup of pencils that he offered in exchange for spare change from passersby. She paused, but then turned away and decided she would purchase one of his pencils when she returned.

Genevieve could still see the young man over her shoulder as she turned off Fifth Avenue and walked under the gilded canopy that protected the guests of the opulent St. Regis Hotel, six red-carpeted steps above, from inclement weather as they descended to limousines waiting at the curb. She continued across Madison and Park Avenues, finally reaching Lexington Avenue, where she approached the entrance to the hospital.

Mrs. Blumenthal was holding the door open, patiently ushering an elderly man and woman out to the street when she noticed Genevieve, who had stopped and was standing between the hospital entrance and the street corner. Looking at her with concern, she held up her forefinger as if to tell Genevieve, "Just one minute," as she helped the couple into a taxi. When the cab pulled away from the curb, Mrs. Blumenthal turned to face her, beckoning Genevieve into the lobby.

"Is everything all right, Genevieve? I didn't think you were expected here today. Do you need to see the doctor or his nurse?"

"Oh, no," Genevieve said. "I'm fine. No, I don't have an appointment." She paused then said, "I was hoping that you would be here and that I could talk to you. I'm sorry for just appearing."

"Give me just a minute, dear." Genevieve had never noticed the door to the left of the elevator that Mrs. Blumenthal disappeared through. She looked at Mrs. Blumenthal's neatly organized desk and then at the credenza behind it. A tall vase, ivory, its edges tipped in gold, was filled with branches of pussy willow and forsythia. Genevieve was thinking perhaps springtime was closer than she had realized when Mrs. Blumenthal returned with another woman, who smiled politely and sat down at the desk. "Please, come with me, Genevieve." Mrs. Blumenthal motioned for Genevieve to follow her back through the door.

She followed the older woman into a small room, and the two sat across from one another over a small round table. Genevieve said, "Oh, gosh, I didn't mean for you to go to all this trouble. I just needed to talk to someone—to talk out loud. You've been so nice." She paused. "And you seem so wise."

"I am not so sure how wise I am, Genevieve." Mrs. Blumenthal smiled. "But, if I have helped you at all, I'm glad. What do you need to talk about?"

Genevieve relaxed, feeling almost as comfortable as if she was talking with her mother. "I feel so, so big. This morning I almost didn't fit into my seat on the bus." She giggled. Mrs. Blumenthal waited, and Genevieve became serious. "I've made a decision, and I'm going to tell my sister and her husband about it when I meet them for lunch today. You've met them. They've been helping me. They're the only ones who know. No one else knows."

"It's frightfully difficult to be keeping something like this a secret." Mrs. Blumenthal said this as if she had experienced the need to keep an important secret of her own before.

Grateful to be understood, Genevieve responded, "It's very hard. I'm hiding this from the people I would like to talk with the most. Eleanore and Charles, my sister and brother-in-law, are wonderful, but they say I'm the one who has to make these decisions. They'll help me do what I need to, but I have to decide what that is."

Looking into Genevieve's eyes, Mrs. Blumenthal leaned forward. Genevieve recalled how she felt those eyes had looked right through her the first time she had come here. Now they were filled with concern. "You are lucky to have them. What are you going to ask them to help you with? What have you decided, dear?"

"I've known since you and I talked. Do you remember? When you said that some gifts are better to give than to receive?"

Mrs. Blumenthal nodded. "I do, yes, Genevieve." The silence that followed invited the young woman to continue.

"A gift. A gift for my baby," Genevieve repeated, almost whispering. "I'm going to give my baby up for adoption—to someone who can take care of him or her better than I can." The two sat in silence, Genevieve's lips in a tight line, quivering, as she awaited the older woman's response.

Mrs. Blumenthal sighed. "You are a brave young woman, Genevieve, and loving as well to give your baby such a gift."

"I think I've known for weeks, but I've been so confused. I knew for sure when I went to church on Easter Sunday. All the doubt and all the questions went away. All that's important is that my baby should have everything it deserves."

Mrs. Blumenthal smiled, regarding Genevieve the way a proud mother might. "May I give you one more piece of my wisdom, as you so kindly put it?" she asked. Without waiting for Genevieve's response, she said, "Decide what it is your baby deserves. Decide what you want for your baby, what you would give him or her if you were able. There are many good people who want to adopt babies. Make your list, then find the mother and the father who will give your baby everything you want for it."

Again, the two sat quietly. Genevieve was grateful. Mrs. Blumenthal had given her the advice that she wished she could have asked her own mother for if she didn't think the questions would break Josephine's heart. She drew a deep breath, and as she exhaled, her face brightened. "Thank you. I still have more decisions to make then." Genevieve slowly, pensively, shook her head. "And you are wise," she added, smiling, reaffirming her earlier statement. "And kind," she said softly.

With Eleanore and Charles

Schrafft's Restaurant, West 57th Street, New York City

Retracing her footsteps, Genevieve walked to Fifth Avenue which, as it ran north to south, divided the city into its east and west sides. Looking to her right, the young man with the pencils was no longer there. Regretting that she had not stopped earlier, Genevieve crossed the avenue. East Fifty-Fifth Street became West Fifty-Fifth Street, lined with narrow, once elegant brownstone residences, many of which had been converted to offices with retail stores on the ground floor. She crossed Sixth Avenue—Mayor LaGuardia had insisted on renaming the boulevard Avenue of the Americas to the consternation of New Yorkers—passing an elegant residential hotel with a uniformed doorman on the corner.

Midway down the block was City Center, home to both the city's symphony orchestra and its opera company. Genevieve paused to read the notices in the display case in front of the building beside the closed box office. Genevieve wondered if she had not decided to be an ice skater if she might have pursued a career in dance. How different today might have been.

When she reached the restaurant, Eleanore and Charles were waiting outside. It was a few minutes past noon. She had been lost in thought along the way, paying little attention to time as she considered Mrs. Blumenthal's advice to determine precisely what it was she wanted for her baby. Eleanore hugged her younger sister and then held her at arm's length. Looking her up and down, she turned to Charles and said, "My little sister is still beautiful, but she certainly looks like a mother-to-be."

Genevieve blushed in response to her sister's comment as Charles enveloped her in a reassuring embrace. "We'll just stick with beautiful," he said. "Let's go inside."

Schrafft's was a large restaurant with round, dark-stained tables and matching chairs in the center, surrounded by booths along the wall. All of them were covered with white table cloths and contrasting red napkins that matched the color of the carpet and were set with shining utensils and glistening water glasses. Even though it was lunch hour, only half the tables were occupied. Charles quickly surveyed the restaurant and asked the hostess to seat them at a booth toward the rear of the restaurant, away from other diners.

As menus were passed out, the three settled into the booth and waited as the water goblets sitting upside down on the table were righted and filled. Eleanore, seated between her sister and her husband, watched the hostess impatiently, and as soon as she walked away, she leaned forward and asked, "So what is it? You said it was important to meet. Is everything okay?"

"Yes, everything is fine. I didn't want to alarm you. I just knew you couldn't talk while Mommy and Daddy were around you on Easter."

She could feel Charles looking at her. "So, are you going to tell us now?" His voice was kind, but Genevieve could tell he was as impatient as Eleanore.

"I'm sorry," Genevieve said. "I've finally made a decision." She paused, and then added, "About the baby," as if there was any other decision needing to be made at the moment.

"And?" Eleanore prompted her, a bit of frustration creeping into her tone.

"I've been talking to the lady at the hospital, Mrs. Blumenthal. It's like talking with Mommy, and—"

Eleanore, exasperated, interrupted, trying to keep her voice level and calm. "Gennie, you can tell us about Mrs. Blumenthal later. What have you decided?"

Their waiter approached the table but retreated as Charles shook his head. Genevieve looked at his back as he walked away. "My baby. I'm going to give my baby up for adoption—to people who deserve and can take care of him or her." She spoke slowly and softly but deliberately, emphasizing each word.

Neither Eleanore nor Charles said anything for a moment as they looked at one another. Eleanore reached out, her fingertips brushing her sister's arm and then said, "As long as you're sure."

Genevieve placed her other hand on Eleanore's and squeezed it. "I'm very sure. It's the right thing to do. The only thing." Then with a sigh and a mischievous smile, she picked up and opened the menu saying, "I'm starved." The waiter who had been watching from across the room returned to take their order.

Genevieve was about to bring up her telephone call with Carl Snyder. She remained confused about whether or not she deserved such good fortune so soon after making the decision about her baby. She knew that one thing had nothing to do with the other but was concerned by how it would all appear. She wanted reassurance; she wanted it understood that what she was doing was for her baby's sake and not for hers.

Before she could begin, Charles spoke. "I had lunch with a friend from the studio in Astoria last week. He mentioned that he knew a couple who want to adopt a baby." He waited, watching for Genevieve's reaction before he continued. "Someone he knew from his Signal Corps days. It just came up in conversation. I hadn't even mentioned you to him."

For what seemed a long time, Genevieve sat still and said nothing. The unexpected call from Carl Snyder had come and now Charles had heard of people wanting to adopt a baby. It all seemed too convenient. She thought about how she had told Dr. Soresi that there were no convenient solutions. "Do you know who the people are?"

"I didn't ask any questions. I didn't want to talk about you until you and I spoke first. I wasn't sure what you were going to do. Do you want me to find out more about them?"

Just as Genevieve was about to respond, the waiter appeared, a large tray with their meals balanced on one hand. As they were served, both sisters leaned toward their plates and inhaled the aroma of their meals before the pungent smell of Charles's corned beef and cabbage reached Eleanore. She wrinkled her nose in distaste. They ate silently for several minutes, Charles' last question unanswered.

Mixing her rice with the gravy on her plate, Genevieve finally looked up, first to her sister and then to Charles. "I don't know who the people are who will adopt my baby," she said, "but I know who I want them to be. That's why I was talking about Mrs. Blumenthal before."

Charles looked questioningly at Eleanore, who asked, "What do you mean about who you want them to be?"

Genevieve speared a mushroom with her fork. "I know exactly what I want for my baby. What they need to be able to give him or her."

"They? Oh, the people who would adopt your baby," Eleanore said. "I don't know if you get lots of choices in these things." From the corner of her eye, Eleanore looked toward Charles for support.

"Do you want me to find out more about them?" Charles asked. "Do you want me to see if they are people who could offer at least some of the things you want for the baby?"

Genevieve used her knife to scrape grains of rice onto her fork as she considered her brother-in-law's question. "All of the things," she said flatly. "It's not a long list, but it has to be all of them."

Eleanore sighed. She had seen this determined and focused side of her younger sister before. These traits did not always make things easy or lead to quick outcomes, but she knew that Genevieve usually got precisely what she wanted. "Do you want to tell us what your list contains?"

"They have to be Catholic," Genevieve began. "And they need to baptize the baby when they bring it home. That's the first thing that Mommy and Daddy and Grandpa and Grandma would want if they knew about this."

"Okay," Charles said as he began to record a mental list.

"And they need to have been married for more than just a little while. My baby needs parents who have been together and will stay together."

"More than just a little while," Eleanore said. "What does that mean?"

Genevieve hadn't given this specific thought. She had assumed that they would understand. "I don't know. At least five years. Ten years would even be better. The husband has to have a good job, and the wife needs to want to be home to raise the baby."

The waiter returned to take away their plates and deliver dessert to the two sisters. Eleanore, not wanting the conversation interrupted, continued as the server brushed the crumbs from the table before placing dessert in front of them. "What else?"

"Do you know how Daddy always says he moved us to Flushing even though it was more convenient to live in Astoria?"

Charles smiled. "You want them to have a house."

Genevieve returned his smile.

"Is there more?" Eleanore asked, fearing the longer her sister's list, the more difficult it would be to find a couple who met all the criteria.

"Only one more thing; they should be people who can't have children of their own. I want my baby to be a treasure to them." Genevieve took a spoon of her tapioca, and as she flattened a sweet pearl against the roof of her mouth with her tongue, she looked from her sister to her brother-in-law.

Charles took the napkin from his lap, folded it, and put it on the table. "If my friend knows these people from the Signal Corps, it's likely they have been married at least five years. But let me find out about the rest. I'll leave a message for him when I get back to the office. All we can do is ask, and then proceed from there if all the other answers are right."

THE GIFT BEST GIVEN

The Residence of Eddie Senz

West 57th Street, New York City

Eddie Senz lived in the penthouse apartment of what had once been a privately owned mansion built early in the twentieth century. On Fifty-Seventh Street, just to the west of Fifth Avenue, the building was still elegant, though its previous grandeur had faded, and it was where Charles told Genevieve to meet him early the following week.

Senz was a highly regarded hairstylist and makeup artist with significant movie and theater credits on his resume, and his services were highly sought after by the grand dames of New York society. He and Charles had become acquainted during the war, at the Paramount Studios in Astoria, which the army had appropriated for use by the Signal Corps. Charles's sometimes secretive work for the Office of War Information and Senz's efforts on behalf of the government's Office of Special Services had caused their paths to intersect over the past years. It was Senz who had casually mentioned two weeks prior that friends of his were hoping to adopt a baby.

Genevieve waited impatiently for Charles to arrive as she stood in front of the ornate building. Its ground floor contained a corset shop, and she felt awkward, certain that everyone who passed was looking first at her and then at the lingerie in the store's window as they tried to reconcile her presence there. She was grateful to see her brother-in-law hurrying down the street from Sixth Avenue.

With its rose-colored marble floor, mahogany wainscoting, and beveled mirror walls, the building's lobby recalled another era. Charles pressed the call button for the elevator, and the grinding sound of gears and pulleys and weights announced its descent to the lobby. Above the elevator door, Genevieve saw a semi-circle styled after the upper half of a sundial, with rays of sunlight at every hour. Instead of hours, however, there were markers for each of the structure's seven floors. She watched as the brass hand traveled slowly from right to left until the elevator stopped with a jolt in the lobby. The interior of the elevator's car reflected the lobby's decor. For each floor, an onyx button, polished by the touch of fifty years of visitors, stood out against a tarnished brass backplate. Nervously anticipating the meeting that was about to take place, she watched as her brother-in-law reached out to press the button beside the letters PH. As the elevator began its slow ascent, Genevieve noticed that the button for the third floor was chipped.

As the car stopped at the penthouse level, Charles drew the gate aside. Before he could reach for the door, it was pulled open from within the apartment, and they were greeted by a man of medium height and slender build with dark hair and a mustache. He wore light gray pleated trousers held up by suspenders, highly polished shiny black shoes, and a white dress shirt buttoned at the collar but with no tie. The sleeves of the shirt were rolled back, revealing a silver watch with a black alligator band. Beside him was an enormous, black French Poodle that sat obediently, though its body trembled and its tail thumped rhythmically with apparent excitement over new guests. Its eyes were large, dark, and wide-spread and appeared to be as friendly as his owner's, Genevieve thought.

"Come in, please," he said, reaching out to Genevieve. "I am Eddie Senz, and this is Horse." As she turned toward the dog, he offered his paw, and Genevieve, without thinking, reached to shake it. She laughed, and her nervousness about having come here with Charles vanished.

The air in the room was fragrant and sweet, and as Genevieve looked around, her eyes were drawn to a wisp of smoke coming from a still-burning pipe in an ashtray on the small table beside the elevator door. Across from where they stood was a fireplace with a heavy, carved mantle and a hearth of the same pink marble as the lobby floor. The wainscoting that bordered the room had been painted white, and the walls above were painted in a deep red, against which numerous gold-leaf framed oil paintings stood out. To her right, the wall over West Fifty-Seventh Street was mostly occupied by floor-to-ceiling windows between narrow bookcases on either side. Three pigeons were perched on the ledge outside. The high ceiling was adorned with white castings of vines and leaves and flowers. They reminded Genevieve of the iced decorations on a wedding cake.

Senz reached to help Genevieve out of her coat and then took Charles's from him. He said, "I am very pleased that you agreed to come with Charles today. I am sure that this is not easy for you." Senz's voice was mellow and soothing, and though he had been born in Austria, there was no trace of an accent. As he directed the two of them to one of the two couches that stood at right angles from the fireplace, he continued, "Charles has told you that I am friends with a couple hoping to adopt a baby. He has told me that you plan to give your baby up and that you have a rather specific description of who you would like the parents of your baby to be."

Sitting upright on the edge of the deeply cushioned sofa, hands crossed in her lap, Genevieve moistened her lips. She smiled when she saw that the poodle had sat down on the floor beside her. "Yes, I want certain things for my baby. I need to know that he is going to have the best home." Genevieve paused for a moment and then added, "Or her. I don't know if I'm going to have a boy or a girl."

Senz looked directly at her, but rather than being uncomfortable, Genevieve sensed kindness and understanding in his eyes. "Every baby deserves a good home," he said. Then, thoughtfully, "Sadly, not every baby gets one. I can assure you that no child would be better loved than one raised by these people who are my friends."

Genevieve turned to Charles sitting beside her. He said nothing but smiled back at her. She knew that he had spoken to Senz about the list she had made and assumed he would not have brought her here to meet him if there was not a good chance that the couple met her requirements. She turned back to Senz. "Please, tell me about them. How long have you known them?"

"I met them both in 1942 when the army took over the Paramount Studios in Astoria. I had already worked there for several years. They came together. He was an enlisted man, and she was a salaried worker. She is a very talented woman, very artistic—they both are talented people. She would edit the training films so the same film could be distributed in different languages. He worked producing training films for the army. We have remained very good friends."

Remembering the list that Charles had provided him, Senz added, "They were already married for five years when I first met them. So, that means they have now been married for eleven years."

Genevieve was reassured when she heard this. "They have no other children?"

EDDIE SENZ. Eddie Senz was a highly regarded hair stylist and make-up artist. Here with Rise Stevens, co-star of Going My Way with Bing Crosby.

EDDIE SENZ. Eddie Senz residence (center) on West 57th Street, Manhattan.

"No, no children. Not that they have not tried. From what I understand, three different doctors have told them it is unlikely they will ever have a child of their own."

"How sad," Genevieve responded, thinking how unfair it was that an accident had given her what they so desperately wanted. "Do they both work now?"

"Both still work, yes. He has steady employment in the motion picture industry and a very promising career. She also works but plans to stop immediately when," he hesitated for a moment, "if they are able to adopt."

"Their being Catholic is important to me. I want to know that my baby will be baptized." She looked to Senz expectantly.

Senz paused to compose his thoughts and to carefully choose his words. "He was born and raised as a Catholic. She was converted to Catholicism as a teenager. Her parents are Ukrainian—Russian Orthodox. It's an unusual story, but yes, she is now a Catholic too. When my friends married, they eloped and were married by a justice of the peace. They have already inquired of their local church and have been told the baby cannot be baptized unless they are married in the church. They want you to know that if you choose them as your baby's parents, they will do that."

The room was quiet, surprisingly quiet given the traffic on the street below the window. Genevieve looked down, and Horse looked back at her, his eyes eager and his tail slowly beating, as if anticipating her next words. She spoke softly. "My baby being baptized is important—very important." Charles nodded as she again looked to him.

Senz waited a moment before responding. "They are aware that you want your baby to be baptized. As I said, they have already inquired with the church, but I can reiterate this if you would like me to."

Genevieve nodded without saying anything, reviewing in her mind the list she had formulated. "Oh," she remembered. "Where do they live?"

"They live in Astoria."

"Genevieve's family lived in Astoria before they moved to Flushing," Charles interjected.

"Daddy moved us to Flushing because he thought that Astoria was too crowded for us. We had a house, but he moved us anyway. Do they have a house?" She waited for his answer, concerned by how slowly he responded.

Again, Senz paused to choose his words with care. He was aware of Genevieve's desires. "They currently live in an apartment; one of the nicer and newer apartment buildings. I have been there. But they have a piece of property on Long Island, opposite her parents' home. They plan to build a house there. Her brother and her sister also plan to build there. A baby would grow up surrounded by family."

"When? When will they build this house? My baby should grow up in a house, not an apartment."

"Of course. I understand that they already have the plans for this house approved and will start to build soon. When I talk to them about how important baptism is to you, I can also find out when they expect this house to be completed." Senz looked quickly to Charles and then back to Genevieve for her answer.

She looked down again. She found unexpected reassurance in the deep black eyes and the metronome-like tapping of the poodle's tail. Her voice softened. "Yes, please. Both of those things are very important. I need to know."

Senz assured Genevieve that he would contact the couple as soon as possible and then contact Charles. Genevieve stood and walked to the window to look out. The pigeons were undisturbed by her presence. Both men stood behind her, and Senz, as he motioned to the building directly across the street said, "This part of Fifty-Seventh Street is called Piano Row. All the best piano makers have their showrooms here. That one is the Sohmer Building."

Turning immediately to Charles, Genevieve, a trace of excitement in her voice, said, "Sohmer, that's who grandpa worked for."

His eyebrows arched questioningly, Senz looked to Charles and said hopefully, "Perhaps this is a good omen then."

With Mrs. Blumenthal

Lexington Hospital

Ten days later, Genevieve arrived at the hospital for her examination. The frequency of her visits with the doctor had been increased to two-week intervals, and with this most recent one, weekly. When she had returned to the lobby, Mrs. Blumenthal led Genevieve to an elevator other than the one she had ridden previously and took her to the seventh floor, the building's top level. There were four spacious rooms there, each with a private bath, and each more like a hotel suite than a hospital room. This special area of the hospital was where Genevieve had arranged to stay beginning early in May and until her baby arrived. After her baby was delivered, she would be attended to there until she was able to return home.

"So, I ask you this each time I see you, Genevieve," Mrs. Blumenthal asked, "the doctor is satisfied with your progress?"

"He seems very satisfied, yes. He's started doing … um … measurements, and he predicts the baby will arrive by the middle of the month. He says he thinks it's a big baby. He said that my weight gain has been perfect, and each time he listens to the baby's heart he tells me it's as it should be. He lets me listen each time. It makes me smile."

Mrs. Blumenthal opened the door to one of the four rooms. Only one other room on the floor was occupied. "I was happy to hear that you have decided to stay here the days before you are due to give birth. You should not be alone. You are going to be very comfortable here, I assure you."

"Eleanore is happy I'm staying here. She's been worried about my being alone."

"Rightfully so, Genevieve," Mrs. Blumenthal nodded. "I think you have made a wise decision. There will always be someone close by. You will never be alone. When the time comes, you will be taken downstairs. After your baby has been delivered and you are comfortable, you will be returned here."

"This is lovely," Genevieve said as she stood in the middle of the room. "I've made another decision," she continued.

The older woman said nothing as she watched Genevieve move around the room. She had recognized over the prior months that Genevieve chose her words thoughtfully and carefully and needed no prompting.

"About my baby's parents. Charles has a friend who knew of a couple wanting to adopt. We met with his friend, and he told me about them. They sounded almost perfect from the start. I had some questions, and when Charles's friend brought me the answers, they were perfect." Genevieve looked toward Mrs. Blumenthal for her response.

"That is wonderful news, dear. I am truly pleased for you. You had a list that described who the parents should be. They met all your wants?" she asked, concerned.

"Every one of them, yes," Genevieve stated, smiling as the question reminded her of her good fortune that the couple she had hoped for had so quickly—almost magically—appeared. "There's one paper that's so long and detailed and personal. It tells everything about them. They completed it, and their lawyer gave a copy to Charles to show to me before I agreed to anything." Genevieve's voice quavered. "I'm sure they'll give my baby a good home."

Mrs. Blumenthal watched as Genevieve walked to look out the room's window. She heard Genevieve clear her throat. From behind her, she saw Genevieve, first with one hand and then with the other, reaching to her cheeks. Mrs. Blumenthal knew she was wiping away tears. "I have told you this before, Genevieve. You are very brave, and you are very generous. You are giving your baby and this couple a great gift."

Genevieve turned, her hands cradling her abdomen. Her cheeks were wet, but she smiled. "It's the right thing. It's what I have to do for my baby. I'll pray that they'll love him or her as much as I do."

CHAPTER SIXTEEN
The First Weeks of May

Pity Party

Genevieve's Apartment, Riverside Drive

It was the last day of April, a Friday. For the first time, Genevieve felt sorry for herself. As she had been doing for days—dusting shelves that she had already dusted, mopping floors that she had already mopped—she resumed cleaning and organizing the apartment for when she returned after giving birth to her baby.

For the past two weeks, Genevieve had been awash in emotions as she thought about being in the situation that she was. She had done her best to manage it, trying to distract herself, but she couldn't help being angry at the man who had been so insistent, and at herself for finally relenting, putting herself where she was now. She tried not to think that she would soon give away the baby she was carrying, and she felt guilty for even daring to think beyond that moment, about the situation that Carl Snyder had suggested to her. She knew that Charles and Eleanore would have sympathetically listened, but they had already done so much for her that she didn't want to burden them more. "Besides," she thought to herself, "they couldn't possibly understand all that I'm going through." And with that, she cried, feeling guilty that she had dismissed their concern for her, even for a moment.

With springtime having arrived in New York, over the following days Genevieve made a conscious effort to take her mind off her situation and the negative thoughts it brought. She walked along Riverside Drive, where the forsythia that reached over the dark granite wall separating the sidewalk from the park below and the river beyond was in bloom. She looked in the shop windows along

Broadway, and Columbus Avenue as she made her way to Central Park, which was alive with red, pink and white azaleas and blossoming cherry trees. By the day, her outings required more exertion and became shorter, but her spirits were elevated when she returned to the doctor the following Friday.

Genevieve had finished dressing when the doctor returned to the examining room. She looked at him expectantly. As had been his practice, he had said little during the examination. "I suggest you pack a suitcase this weekend and plan on joining us next week, Miss Knorowski. You've started to dilate. By my experience, I anticipate your baby will arrive within the next two weeks. I would rather that you be cautious than to go into labor unexpectedly while you're alone. Here, we can monitor you by the day."

The doctor's suggestion took her by surprise. She nodded her head as she quickly thought of transitioning from the apartment to the hospital and all that it implied. "Monday. I can be here Monday. Is that all right?"

"I'll make sure that everyone is aware," the doctor said. "Monday is fine."

Mrs. Blumenthal was at her desk in the lobby, and the two chatted briefly as Genevieve prepared to depart after her visit. She was on the way to meet Eleanore and Charles at P. J. Clarkes where the three had eaten lunch months prior after learning that she was pregnant. "The doctor wants me to stay here beginning next week. He says my baby will most likely come in the next two weeks. I told him I'll be here on Monday to stay."

Mrs. Blumenthal could sense Genevieve's surprise that the need to move to the hospital had so abruptly arrived. As she had done in the past, she reached out to take Genevieve's hand and squeezed it reassuringly. "We will take good care of you, Genevieve. You will not be alone here."

Genevieve found Eleanore and Charles at the same table that they had previously shared near the back of the restaurant. Both rose to greet her, and Eleanore giggled. "I can't get my arms around you to hug you!" Genevieve blushed and quickly sat down, feeling very conspicuous. She proceeded to tell them of her anticipated move to the private suite at the hospital the following Monday and that the doctor thought her baby would arrive in the next two weeks.

Eleanore, now serious, seemed relieved to hear that her sister would be in a situation where care would be close at hand. Taking a deep breath, she looked to Charles and then back to Genevieve. "We were thinking. There's still time to tell Mommy and Daddy so you won't have to go through this alone. We could—"

"No," Genevieve bluntly interrupted. The three were silent for a moment. "Even if they could understand my being in this situation, they would be so hurt that I've hidden all this from them. They wouldn't understand this whole charade. I won't do anything to hurt them. I'll reappear in a month or so, and no one except for the three of us will ever know."

Charles began to speak. "Eleanore just thought—"

"No," Genevieve interrupted. "I won't do that to them. I love the two of you so much. I owe you so much for seeing me through this, but I wish that you didn't have to be involved either. It's for me to deal with, and soon it will be in my past."

Eleanore and Charles looked at each other with resignation. They had anticipated Genevieve's response and knew better than to pursue the discussion further. Charles reached down next to his chair and produced a thick manila envelope. "These are all the papers for the adoption. You are going to need to sign them." Genevieve reached for the envelope as Charles continued. "They are all very clear. They say that you know precisely what you are doing and that you know what your rights are. They need to be witnessed and notarized. You need to look through them before you sign them."

Genevieve opened the metal clasp on the envelope, looking inside without removing the documents. "So many papers." She appeared to speak to the envelope's contents rather than to her sister and brother-in-law. Looking up, she asked, "When do I need to sign them?"

"The parents are paying all the legal and filing fees. We need to go to their lawyer's office next week," Charles answered. "His office is on Forty-First Street, down the street from the library."

Genevieve looked suddenly alarmed. "Are they going to be there?"

"No," Charles reassured her. "It will be just you and me. The lawyer and his notary will be there. The couple will come to his office separately."

Genevieve picked up the menu that was before her on the table and stared at it. "Part of me would like to meet them to be sure my baby will be safe with them. But it's better for everyone if that doesn't happen. I have to trust my judgment and what I've been told."

A Home for the Moment

Lexington Hospital

The following Monday, Genevieve prepared to leave the apartment. With her suitcase placed beside the door, she walked through the three rooms that she had left spotless and tidy. She smoothed the comforter on the bed, checked that the empty refrigerator was unplugged, turned the bathroom faucet tight to slow a drip that she had meant to get fixed but hadn't, and lowered the shades on the west-facing windows to keep out the afternoon sun. All the while,

Peter and the Wolf once more played on the Victrola. Lifting the needle from the vinyl disk, she returned the record to its sleeve. In the living room where she and her baby had spent so much time together, she spoke out loud. "We'll be back in a few weeks," she said. Then, as she picked up her suitcase and stepped out the door, she corrected herself. "I will be back in a few weeks."

Genevieve took a taxi from the apartment to the hospital, the first one in which she had ridden since returning to New York in January. As it pulled to the curb, the hospital's heavy door opened, and Mrs. Blumenthal stepped out to greet her. It was as if she had been waiting for Genevieve. She looked different, Genevieve thought, realizing that this was the first time she'd seen the older woman in a dress. The pale-blue fabric of the dress with its belted waist and full skirt below was in sharp contrast with her usual tailored business suits. Rather than tightly pulled back, her hair was down, held in place behind her head by a silver filigree barrette. As Genevieve paid her fare, Mrs. Blumenthal gathered her small suitcase and led the way back into the building. Another woman, one Genevieve recalled from a previous visit, was sitting at the desk in the lobby and was on the telephone. The woman looked up and smiled as Mrs. Blumenthal led Genevieve to the elevator to the seventh floor.

The room was located to the left of the elevator as they stepped off. A woman wearing a traditional, all-white nurse's uniform stepped out from one of the rooms, gently closing its door behind her. She smiled as Genevieve was introduced, taking the suitcase from Mrs. Blumenthal, who excused herself by saying to Genevieve, "I must return to the lobby. I leave you in very good hands."

Guiding Genevieve to the room that she would occupy for the next weeks, the nurse said "Don't hesitate to ask for anything you need. There's a card with the hospital extensions next to the telephone, and the operator can help you make outside calls if you like. There is always a nurse on this floor. I will be here until four o'clock, my relief will be here until midnight, and then another will be here all night." Pointing to a call button wired into the wall beside the bed, the nurse said, "If you feel you need help, we want you to press this button. Don't hesitate."

"Thank you. Only if I really need to," Genevieve said. "I don't want to be a bother."

"Don't ever worry about bothering us. We're here to take care of you." Smiling and looking Genevieve up and down, noting how Genevieve's baby had changed position, dropping lower toward her pelvis, she added, "You and your baby. The doctor has on your chart that he expects it will arrive sometime in the next two weeks. I think his prediction will be right on target." Lowering her voice, the nurse said, "We've all been looking forward to you being here. Taking care of a mother and her baby is much more rewarding than dealing with cranky celebrities' gall bladders." Then, remembering that she would be caring only for Genevieve but not her baby, the woman abruptly fell silent.

Genevieve smiled forgivingly, dismissing the nurse's unintended remark, and responded, "Yes, he told me that as well. I'm not sure what I'll do with my time. He wanted me here because I don't have anyone else around. Just in case."

The woman opened the door to a clothes closet, pulled out an empty, cedar-scented drawer of the small dresser and pointed to Genevieve's suitcase. "Make yourself at home." She smiled as she left the room.

As she sat on the edge of the cleverly disguised mechanical bed, she picked up the directory card by the telephone, studied it, and then called the operator to request an outside line.

She wanted to let Charles know that she had arrived at the hospital and was settled in. Genevieve also knew that she and Charles were expected to meet with the attorney for her baby's new parents. She needed to know where and when. She had read through all the court papers that Charles had brought in the thick envelope. All of them demanded her signature. They contained so many details, so much terminology, so many assurances, and so many warnings.

To an outsider reading them, the papers would seem so impersonal, just words on a sheet of paper. When she read them, though, all she could think was, "They're talking about my baby." She read them once, then again, and then one more time the following day before she returned them to the envelope. She prayed that when the new parents—her baby's parents—read them, the papers would contain much more than legal details, terms, assurances, and warnings for them. Cupping her hands under her tummy, feeling its weight, she had prayed that they would think, "These papers are talking about the baby we've waited so long for."

When Charles came to the phone, Genevieve let him know that she was settled in at the hospital and reassured him that she was feeling well. There was a pad of paper with a pen beside the telephone on which she wrote down the details for the meeting with the attorney. "Wednesday, ten a.m., 12 East Forty-First Street, the law offices of Francis Edward Carberry," he told her. She read them back to him. She added the telephone number he provided at the last minute, Lexington 2-5696. Again assuring Charles that she was fine, they disconnected. Genevieve sat there with the receiver in her hand until the operator came on the line and asked if there was anything else she needed. "No. No, thank you, nothing," she said as she hung up the telephone.

Over the next day and a half, Genevieve met the other nurses who attended the floor around the clock. In the solarium, she encountered the two other patients also staying on the floor, one an aging soprano long ago retired from the Metropolitan Opera, the other a doughy, dour man, an author of modest renown, although he had not written a best-selling book in over ten years. Genevieve was relieved that they seemed to have no time left, after talking about their recent gallbladder surgeries and sparring over who had enjoyed the more important career, to show interest in her.

The Law Offices of Francis E. Carberry

East 41st Street, New York City

On Wednesday morning, two days after her arrival at the hospital, Genevieve bathed, dressed, and ate breakfast in her room. In the lobby, Mrs. Blumenthal was filling the tall crystal vase she often used with clusters of bright orange flowers bursting from pods at the end of long stems with curled green leaves. The prickly buds looked like thistles, but Genevieve had never seen thistles that color.

"Good morning, Genevieve," she smiled. "Safflowers," she said, noting the young woman's curiosity.

"They're so pretty. I've never seen anything like them before." Genevieve was in a hurry, but she leaned over them and inhaled.

"They do not have a smell, do they?" the older woman asked. "I have always wondered what they would smell like if they did."

"They would smell like oranges," Genevieve offered without even thinking. She turned to look out the door and could see the sunlight streaming down between the buildings on either side of Fifty-Fifth Street. "And cloves," she added. Then, lowering her voice though there was no one else around, she said, "I'm on the way to the lawyer's office now. This morning I need to sign all the papers."

Mrs. Blumenthal drew a deep breath, saying nothing, asking only, "Shall I hail a taxi for you? The sidewalks are crowded and busy in the morning."

"Thank you. I'll be fine. It's not far." Genevieve followed as Mrs. Blumenthal walked ahead to open the door. "I'll be fine, thank you," she repeated.

The sidewalk along Lexington Avenue was busy with the last streams of businesspeople as they hurried to work. When she reached Grand Central Terminal, she stepped into an arch-ceiling walkway illuminated by brass chandeliers and sconces that led to the station's main concourse. She paused for a moment near the information booth then turned to her right to look at the sliding brass doors that opened and closed as trains arrived and departed. To her left, the boards indicating departures and arrivals rattled above the two walls of brass-fronted ticket booths. She had stood in this very spot when her family brought her here as she set off to Vancouver to begin her career. So much had changed since then.

As Genevieve emerged from the terminal, it was only a short walk to the attorney's office. Turning on East Forty-First Street, she could see the main branch of New York's public library ahead of her, across Fifth Avenue. A large building that spanned two city blocks, it contained millions of books and, flanked by a pair of imposing statues of male lions, three broad flights of stairs climbed from the street to its pillared entrance. The office building she was looking for was on the left. Genevieve entered the lobby through a brass revolving door set between two street-level storefronts and took the elevator twelve floors to the lawyer's suite. From the directory in the lobby, it appeared he was one of a number of attorneys who worked for a large firm.

Other than a bored-looking woman sitting at a reception desk, there was no one else in the waiting area as Genevieve entered the office. Before Genevieve could speak, the woman offered a shallow smile that quickly dissolved and said, "Mr. Hans is already here. He's waiting in the conference room. Someone will be right out to bring you back there and to let Mr. Carberry know that you've arrived." With that, the receptionist picked up her phone, dialed a two-digit extension and curtly announced, "She's here." Genevieve neither responded nor smiled. She turned her back to the woman and examined the framed antique maps on the reception area's walls. She knew it was terribly obvious that she was pregnant, but she resented the fact that the woman had not even greeted her and then had assumed the purpose of her visit as she had.

A young man in a white shirt and navy-blue striped tie, his suit jacket buttoned—Genevieve thought he was only a little bit older than her—quickly appeared and explained that he was Mr. Carberry's assistant. His smile was friendly, and he made polite small talk as he led her down a long hallway past large-windowed offices to a wood-paneled conference room where Charles was seated. "I'll let Mr. Carberry know that you're here," he said as he left the room.

Charles seemed serious. "This is a big day. Are you ready for it? If you're having any second thoughts, it's not too late for you to change your mind."

"I'm fine," Genevieve stated, almost in a whisper. "I'm fine with my decision. It's best for everyone."

As Charles nodded, a man in his mid-thirties, his pleated trousers held up by suspenders, a deep maroon tie with gold stripes accenting his crisp white shirt, entered the room. He appeared to be about six feet tall, and had dark hair and a fair complexion. Behind his horn-rimmed glasses, his eyes were blue. He was followed by the younger man who had brought Genevieve to the conference room. "You must be Miss Knorowski," he greeted her. "I'm Francis Carberry." He looked her in the eyes with a smile that put her at ease.

Genevieve smiled nervously and responded, "I'm pleased to meet you." The touch of Charles's hand on hers reassured her.

"There are a number of documents that you need to sign today, Miss Knorowski. Your brother-in-law has told me that you have reviewed them, but to ensure that you fully understand each of them, I need to go over them with you." Carberry waited patiently for Genevieve's response.

Genevieve said nothing, not realizing that a response was expected. The lawyer motioned to the younger man seated beside him and continued, "As we review each document, I will ask you to sign it, and my assistant will notarize your signature. Once all of them have been signed and notarized, they will be filed in Superior Court in Queens County, and also with the Department of Social Services. They will play a role in overseeing and finalizing the adoption. Do you have any questions?"

Genevieve looked from the papers in front of the lawyer to the notary stamp that the young man held in his hand. She swallowed, took a deep breath, and answered, "I have no questions. I understand."

One by one, Carberry took the documents from the pile of papers that lay on the table in front of him. They were the ones that Genevieve had already read. He spoke slowly, his tone of voice patient and sympathetic as he explained what each was called and what signing it implied. She listened attentively, but she knew what signing each of them meant; she was agreeing to give up her baby. With each document, the attorney asked if Genevieve understood, and one after the other, she nodded and signed as the assistant notarized.

"I have one last form for you to sign, Miss Knorowski, and it is a particularly important one." There was a greater degree of seriousness to Carberry's demeanor as he leaned toward her. "This form is called an Extra Judicial Consent. It says that if within forty-five days you have second thoughts about giving your child up for adoption, you can request a hearing to have the baby returned to you." Genevieve was silent as he continued. "However, it also says that if the adoptive parents are not willing to return the child, they may keep it until a hearing is held and a judge makes a determination. Do you understand?"

Other than the sound of a car horn on the street below, there was no sound in the room. Genevieve closed her eyes then covered them with her hand. She bit her lower lip. Finally, shaking her head slowly from side to side, she took her hand away, reached out, and took the document from Carberry's hand. As she signed it, she whispered with a quavering voice, "I would never do that to them. I would never do that to my baby."

Genevieve felt exhausted both emotionally and physically as the assistant led her and Charles back to the reception area. Mr. Carberry had been patient and professional. But listening to him explain each form's purpose, having to sign them one after the other, and then to watch them get notarized had drained her. Genevieve made no effort to respond to the receptionist's, "Have a nice day," as they stepped out into the elevator lobby.

"Lunch?" Charles asked, stepping out of the building onto the street. He often teased Genevieve about her boundless appetite.

"No, I'm really tired." Charles noticed for the first time how pale his sister-in-law looked. "The hospital will make lunch for us if you want to come back."

"Are we going to walk?" Charles knew that Genevieve walked whenever she could.

To his surprise, Genevieve said she would prefer that they take a taxi back to the hospital. He recognized the toll that the morning's proceedings had taken on her. He flagged down a passing cab, and they made the short trip in silence.

Genevieve was guided to her doctor's office on the fifth floor the next morning. Despite the fact she had grown increasingly weary by the day, she was having trouble getting comfortable enough to sleep well. As always, he measured her vital signs and asked the routine questions about how she was feeling. He was reassured by the fact that her responses matched the observations of the nurses who were now tending to her.

"Given that your baby has dropped," he stopped himself mid-sentence, and asked, "Do you understand what that means?"

Genevieve paused before answering, and then nodded, "Yes, the baby is positioning itself to be born?"

"Exactly. That and the fact that you've been increasingly fatigued indicates that I need to begin measuring to see how dilated you are. It's not perfect, but it's the best indication of how close you are to giving birth, how ready your body is to send your baby out into the world." He smiled reassuringly.

Trying to respond to his smile with one of her own, Genevieve resigned herself to the fact that examinations would become frequent, if not daily, until her baby arrived. All other arrangements were in place. "Let it come soon," she thought to herself.

At the doctor's suggestion, Genevieve changed the routine she had been keeping since she had arrived at the hospital at the beginning of the week. Rather than twice a day, she limited her outings to once in the early afternoon after lunch. She would stay in bed as long as she was comfortable in the morning then have breakfast before moving to the solarium. She was pleased that the opera singer had been discharged. Other than offering a grunt to acknowledge her presence, the author evidenced no interest in her.

The solarium held a selection of recently published books. She was delighted when she found a book called *The Black Stallion*. As she opened it and thumbed through it, she was delighted when she found that the story was based in Flushing, where she had grown up. She could recall the trough for watering horses opposite the town hall on what was now Northern Boulevard. Though it was a children's novel, she couldn't resist it and quickly devoured the book. She had always loved animals, and it provided a welcomed retreat for her. She quickly finished reading another small book by John Steinbeck called *The Pearl* and dreamed of one day visiting the Gulf of California where the book was set. When she saw another book by him, *The Wayward Bus*, she began reading that one next. The author's descriptive prose reminded her of when she had traveled by bus through the mountain canyons and across the parched and barren desert from Los Angeles to Las Vegas with McGowan and Mack five years before. As much as she tried to rest, Genevieve's fatigue continued to increase. "It's natural, Genevieve," the doctor told her. "All part of the miracle of birth."

Shopping

Bloomingdale's, Lexington Avenue, New York City

Having access to the telephone comforted Genevieve. She had felt isolated in the apartment, but now she received daily calls from Charles, as well as from Eleanore whenever her sister could find privacy. The Tuesday after he had joined her at the lawyer's office, during Genevieve's second week in the hospital, Charles came to take her to P.J. Clarke's. Eleanore came to the hospital two days later to join her sister for lunch in her room and was surprised afterward when Genevieve, after expressing frustration at constantly being tired, suggested she wanted to go shopping.

"Shopping? Shopping for what?" Eleanore asked.

"All I have here are clothes for a pregnant mother. Something for when I leave here. Mrs. Blumenthal is going to take care of donating all these maternity things."

"I can bring you something from the apartment," responded Eleanore. "You've been telling me how tired you are; you're supposed to rest."

"I haven't been out yet today. The doctor says that exercise is good. It will make things easier." Genevieve grew quiet, but before Eleanore could speak, she continued in a serious voice. "When I leave here, I want to leave all this behind me. I need to start over. I don't want to look like I did when I came here." As she spoke, she wondered if there would ever be a way to leave all of this experience behind her or if she would always carry a piece of it with her.

Eleanore understood how stubborn her sister could be. "Where? Where are you thinking of shopping? Everything is a long walk from here."

Genevieve had already considered the options. "It's only five blocks away. I walk more than that each day. And we won't be out long. It's not like I can try anything on." She hesitated and looked at Eleanore with raised eyes. "Bloomingdale's. Please?"

The two stepped out of the building, turning up Lexington Avenue toward Bloomingdale's, which occupied a square city block bounded by Fifty-Ninth and Sixtieth streets and Lexington and Third avenues. The midday sun was shining, and even though she was tired, Genevieve was relieved to be outside.

She walked slowly next to her sister, and as they reached Fifty-Seventh Street, she giggled, saying, "I feel like a duck."

Holding Genevieve's arm as they crossed the four lanes of cars stopped at the intersection, Eleanore unconsciously let out an uninhibited snort as she often did when she was amused. For the first time, she found humor in Genevieve's situation. "My dear sister, you look like a duck! Hurry and waddle across!" Both were laughing as they reached the far sidewalk.

The two sat on a bench inside the entrance to the store. The walk had tired her, but she was glad to be there. "Are you sure you're okay?" Eleanore resumed her role as the big sister.

As if to reassure her that she was all right, Genevieve stood and held out her hand to Eleanore. "The second floor. That's where the things in my size are."

Stepping off the escalator on the second of the huge store's seven floors, Genevieve found the displays of summer dresses in the size appropriate for her usual five feet, two inch and 105-pound frame. A saleswoman approached from across the floor and asked tentatively, "May I direct you? The maternity department is two floors up."

Eleanore looked to Genevieve, who smiled back mischievously and said to the woman, "No, thank you. I think I've found my size."

Looking at Genevieve, who was already holding up a dress she'd taken from the rack, the salesperson stammered, "Well, yes, of course. That dress is umm—"

"This is the 'before' me," Genevieve interrupted, spreading her arms as she unsuccessfully attempted to curtsy. Eleanore turned away, stifling a laugh. "I am shopping for the 'after' me." Genevieve's smile indicated she understood the woman's initial thoughts.

Although flustered, the woman was relieved that it didn't appear that she had offended Genevieve, and with an offer of, "Please let me know if there's any way that I can help you," she quickly retreated.

Keeping her promise to Eleanore, Genevieve shopped quickly, moving through the department, finally selecting three different dresses. Watching her sister hold the first one up to herself, Eleanore tried unsuccessfully to refrain from laughing. "That looks like a postage stamp that's been pasted on a big manila envelope!"

Genevieve liked to make her sister laugh. Offering a curt "Humph," she pretended to be offended and held the second dress up as she had the first.

"My goodness, no! The stamp is getting smaller, and the envelope is getting larger!" Eleanore was laughing harder.

The sales lady watched with curiosity from across the floor as Genevieve, haughtily raising her nose in the air, assumed a very proper accent as she lifted the third dress and asked her sister, "Perhaps this is more to madam's liking."

Eleanore tried to hold back, but another amused snort burst forth. She shook her head side to side and then took a deep breath to compose herself. "They're all beautiful. You're beautiful. Pick the one that's the color that you like best. We should be getting you back."

The two sisters walked slowly and cautiously back to the hospital. The outing had tired Genevieve more than she had anticipated. As she entered the lobby, Mrs. Blumenthal quickly looked at her and then to Eleanore. "Your sister burns the candle from both ends."

Looking over her shoulder, Eleanore replied, "She's always been this way. She's never known any better." Genevieve smiled wearily but said nothing as Eleanore followed her to the elevator.

As her sister hung the newly purchased dress in the closet, Genevieve lowered herself into the upholstered chair in the corner of the room. She was grateful for its comfort; it was good to be off her feet. She closed her eyes and emitted a short groan that surprised even her.

Eleanore turned quickly. "Are you all right?"

Genevieve shifted in the chair, trying to find a comfortable position. Her jaw was clenched. "A little bit of a cramp. It's okay now. It's passed." She took a deep breath.

"Are you sure?" Eleanore was watching Genevieve carefully. "I'll let the nurse know when I leave. Promise me if you feel any more cramps like that, you'll say something."

After briefly holding her eyes closed, she opened them and smiled at her sister. "I promise I will. Please don't worry about me." Genevieve silently wished Eleanore could stay with her at the hospital. Knowing that the thought would only make Eleanore feel bad, she said nothing.

Eleanore thought her younger sister, her little sister, suddenly looked vulnerable and alone. She leaned down to her and kissed her on the forehead. "I have to go now. I'll call you whenever I can. I'll be back as soon as I'm able." She held her eyes shut for a moment and said, "I feel like I'm abandoning you here. I hate it."

"You're not abandoning me, and I'm going to be fine. There are lots of people around." Genevieve hoisted herself straighter in her chair and reached to hug her sister. "Go. You have to get home. We don't want Mommy wondering where you've been."

CHAPTER SEVENTEEN
The Home Stretch

Waiting – Impatiently

The Seventh Floor Solarium, Lexington Hospital

She had been restless all night, unable to find a comfortable position in which to sleep. The afternoon nurse had been particularly attentive to her, and as she slept fitfully, Genevieve was aware of the overnight nurse's vigilance. Hourly, the door to her room would quietly crack open then close again, shutting out the dimmed lights of the solarium, returning her room to darkness.

Immediately after breakfast, Genevieve once again met with the doctor. The brief trips to his examining room had become routine and no longer bothered Genevieve as they had when they first began. As she had suspected, the doctor confirmed that she was experiencing contractions. She gritted her teeth as he lifted her gown to examine her then ran his hands over her abdomen, assessing the position of her baby. As she lay back, Genevieve recalled when he had first listened to her baby's heartbeat and how he had recited a number to his nurse. One five two. Now he was dictating numbers in centimeters and in plusses and minuses. As he had months before, he left it to Genevieve to initiate the conversation.

"What do those numbers mean?" she asked.

His hands continued to gently press against her abdomen. "The first number I gave the nurse is the extent to which your cervix is dilated. Dilation sometimes can take a long time; other times it may occur very quickly," he offered.

Genevieve looked up at him thinking, "Go on, go on." He spoke so slowly and methodically. She wondered if her heightened impatience was unusual.

"The other number," he continued, "refers to the position of your baby in your pelvis. You recall how we talked about how it had dropped?"

Genevieve took a deep breath. "I do, yes." Genevieve looked up, trying not to show her frustration. "Where am I on the scale then?" she asked as she drew a deep breath.

"Here, let me help you sit up," he said as he offered her his hands to lift her upright and help her to the edge of the examining table. "All in all, between beginning to experience contractions, the fact that you are showing signs of dilation, and that your baby has continued to drop, my educated guess—and though it is educated it is just a guess—is that you will be in labor within the next forty-eight hours. I don't plan to be far away from the hospital this weekend." He smiled.

Genevieve sat on the edge of the table, both her hands grasping the hem of the gown she was wearing. She felt embarrassed to be asking what she thought must be an obvious question. Her lips moved silently before she asked, "When it's time, what will happen? Will I be put to sleep? And when I wake up will I have had my baby?"

The doctor nodded sympathetically. "We should have had this conversation earlier. I'm sorry. Of course, you want to know. No, we don't put you to sleep."

He noted the look of alarm on Genevieve's face, and before she could interrupt he continued. "There are risks to general anesthesia, and afterward, there is almost always discomfort associated with it as your body tries to purge itself of the medication used. Dr. Soresi is a pioneer of something that is called epidural anesthesia. It's been perfected over the past ten years. He is confident that it will become the preferred form of anesthesia over the coming years."

"I'll be awake? Am I going to feel pain?" It was obvious she needed an explanation.

"You will be awake, yes, but the epidural will block the pain. You will feel the contractions, and you will be fully alert as you give birth. I can explain the details if you'd like." The doctor paused for Genevieve to respond.

"There's no risk to my baby? That's what's most important." Genevieve looked to the doctor for reassurance.

"No more risk than with any other type of anesthesia. There is probably less risk, though that has not yet been quantified." The doctor waited again.

Genevieve appeared pensive as she looked toward the floor. Then she lifted her head, her eyes meeting the doctor's, and nodded, satisfied with his explanation.

He went on to explain that during birth, although she wouldn't have feeling in her legs, she would be able to help—to push with each contraction—and that there would be no pain. He continued, carefully observing Genevieve's reaction, and when she grimaced, he stopped and again assured her that the process would all be painless.

Bravely, she tried to smile. "Maybe I didn't need all the details after all. But I trust you if you say that it's the best way."

Genevieve returned to the seventh floor and adhered to the doctor's order that she refrain from any further forays outside. She attempted to sit and read. She was drawing close to the end of *The Wayward Bus*, but she found it difficult to stay comfortable or to concentrate for very long. Genevieve was delighted when her telephone rang and it was Mrs. Blumenthal calling to ask if she might like company for lunch.

All night and through the morning Genevieve had tried to push aside thoughts of how alone she was, so she was grateful for the companionship as the two sat at the small table in her room. The older woman had brought a small vase with a bouquet of Black-eyed

Susans, their dark centers punctuating the rings of yellow petals that surrounded them. She told Genevieve that the Preakness Stakes, a famous horse race, would take place the next day. Other than the book about the black stallion she had just read, Genevieve's only exposure to horses was the one that used to pull the plow before her grandfather could afford a tractor. She listened as Mrs. Blumenthal went on, telling her that a horse called Citation was expected to win again, but no matter which horse won, she said, it would be rewarded with a blanket of Black-eyed Susans.

After lunch, Genevieve turned on her radio and lay on her bed listening to music. The Nat King Cole Trio's "Nature Boy" had just supplanted Peggy Lee's "Manana" as the number one song on the radio charts. The only thing interrupting their seemingly continuous play was news that a new state on the Mediterranean Sea in the Middle East, Israel, had declared its independence and that war had immediately broken out in response. Wondering how so quickly after the world had finished one war another could break out, she moved to the solarium and slowly paced back and forth, stopping occasionally to look out over the city. The author who had been in residence in the room farthest from hers had been discharged that morning. She was now the only patient on the floor. She welcomed the unexpected privacy, though she knew the nurse was always present, observing from a distance.

That night was another restless one, and Genevieve moved from her bed to the chair in her room and then walked back and forth through the solarium as she tried to get comfortable. It seemed that it was only when she dozed off that the nurse would come to check on her and interrupt her sleep. She turned the radio on in the morning as the sun was rising over the city. In one breath, the announcer said the United States had recognized the new country, and then in the next, he stated that reports were in that Egypt had bombed its capital.

She had a light breakfast of tea and toast, and shortly afterward, her doctor knocked on her door and stepped into her room. Genevieve was surprised to see him on a Saturday morning, his white coat over clothing more casual than his usual weekday attire. The previous day's examination indicated that she might soon go into labor, so he had come to check on his patient. The nurse came in from the floor as the doctor examined Genevieve in her room, sparing her having to move to his examining room downstairs. As he had done the day prior, he measured and palpated as she watched his face for some indication of what he had found.

He nodded to the nurse and then smiled at Genevieve. "Very good," he said.

Genevieve waited but he offered no more information. "How long? Can you tell how long until my baby will arrive?" she asked impatiently.

"Much of this is our best guess, Miss Knorowski. I think I have said that before." His smile was sympathetic, knowing that she wanted an answer more specific than he could provide. "We have just so much control over nature. Sometimes women move along quite quickly. Other times their progress slows, and it takes longer than we expect."

The nights of interrupted sleep, the long days, were increasingly wearing on Genevieve. "I understand about nature, but what is your best guess?"

"Best guess? Two days, perhaps three. I've alerted everyone, the nurses and the anesthesiologist, to be available on short notice." He smiled at her and nodded, "Sooner rather than later if I'm right, Miss Knorowski."

Genevieve was surprised when, after lunch, Eleanore and Charles appeared. She was elated over their unexpected visit. The two were in the city to shop for clothes for their daughter and son, who were being watched by their grandmother, a stoic woman who, to everyone's surprise, had increasingly come to relish the time alone with the children. Genevieve told them about the doctor's visit earlier in the day and his prediction as to when her baby might arrive. She continued matter-of-factly telling them of the plans for her anesthesia.

Afterward, the three rose and paced back and forth through the solarium for several minutes before Genevieve accompanied them to the elevator to hug them goodbye. Eleanore held her sister tightly then stepped back. She tenderly touched her fingertips to her sister's belly then removed them, raising them to her lips. She placed a kiss upon them and gently pressed them again to Genevieve's abdomen. With Charles looking on, both sisters held back tears as the elevator door closed, once more leaving Genevieve alone.

It was late in the afternoon when the Black-eyed Susans that Mrs. Blumenthal had brought her the day before caught Genevieve's attention. She was reminded that the Preakness Stakes was taking place that afternoon. She had no particular interest in horse racing, but if she could find it on the radio, it would interrupt the quiet and distract her from the contractions that were increasing in frequency.

She turned on the radio and began to slowly twist the dial of the tuner, searching for the broadcast. Sure she heard crowd noise, Genevieve stopped at the 1050 mark on the dial, but she quickly realized that she had come across a baseball game. Red Barber, in his southern accent, was telling listeners that it was the bottom of the ninth inning, and the visiting Boston Braves were leading the Dodgers one to nothing at Ebbets Field in Brooklyn. Wondering if Aleksander, her grandfather, was listening to the game, she resumed turning the dial.

Finally, just as she located the race, the nurse entered the room, and

Genevieve urged her to sit down to join her. For the first time, the announcer said, the Columbia Broadcasting System was simultaneously broadcasting over the radio as well as on television. Both were amused as they listened to announcer Brian Field's accent fluidly shift from British to Irish to one that was decidedly New York. The horses were ready to be loaded into the starting gate. There were only four he said, and Fields described how each behaved as they entered the gate.

Leaning toward the radio, Genevieve and the nurse heard the metallic clanging of a bell and the swell of the crowd noise as the race began. His accent constantly changing, Fields was animated as he described how the horses all ran together until the final turn, where Citation pulled away from the field, crossing beneath the finish wire alone and winning the race as the crowd cheered. Genevieve blushed with embarrassment as she realized that she was clapping, feeling more energetic than she had in the past several days.

The burst of energy she experienced after the race was to be her last. That evening, Genevieve paced the solarium, had a light dinner, and then finished reading the Steinbeck book. She slept for only short periods of time, and when she awoke, thoughts of the book were in her mind. First, she pondered the story of Juan, the driver who had steered his bus and its passengers into a ditch and leaving to get help, though he never intended to return. When she stirred next, her thoughts turned to Mildred, the young college girl traveling with her parents. She was so attracted to Juan that she followed him. Based on nothing more than the physical attraction, Mildred had given herself to him only to realize afterward that it was an empty and cold act she knew she would forever regret. Genevieve reminded herself that Mildred was only a character in a book and would never need to experience what she had.

The following morning, the doctor, accompanied by the overnight nurse who was nearing the end of her shift, appeared in her room.

Genevieve had not yet had breakfast. There was no longer any embarrassment on Genevieve's part as the doctor assessed her baby's position and measured her dilation. She was about to speak, about to ask if anything had changed when she was forced to clench her teeth hard as a contraction gripped her, and for what felt like an eternity, though it was probably only thirty seconds or so, her insides felt as if they were being tied in a knot.

"You are in the early stages of labor. Your baby has continued to move down, and you've begun to truly dilate. Your contractions will become more frequent and will last longer as you progress." Nodding toward the nurse standing on the other side of the bed, he continued, "Everyone will do all they can to keep you comfortable. I suggest you eat lightly if you can and continue to walk as you're able."

"How much longer do you think ... until my baby arrives?" Then, using the doctor's caveat, she added, "In your educated opinion."

He smiled slightly as he responded. "The closer we get and the more indications that I can see, the more educated my opinion becomes. I would say between twenty-four and thirty-six hours."

Genevieve had sat up as the doctor was speaking and her legs dangled over the side of the bed. "I'm ready, I think. For breakfast, anyway," she added.

She had the same breakfast that she had been consuming over the past few days—a scrambled egg, toast, and tea. At about eleven o'clock, just as the nurse was about to take her vital signs, something the doctor had ordered to be done hourly, the telephone in her room rang. Knowing it might be her only opportunity to talk with her sister for the next few days, Eleanore had chosen to stay at home with her toddler son while the rest of the family was at church. Genevieve reassured her that she was all right and then told her about the doctor's visit. She felt bad for Eleanore, who continued to express that she felt like she was abandoning her sister when she most needed her. She knew that Eleanore was biting her tongue, refraining from once more suggesting that their parents be informed so that Genevieve would have people around her for the birth.

"Charles will come to the hospital tomorrow. They have his office telephone, in case something happens."

Genevieve did her best to sound confident. Her sister worrying about her was natural, but it wouldn't help anything. "They do have his telephone number, yes. I checked yesterday." Then she added, "And we do know what's going to happen, don't we?"

There was the sound of a child fussing in the background on the other end of the line. "I have to go, Gennie. God, I love you. I hate I can't be there with you."

"I'll be fine. Everything will be fine." Genevieve tried to sound convincing. "I love you too. You need to go. Tell Charles that I'll see him tomorrow." There was silence on the other end of the line and she silently counted, "One, two, three, four," before she heard the click of Eleanore hanging up the telephone.

Genevieve walked up and down in the solarium, and then she walked still more. The rest of the day passed slowly. She remained the only patient on the seventh floor.

Monday, May 17, 1948

Lexington Hospital

By six o'clock the next morning, there was a flurry of activity in Genevieve's room. The nurse had alerted the doctor that Genevieve's contractions had increased overnight, and by the time he arrived, they were coming at five-minute intervals. He smiled, patted her arm, and told her that everything was as it should be. Then he turned to engage in a hushed conversation with the anesthesiologist who had followed him into the room.

"We will keep you in your room for another couple of hours. The nurse will be watching you closely. If the pain and frequency of your contractions become too great, we'll get you downstairs to start you on the epidural we talked about. Do you recall?"

Genevieve nodded and tried to make light of his comment. "If the pain gets too great? It's going to get worse?"

"Well, more frequent anyway," the doctor responded. "Once the anesthetic is administered, you won't feel any discomfort."

She had lost track of time. Genevieve found herself on a cushioned table under an overhead lamp in an otherwise dimly lit, chilly room. The doctor had been right. Once the catheter had been inserted and the anesthetic began to drip, the pain diminished then disappeared, even as the contractions became more frequent and lasted longer. She was grateful for the relief. The nurse who had been with her during her examinations from the first time she had come to the hospital was at her side. Genevieve stared at the ceiling, aware of the nurse who held her hand, the anesthesiologist who monitored her, and the doctor who had entered the room. All were in surgical scrubs, masks, and caps.

As her contractions became regular, she instinctively began to push as each occurred. It felt like she had been pushing for hours. The edges of the light above her blurred against the ceiling as the nurse leaned over her.

"You're doing wonderfully, Genevieve," she reassured her. "It's time for you to work now. You need to breathe then push. Push hard." She continued to firmly hold Genevieve's hand. Genevieve grasped it in return.

THE GIFT BEST GIVEN

"You're fully dilated, and your baby has moved all the way down." The doctor's voice sounded distant and was matter-of-fact.

Genevieve grunted as another contraction washed over her, and she squeezed her eyes shut, responding to the nurse urging her to push. "Breath now, Genevieve." Her eyes opened as the contraction dissipated. "Breathe … breathe … now push!" Her eyes closed again as she summoned her strength.

"I can see your baby's head." The doctor's voice was calm. "Another few pushes. Push hard."

Genevieve squeezed tightly on the nurse's hand, grimacing as she pushed. "That's it, Genevieve. Squeeze. Push hard."

Genevieve gasped for air as she heard the doctor, his voice excited. "Head is out. One more time, push."

Despite the anesthesia and her focused exertion as she pushed, the shudder that she experienced and the long guttural noise that escaped her body surprised Genevieve. She lay still, staring at the ceiling, then turned her head to the nurse who nodded back at her. "All done, Genevieve." She heard her baby's cry in the background.

Gathering her senses, Genevieve looked around and became aware of two other nurses in the room. One was caring for her as she heard the other say, "Twelve ten p.m., male child, twenty-one and a half inches, eight pounds and six ounces."

Her head was back; her eyes were closed. She was giving her baby away. She was not sure that she wanted to know those details. Then she looked up and the nurse was standing over her with the baby swaddled in a blue blanket. The room was silent. "Miss Knorowski—Genevieve—do you want to hold your baby?"

If she took her baby, if she held him, Genevieve was afraid that she wouldn't be able to let him go. She closed her eyes again and turned her head, but then she raised herself up and held out her arms. The nurse placed the newborn on her chest. Genevieve looked at the doctor and asked, "Can I be alone for just a minute? Just a minute, please."

The doctor nodded. "Yes, for a minute. We need to be taking care of you both." He signaled to the others, and they followed him from the room.

The light overhead had been dimmed, and Genevieve was left alone with her baby boy in the cool, quiet room. As he lay across her chest, she was sure she could feel his heart racing. Hers beat back in response. She held him and kissed the top of his head. Through her tears, she said, "You go and love them. Love them as much as I love you."

Charles arrived at the hospital shortly after Genevieve had given birth. Mrs. Blumenthal intercepted him before he could enter the elevator and told him the news. Though she reassured him that his sister-in-law and her baby were both fine, he was dismayed that she had been alone.

"Genevieve will need you more today than any other day of her life, Mr. Hans. Be strong for her."

Charles waited anxiously in the solarium for Genevieve to be returned to her room. He wanted to call Eleanore to let her know but feared she would lose her composure if he told her over the telephone while others were around her, so he did nothing. An hour later, when she was wheeled from the elevator, Genevieve reached for his hand. She was exhausted and her face was solemn. "It's a boy, Charles. Go see him so you can tell Eleanore. Then come back."

One of the nurses who had accompanied Genevieve back to her room offered to guide Charles to the hospital's small nursery. "She was very brave," the nurse said. "She's so tiny, but she was so strong."

Charles nodded as he was left alone in front of a viewing window separating a small nursery from the hallway. Another nurse was standing beside a bassinette with a card attached to it marked Male Knorowski. It was not an ordinary task for him, but he stood and observed, trying to take in every detail. Eleanore would want to know. He mentally noted a full head of light curly hair, and that the baby's brown eyes were wide open, as if taking in his surroundings. In a small notebook that he took from his breast pocket, he noted the height and weight indicated on the card. Below those numbers, he wrote, "Looks like a happy healthy baby."

When he returned to her room, Charles found Genevieve in bed with her eyes closed. She opened them as soon as he entered and looked at him questioningly. Charles swallowed then smiled as she once again reached out for him. She looked like a small and innocent child as she lay there. "Tell me. I saw him and I held him and I kissed him, but it already seems like it was just a dream. Is he all right?"

His sister-in-law was every bit as brave, every bit as strong as the nurse had said. "Yes, he's fine. He's beautiful." He paused. "Just like you."

Genevieve smiled weakly. "Tomorrow he'll be gone from here, Charles. I already miss him."

Feeling helpless, not releasing his grasp on his sister-in-law's hand, he wiped his tears away with the back of his hand. There was nothing that he could say that could make a difference at that moment.

This time it was Genevieve who summoned her strength and squeezed Charles's hand. "Eleanore is going to be sad too. Tell her not to be. Today will be our pity party, mine, and yours, and hers. But tell her tomorrow we all have to move on." Genevieve looked at Charles and, as her eyes began to close, said, "Thank you, Charles. And thank Eleanore too—for everything."

Through the rest of the afternoon, Genevieve slept an exhausted sleep. She was barely aware of the nurse periodically entering the room to check on her, but each time she stirred, she thought of kissing her baby's still-wet head. The recollection of the few brief moments brought her comfort.

When she awoke, the clock opposite her bed said six o'clock. Genevieve looked to the window trying to determine if it was morning or evening. Mrs. Blumenthal was sitting beside the window in a straight-backed chair. Seeing Genevieve's eyes open, she smiled as she rose and walked to the side of the bed.

"You had a good nap, Genevieve. You worked hard for it today."

"I held him … my baby." She closed her eyes as the memory returned to her. "Charles went to see him. He said that he was beautiful. Have you seen him?"

Mrs. Blumenthal leaned close. "I have been to see him, yes. He is an angel. You are giving them the gift of an angel." She looked into Genevieve's eyes as they began to fill with tears. "And you will always be an angel to them as well."

Genevieve shook her head side to side, tears freely flowing. "I'm sorry," she said as she gently sobbed. "I can't help it." Then, from someplace deep within her, Genevieve found the strength to laugh for a moment. "I told Charles that today is the day I'll pity myself. Tomorrow will be a new day."

"It will be a new day for all of you, Genevieve. A new life beginning for all of you: you, your baby, and your baby's new parents."

The Days After

In the middle of the afternoon, the day after he was born, Genevieve's baby's adoptive parents arrived by taxi at Lexington Hospital. They were accompanied by the new father's sister, herself a mother of three, along to provide moral support. Mother, father, and baby returned to the family's apartment in Astoria where they lived until construction soon began on a brick home on a half-acre lot in West Islip, on Long Island, where the baby would be surrounded by his aunts, uncles, and grandparents.

The week after giving birth, dressed in the pale yellow pin-dotted dress that she had purchased at Bloomingdale's, Genevieve, accompanied by Charles, left Lexington Hospital to return to the sublet apartment on Riverside Drive. Mrs. Blumenthal had come to her room to visit earlier that morning but was absent from the lobby as Genevieve departed. A bouquet of pale-blue hydrangeas was on the credenza behind her vacant desk.

At the end of the same week that Genevieve left the hospital, Charles returned to the apartment with Eleanore, who prepared dinner for the three. Charles told Genevieve that he had received a telephone call from Eddie Senz that afternoon. Senz wanted her to know that her baby's adoptive parents had been married on the altar of Most Precious Blood Church in Astoria the day before. This morning, respecting her wishes, their son—Genevieve's baby—had been baptized in the same church. They named him Edward, recognizing the role that Eddie Senz had played in his adoption.

Genevieve cautiously resumed daily activities, taking morning and afternoon walks that slowly increased in length. She returned to Broadway and West End Avenue to do her shopping. Only once did a friendly but unknowing shop keeper ask, "Who's looking after your baby?" She smiled, said nothing, and returned back to the apartment. It was the only time since she had given birth that she would take the record of *Peter and the Wolf* from its jacket to place it on the Victrola. Standing at the window, listening to it as she looked over the river, she wondered if someday her baby might hear the music and wonder at its familiarity.

Through all that had occurred, Genevieve never missed the Sunday call home that was expected of her. Each call had made her feel bad about misleading her family and about what she was hiding from them. The most difficult call was the one she made the Sunday that she was going into labor. The call she made on the third Sunday of June, however, was the easiest. She announced that she would soon be returning home and promised that as soon as she knew when that would be, she would let her family know so they could greet her at the station. At the same time, she conspired with Charles to deliver her to the house in Flushing, feigning a desire to surprise her family. She arrived there ten days later, on a Wednesday, to laughter, tears, kisses, and hugs.

By July, less than two months after giving birth, Genevieve resumed skating at Iceland. As he had promised, Carl Snyder introduced her to a new partner, Bob Payne. Together, they appeared as featured performers, first with Ice Vogues and then Holiday on Ice, skating in the United States as well as Latin America and Europe until a back injury ended Payne's career in 1953.

Other than Eleanore and Charles, no one ever knew what Genevieve had experienced. Ever grateful for all they had done for her, Genevieve gave them three thousand dollars, which they ultimately paid back, for the down-payment on their first home on Long Island. Eleanore died of cancer in 1971 at the age of fifty-seven. Charles later married his wife's cousin and lived to the age of ninety-one.

Genevieve married Ted Meza, a former performer turned set designer, in 1955. She retired from performing to give birth to their first son in 1956. In her final appearances as a professional, she was paired with Phil Hiser, the skater who had first noticed her abilities at Iceland in 1942, almost fifteen years before.

AFTERWARDS. Genevieve with Phil Hiser in 1956 with Holiday on Ice. It was Hiser who met Genevieve 15 years earlier and encouraged her to skate professionally. Photo courtesty of Ted Meza.

AFTERWARDS. Genevieve's son, Ted, born in December, 1956, with his wife, Sheryl in August, 2019.

CHAPTER EIGHTEEN
Kin

Serendipity and the Power of Prayer
Weaver Street Market, Hillsborough, North Carolina

August 4, 2017

From the time I began this journey I've kept detailed notes of every fact discovered, every letter written, every phone call received, and every sliver of possibly useful information that would be worthy of later investigation. I've recorded these bits of information in a notebook that those of a certain age—that age being "older"—will readily recognize from their days in elementary school. A book of white lined pages, its black cardboard cover is arrayed with white speckles but, in this case, updated. When you look carefully, rather than random shapes as they were years ago, the speckles are four-pointed stars placed in orderly rows across the cover, interrupted only by the white label indicating "Composition, 100 sheets, 200 pages, college ruled." Although I've recently learned that composition books have never gone away, thinking that I had discovered an item revived from years past, I had purchased this book two or three years before, for no particular reason I can recall. Never put to use, it sat on a shelf until last March, as if patiently and knowingly waiting to be called upon.

The first pages are filled with notes of joyous discoveries: the names of Genevieve's sisters, her brother, parents, grandparents (my biological great-grandparents—I had never known of great-grandparents before), addresses of cousins into whose lives I would later attempt to delicately insert myself in search of still more information. Traces of Genevieve's career from the time she was young. Did she really leave what I assumed was a conservative Polish Catholic household in New York at the age of eighteen to live and perform in ice shows in Cincinnati? I found later she had actually left home a full year earlier—in the midst of World War II—to travel across the continent alone by train to join a skating company in Vancouver.

I learned in 1955 she had married another skater, Ted Meza, a former vaudeville performer, a man nineteen years older than her, between shows while on tour with Holiday on Ice in Norfolk, Virginia. I had wondered if he could be my father, only to find out later that he was not and wondered if he had ever been aware that Genevieve had brought me into the world.

Another year of touring, another list of tour dates for me to record in my notes. Pregnant with their first child, they retired from performing and settled in Atlanta to write the next chapter in their lives as they opened a business that produced theatrical props. A second child arrived, another son, and their business flourished until 1965, when they were forced to relocate as Atlanta's Hartsfield Airport expanded consuming their studio property in the process. Leaving Atlanta, a budding cosmopolitan city even then, Genevieve and Ted purchased a farm of almost 500 acres in Griffin, Georgia, a rural textile mill town fifty miles to the south. There, they built a home, relocated their business and became part of the community.

I filled one page of my notebook after another. I continue to do so and have now purchased my third composition book, having filled the first two. Not every discovery has been a happy one. Genevieve lost Eleanore, her oldest sister, to cancer in the 1970s and the next oldest, also to cancer, in the 1980s. Her husband died in 1994 following a stroke at the age of eighty-eight. Over time, I encountered information on the death of their second son, Tim. Details are perhaps for another time, but depending on perspective and how much is truly understood, his loss could be termed tragic, or at least inevitable. Tim, before his demise, had a child. I wondered how well Genevieve knew her granddaughter. Ted, her first son, married and divorced then married again and had two daughters before divorcing again. I wondered about Genevieve's relationship with them.

Finally, I found that Genevieve had died in 2014 at age eighty-nine, less than three years prior to my decision to connect with my origins. I was disappointed, I suppose, to have not had the chance to meet her, but I'm not sure that I had ever expected that she would have lived long enough for that to be possible. My concern was that a woman who had seemingly lived every little girl's dream—she had received piano lessons, ballet lessons, skating lessons, and had become a celebrity—may have passed mostly unnoticed and with sadness around her.

Though I knew I had living cousins—I had already spoken with one of them—my only remaining direct link to my birth mother was my half-brother Ted. I found telephone numbers on the internet with Ted's name attached, but not wanting to surprise anyone with an abrupt, "Hey, you don't know me but I'm your brother, can we talk?" I decided to write. The first address was for a property on High Falls Lake, a short distance southwest of Jackson, Georgia. Many names were attached, both the family's surname and others. I located it on a satellite map. There was no house visible, but perhaps it was hidden beneath the cover of the dense forest. I found the street view. The photograph showed a rutted dirt drive at the end of a county road, barred by a rusting pipe gate. It was a discomforting picture for some reason. (Having recently stood at that gate, the feelings of discomfort returned as a sunny, hot Georgia afternoon seemed to momentarily turn dark and chilled).

I proceeded to pen and mail a carefully worded letter. I had to wait only a week before it was returned to me as undeliverable. Back to the online sources. I found another address for my brother, this one in Barnesville, Georgia. I took the same letter, transferred it from the returned envelope to a new one, addressed it, and mailed it. Again, the letter was returned, a red stamp indicating, "Addressee Unknown." Finally, a third letter was sent, this one to a post office box listed in Ted's name, and within a week's time it, too, was returned.

Perplexed, I went back through every note I had made and every document I had touched that might point me to Ted. The blog that had gifted Linda and me with our new picker friends and the treasured memorabilia of Genevieve's had a comment section. There, I found only two comments, each posted by the same individual who stated that he had grown up with Ted and his brother as boys in College Park and that his family and Genevieve's family had known each other well. The posts included only a bit of obscure identification for the author, but with help from another contact I had previously made online, I was provided with an email address.

Once again using my hopefully not too intrusive, "Hi, I hope you can help me, I'm exploring a possible family relationship," introduction, I wrote to him. My email was answered, and the individual wrote that he knew where Ted was, that the two had recently spoken, and that I should anticipate a call from Ted. I occupied myself by making a list of questions about my mother and waited for the telephone to ring. Eight days later, having received no call, I again emailed this individual, who has now become a friend, and asked him to please call me. It was time to lay out all the facts for him with the hope that he might more forcefully encourage my brother to call.

The phone rang the next day, and this friend and I had a lengthy conversation during which I learned that Ted had been involved in a traumatic fire on New Year's Eve of 2015, had been hospitalized, and had been in a physical rehabilitation facility since. As I fully explained my interest, he promised he would contact my brother and urge him to call me.

Three days later, I received the call I was hoping for. I was greeted with a gravelly voice and a thick southern drawl. Ted was friendly, verbal, and animated as he told me about what he had experienced with the fire and his subsequent recovery. He explained that he was again married, now to a woman who was also a resident of the assisted care facility in which he was a patient. He had met her earlier while visiting his mother there before his accident. He spoke with evident pride about his parents and told me of the memorabilia of theirs that he had retained.

I explained that Genevieve, his "Momma," as he referred to her, was my birth mother, something that our mutual contact had not told him. There was a moment of hesitation. Looking back on my notes, I wrote: "Kevin hadn't told him about how we were related—I explained—almost didn't seem like it registered." Perhaps I had no right to expect that a piece of news like that should have registered, communicated as it was. As quickly as our conversation had begun, my brother told me he had to hang up but promised to call the next evening when he had more time. Two days later, much to my frustration, Ted reached out, but I missed the call. It wasn't until almost two weeks later that I made contact with him again, and he answered only to say he was going for a walk with his wife and didn't have time to talk.

Before I could connect with Ted again, another month passed, and he told me he was out of the rehab facility, living independently. Although he had undergone hernia surgery the day before, he promised to call me back in thirty minutes. I was concerned that my information about our shared parentage had registered with him, and he was uncomfortable dealing with it. There was no call thirty minutes later, or the next day, or the day after that. I began to question whether I would hear from him again.

Two weeks later, knowing that Ted visited his wife at the rehabilitation facility, I addressed a letter to him there, then again emailed Kevin, our mutual contact, to ask if he would follow-up to confirm that Ted had received and read it. Almost two weeks passed before I heard from Kevin, confirming that the letter had been received and providing me with Ted's telephone number. I made calls throughout the following week and none were answered.

In the seven years we've now lived in North Carolina, Weaver Street has become "my place." It's a co-op supermarket, bakery, coffee bar, wine store, and more. I'm there frequently enough that no one on the staff any longer says, "Have a good day," or "See you tomorrow." More often than not it's, "I'll see you later," and predictably, I'm back that same day. The personnel know my name, and though there are thousands of members, many of the cashiers have my co-op number memorized when I check out. Three days a week I plan my run to start and end at Weaver Street, not because there's no other place to run, but because the run gives me an excuse to breakfast there afterward. On other days, I plan my swim at a nearby sports facility to end in time to make it to Weaver Street for a breakfast of oatmeal with pecans and almonds or a sausage, egg, and cheese biscuit.

I was sitting on the patio outside the store early that first August after I had begun my search. I was frustrated over my inability to make contact with my newfound brother. I had my notebook in hand and was reviewing the past months' entries when I noticed a young man dressed in a jacket and tie approaching the small handful of occupied tables one at a time. At each table, a brief interaction ensued, then ended with the patrons politely shaking their head from side to side. As I mused over Weaver Street being so special a place that it had such a well-dressed, well-groomed panhandler, the young man finally reached my table. "Pardon me, sir, is there anything I can pray for, for you, this morning?"

I was startled. My first thought was, "Why the hell not," but I thought under the circumstances that might be an inappropriate response so simply said, "Yes, please, any prayer will be a good one."

With a satisfied smile, a nod, and an, "I'll say a prayer for you," the young man disappeared around the corner not to be seen again.

I looked down at my composition book, idly turning it over in my hands as I thought to myself, "Say a prayer and make the phone ring." For the first time, I noticed the label on the composition book's back cover:

Item No. 46016

Norcom, Inc.

Griffin, GA 30224

Griffin, Georgia, the rural textile mill town fifty miles south of Atlanta, where half a century before, Genevieve and her husband had moved to run their business and raise their family, and where I conjectured my brother Ted may well have been living at that moment.

That same evening as Linda was doing paperwork at our dining room table, I came in from sitting with Kitty, the magical little cat who had wandered in out of nowhere and adopted us a couple of Aprils prior. More for background noise than anything else, I flipped on the television and found American Pickers, which was just transitioning from one episode to another. For some reason, the aerial shot of their truck traveling down a two-lane road beneath lush green foliage made me turn up the volume. The pickers were in rural Georgia on their way to another pick. Did they really say that? Was I hearing things? The pick was at the old Rushton Mills, a former cotton mill in Griffin! I called Linda to listen and to watch, and she was both amused and surprised by the coincidence, though not nearly so much as I was. I had not mentioned the young man offering prayers at Weaver Street in the morning, or my belated wish that his prayer would make the phone ring. We watched the show until it ended. I made notes—perhaps the mill's proprietor might prove a useful contact in Griffin. Shaking my head, I said, "The only thing that could happen now is that Ted will call."

I went into the bedroom where I had left my cell phone, picked it up, and sure enough, there was a missed call from my brother. Braced to begin another round of fruitless attempts to connect, I hit the redial button. One ring, two, a third, and then the vaguely familiar gravely southern drawl answered, finally pushing open a new door to step through on my journey.

Kin
Forsyth, Georgia

September 5, 2017

Finally, after almost four months of perseverance, four months of days not always patiently spent, four months of letters sent to post office boxes, one address, and then another, and aided by the prayer of an unknown stranger, Ted and I were talking. There was so much I had been wanting to learn, and I was now struggling as I tried to keep up and take notes as Ted talked rapid-fire, telling me where he was living, who his godparents were, how and when and where his parents had died, that he was married again, that his "Momma" was a "kitty cat person," and if it hadn't been for Bill Clinton, the textile mills in Griffin would still be operating.

As Ted spoke, though he seemed to understand that he and I were related by blood, I still was not sure he accepted that we shared the same mother. In retrospect, I recall thinking early on that if I discovered that my mother was still alive, I would need to be delicate in revealing myself to her. I don't recall thinking the same as I reached out to Ted or to the cousins I had discovered. Perhaps I had no reason to assume, though the first cousin I reached out to had cautiously done so, that Ted would immediately, if ever, accept what I was telling him.

I gently suggested to Ted that Linda and I wanted to visit him. Whether I was particularly persuasive or Ted was simply curious—there was no pressure on my part—he agreed without hesitation. Ted's only caveat was that he wanted Kevin to join us, and I had no issue with that. Kevin, his trusted friend, had been the one to bring us together.

A couple of weeks passed as Kevin and I determined dates good for both of us for a visit. In the meantime, Ted and I talked again. Anticipating our trip, Ted told me that his wife had asked him precisely who we were, and he had told her, "Some sort of kin." He promised her when we came to visit that he would find out just how we were related. I smiled, took a deep breath, and stifled a sigh. Once again, I explained that he and I were half-brothers. This time, I was confident that he was hearing and understanding what I was saying, but I knew it was making no sense to him.

In his mind, Genevieve, our mother, and Ted, his father, had always been together. Besides, if what I was saying was correct, certainly Genevieve would have told him. Nonetheless, Ted's questions didn't stand in the way of our planning. We agreed to get together two weeks in the future, immediately after Labor Day weekend. He would join Linda and me for dinner the night we arrived, and then, two days later, we would meet Kevin, and all of us would have lunch with Ted's wife, Sheryl, at the health and rehabilitation facility where she was a resident.

We made the drive to Georgia as planned, traveling south as tens of thousands were heading in the opposite direction, fleeing Florida ahead of the predicted landfall of Hurricane Irma. By the time we reached our hotel that afternoon, its lobby was beginning to fill with snowbirds with rhinestone-collared poodles and pomeranians on leashes, squawking birds in cages, and cats in carriers. The eyes of the desk staff were already beginning to glaze as they checked in those who had had the foresight to make reservations and politely advised others that the hotel was already fully booked. The scene at the hotel would remain that way for most of the next two days as we watched the traffic on I-75 beneath our window slow to a crawl and remain that way overnight.

As planned, we picked up Ted at his apartment that evening to go to dinner. The first meeting wasn't awkward, but there was the mild tension of people assessing one another and deciding whether or not they want a relationship to proceed beyond the first casual meeting. When we met, Ted was sixty-one, about five feet, eight inches, and was blue-eyed with a fair complexion, brushed-back hair that was gray, almost white, and a matching goatee. We left his apartment to head to a Golden Corral restaurant in Macon, once more driving in the direction from which others were fleeing.

Golden Corral is not on our usual list of dining experiences, but it fit our purposes. I had seen an alluring television ad featuring the "chocolate fountain" after we had checked into the hotel, not that it had anything—well, not too much—to do in influencing our decision,. The buffet restaurant was reasonably convenient, there was food for every taste, no worrying about the cost of one item versus another, and it offered the opportunity to get up and leave the table if there was an awkward moment. On every level, the decision was a good one. The three of us ate, talked, and wandered when wandering seemed right. For the most part, we asked Ted about himself and his experiences, and he was open and forthcoming.

After dinner, we returned to the car to go back to Ted's apartment, where he said he had some memorabilia from his mother and father to show us. After a bit of awkward silence Ted said from the back seat, "Sheryl wants to know what kind of kin you are." Sheryl is Ted's wife. I could feel Linda's eyes move toward me, though she didn't turn her head. This was the third time now that the question had been asked.

I explained again that both he and I had the same mother, Genevieve, although we were the sons of different fathers. I waited for Ted's response. In a not at all confrontational or challenging manner, Ted expressed that he didn't know how that could be. He said that his mother and father had performed together. He had posters with their names on them, and besides, his mother would have told him.

I assured him that I had carefully researched and documented this; that I would not have come to see him if I was not confident. I continued that, from all I had discovered, at the time I was conceived in August of 1947 Genevieve was in San Francisco with Ice Follies and had a different partner, while his father was on tour elsewhere with Holiday on Ice. The car was quiet, and I was sure Ted was contemplating what I had said. We drove the rest of the way mostly in silence.

When we got back to Ted's apartment, he momentarily disappeared into his bedroom before returning with a number of rolled-up posters, the type and size seen hanging in the lobbies of movie theaters. Along with them, he had brought a leather-bound scrapbook. What a treasure! It was filled with black and white photographs detailing Genevieve's skating career in chronological order. Before I could look very far in the album, Ted rolled out the posters, themselves a similar collection of treasures.

The posters, mostly from the Ice Capades, were arranged by year, and Ted once again repeated that his mother and father had performed together. He rolled out the 1945 poster and ran his finger down the list of performers: Ted Meza, his father, but as his finger continued down the list of names, Genevieve's was not there. As he unfurled the 1946 poster, I told Ted that my research had indicated his mother had been skating in various hotel shows at that time. Again, he ran his finger down the list of names, and again Ted was there, Genevieve was not.

As I had in the car, I explained that by 1947 Genevieve and her skating partner, Teddy Roman, had joined Ice Follies and that the troupe spent the summer in San Francisco as they performed and rehearsed. I told him also that a DNA test had revealed the identity of my genetic father, and that he was from San Francisco. Ted quietly unrolled the poster for 1947, seeming less sure of what he would find. Again, Ted Meza's name was prominently listed as a featured performer, but the name of Genevieve Norris was absent. Without saying anything, Ted carefully rolled up the posters.

At the same moment, I was turning the pages of the scrapbook and came to pages of black and white snapshots taken as Genevieve traveled during 1946 and 1947. Precisely in the middle of the left-hand page, framed by the others, was a faded color photo of her in a pink suit outside a restaurant. "A date picture," Linda would call it later. The hilly terrain, the way the street rapidly fell away downhill in the background, would have been enough to suggest San

Francisco. On the snapshot's border and in Genevieve's handwriting, as if placed there seventy years ago in anticipation of this moment, was the notation, "San Francisco, August 1947."

I showed the photograph to Ted, trying to avoid conveying any hint of, "I told you so." He studied the picture, then quietly closed the album and returned both it and the posters to his bedroom. There was no more said about it that evening. We shared a beer, made some casual conversation, and then Linda and I returned to our nearby hotel, where the lobby was still filled with yapping little dogs and complaining birds.

On his way to Ted's two days later, Kevin stopped to meet me at the hotel, which was now absent the chaos with the threatening weather mostly passed and the snowbirds on their way home. From the start, I understood why he was so important to Ted. Kevin expressed a lifetime of affection for Ted's family. His concern for all that Ted had experienced over the past few years and for his well-being was apparent. He was open and kind, and from the moment he walked in the door, he was accepting of what I told him about the results of my months of family research, going so far as to say that he saw a greater resemblance to Genevieve in me than he did in either of her other two sons.

We all met at Ted's apartment again a couple of hours later, and I once again asked to see Genevieve's scrapbook. As I turned its pages, Ted again questioned that we shared the same mother, but this time I sensed he was not so much resisting the fact as he was trying to come to terms with the fact that his mother had not told him. I had held back one last thing to use only if it was necessary. I had brought a copy of the signature page of my adoption decree, signed by my parents' attorney and, in her easily identifiable handwriting, by Genevieve.

Again, I reassured Ted I would not have subjected him to a claim like the one I was making if I was not confident. I explained what the paper was and handed it to him as Kevin quietly looked on. Ted examined it carefully, and it was obvious that he immediately recognized his mother's signature. He handed it to Kevin, who reviewed it and then quietly nodded to Ted as if to say, "Looks good to me." Ted began to return the document to me, but I told him it was a photocopy, and that he could keep it if he might have any use for it. Before we left the apartment to join Sheryl for lunch, we took pictures with one or another of us posing with Ted. In looking at the one of Ted and me, he was smiling. I like to think that maybe by then he had started to accept that I was who I had presented myself to be.

If there was any doubt about Ted not accepting just what kind of kin I was—what kind of kin *we* were—when we talked by telephone a couple of evenings later, he told me he had taken the copy of my adoption decree to the assisted care facility where he had spent so many months as a patient and where Sheryl remained a resident. He had shown it to the center's administrator. I waited to hear more, and Ted told me that the administrator had asked if the signature was Genevieve's. There were a few moments of silence, so I asked him what happened next. Ted said he had confirmed that the signature was his mother's. Again, I waited, but Ted said no more. Finally—I don't imagine as much time actually passed as it seemed—I asked, "What did he say?"

With a chuckle, Ted replied, "He said, 'Ted, it looks like you have yourself a brother.'"

KIN. Author with maternal half-brother, Ted Meza, in Forsyth, Georgia, September 2017

CHAPTER NINETEEN
Pieces of the Puzzle

Eighteen Months
Surrogate Court, Queens County, New York

January, 1950

I was adopted at birth in New York City in May of 1948, and I was luckier than most in that my parents received and retained the documentation of my privately arranged adoption. In contrast, the vast majority of adoptees in New York State had no access to information surrounding their adoption as a result of 1935 legislation endorsed by Governor Herbert Lehman to forever seal those records. It was only in 2019 that this legislation was finally repealed.

Lehman and his wife had previously adopted an infant—*purchased* that baby, actually—from Georgia Tann, an accused baby trafficker. Tann used the unlicensed Tennessee Children's Home Society as a front for her black market adoption business, which netted her millions of dollars from the 1920s until the early 1950s, selling babies for $5,000 to affluent customers, largely in New York and California, including celebrities such as Joan Crawford, who adopted three children through her, and June Allyson and Dick Powell. Questions surround Lehman's support for these regulations, but those questions aside, the legislation he signed remained in place, leaving thousands of adoptees with no avenue to determine the identity of their biological parents. On November 14, 2019, New York Governor Andrew Cuomo signed legislation that would allow adoptees, beginning in 2020, the right to obtain their certified birth certificate, finally allowing them access to information regarding both their adoptive and their birth parents.

In examining the document that had so long sat in the white envelope in our metal file box, I realized that it was the decree finalizing my adoption, dated January 6, 1950, eighteen months after I'd left the hospital and gone home with my new parents. Thinking now about those eighteen months makes me shake my head in contemplating not only the steps taken and the sacrifices made by my parents to ensure that my adoption would ultimately be approved, but also the emotions they must have experienced as a state-appointed social worker would make periodic post-placement visits to ensure baby, home, and parents were as they should be.

Within days of my coming home—May 27, precisely—my parents, who had eloped on Valentine's Day in 1937 and neither of whom were particularly religious, were again married, this time at Most Precious Blood Roman Catholic Church near their apartment home in Astoria. I assume—there's no longer anyone to ask, so an educated guess will have to do—that this was to fulfill my birth mother's stipulation that I be baptized, because the next day I received the sacrament and was baptized Edward James Di Gangi in the same church. A week later, my parents along with their attorney, appeared in court, and I was formally designated their foster child, words that seventy-one years after they were spoken still resonate with a threatening level of impermanence.

My father was a city boy—a product of Manhattan's Lower East Side in the early part of the twentieth century, an "urbanite" through and through. He had little patience for standing still and was building a burgeoning career in New York City's motion picture industry, but shortly after I joined him and my mother in their apartment, he accepted title to a half-acre tract of land across the street from my mother's parents who lived in West Islip, then still a Ukrainian enclave on Long Island. In short order, he oversaw the construction of a three bedroom, two bath brick home at 7 South Street, in which we were living by the time my first Christmas arrived. My mother later would point to three rapidly growing pine trees on the property line, each planted after serving as Christmas trees in 1948, 1949, and 1950. Sadly, the three are long gone.

Recalling my father's frustration with commuting from Queens to Manhattan after we later moved closer to the city, I can only shake my head thinking about what he endured driving ninety miles roundtrip each day while living on Long Island and working in the city. My father freelanced. He was his own boss. He'd work a project and then he'd find another one, and in the growing New York City movie and television industry, he was seldom without work. Still, I wonder if there was concern as to how this type of employment, moving employer to employer, would be perceived when it came time to finalize my adoption, and perhaps that question is in itself the answer to another that's forever perplexed me.

Sometime late in the 1940s, after moving to our new home, my father and my mother's brother—Uncle Connie, who would soon build his own house, next door to ours—took over a postage stamp sized general store that those of my generation and most of the generation before referred to always as "Joe's." Located two blocks from our new home, the store had opened in the early 1920s in the house of its original owners, Alexander and Josephine Kazenowski, before the small building that would subsequently house it was constructed at the corner of Hawley Avenue and Higbie Lane. Known for extending credit to the area's Ukrainian farmers and estate workers, the Kazenowskis passed the business on to their daughter, a school teacher, who apparently came to terms with my father and uncle to purchase it. By the time they took control of the store, the area had begun to grow, and in addition to coffee beans and canned goods, black bread and fat back, the store began to offer services as a substation of the nearby Babylon post office, with Uncle Connie's wife, my Aunt Stella, as the first postmistress.

In looking back over this time, as the eighteen months reached their end, I imagine my parents nervously standing with their attorney in front of the Honorable Anthony P. Savarese, Surrogate Court Judge in the imposing courthouse in Jamaica, Queens. "Francis Carberry for the petitioners, your Honor." Their attorney presenting documents to the clerk: copy of termination of parental rights; affidavit of Genevieve Knorowski and Francis Carberry dated June 11, 1948; final report of Donnetta Difiglia, the forty-three-year-old social worker whose visits over the course of the eighteen months must have unhinged my normally calm mother.

A round of perfunctory questions by the judge to my parents, a thought filled sigh, a slight but sincere smile, and finally an offer of best wishes from His Honor. "Petition for the adoption of Edward James Di Gangi is hereby granted."

Were there ever any ambitions on my father's part to be the proprietor of a tiny country store? The question's probably best answered by the fact that almost as soon as Judge Savarese nodded his kindly head and my adoption was finalized, my father retired from his recent occupation, leaving any pretense of being a grocery and dry good merchant with a conventional, steady income behind him and returned to his career full time. I can't imagine it was more than weeks after my parents stood in court that they found a home under construction in Queens. Close to Manhattan, close to the Grand Central Parkway, close to mass transit, opposite a large park that promised endless adventure for a young boy, and just a short walk to a new elementary school, it was there that we lived for the next fourteen years.

So, an eighteen month slice carved from the lives of my parents. All the people are gone, the Christmas trees are gone, Joe's store is gone, all lost to the past. But as long as those eighteen months are recalled, so long as the people, and the trees, and the store are remembered, all live on.

Pieces of the Puzzle
Churton Grove, Hillsborough, North Carolina

March 24, 2018

Like a jigsaw puzzle, every story is made up of pieces; big ones, smaller ones, pieces not easily found, tiny and hiding, essential to complete the picture. Snap together a few large pieces and a crude picture will emerge. If you desire detail—nuance and subtlety—then more pieces, the diminutive ones, need to be found and added.

In the beginning, knowing so little with regard to my having been adopted, my picture was composed of only a couple of very big pieces, and I felt fortunate to have found those. The answer to the question of who my mother was had been preserved for me. Always assuming that I had been the result of a young girl's careless moment with an eager schoolboy, I never anticipated that I would find the "dad piece" to the puzzle. However, I did find that part, and my very simple picture gained a bit more detail and perspective.

Hours on the computer, telephone calls, letters to previously unknown relatives (some wary, all ultimately open and embracing), and dollars sent for copies of archival records all added more pieces to be spread before me and snapped together. The crude sketch of the two unknown faces gained detail. What they did, where they did what they did, what they were like, and who their relatives—now my relatives—were all fell into place. With much of the story known, what remained were the most subtle of the details, the greatest of which was how my adoption was arranged.

In April of 2017, I called my cousin (my adoptive father's niece), Ann, in New York, something I tried to do on a regular basis. At the age of eighty-one, she was the oldest of my cousins, the only female, and thus, by my deduction, the living relative most likely to know anything at all about my adoption. I don't believe the fact that I was adopted was ever intended to be kept a family secret; it was simply something that was never discussed. So, when I called Ann that day, after assuring each other that our families were well, that the weather was still cold but hopefully it would be spring soon, and that getting old is a tiresome process, I came out and asked her, "What do you remember about my adoption?" It was a bit awkward. It shouldn't have been I suppose, but I was concerned she might see this unanticipated question as some sort of betrayal of my adoptive parents, some indication I was forgetting all that they had given me. There was a fear that, by asking the question, it might somehow put a rip, no matter how small, in the relationship I had with her.

Ann was surprisingly unperturbed by my question. Perhaps she had been anticipating it since my adoptive mother had died thirty years before. She told me her recollection was that my biological mother was an ice skater and that her own mother had gone to the hospital with my parents to bring me home. She then told a story, the details of which she was uncertain, about my adoptive mother having been converted to Catholicism in some mysterious group ceremony at a lake near her home in West Islip on Long Island when she was a girl. She added that the conversion was a fortunate thing. My parents, unless both were Catholic, would not have been able to have me baptized, something that was understood to be critically important to my birth mother.

I had hoped for more information from Ann, but that was all she recalled. It wouldn't be until a year later that she would provide one more detail she had recently remembered, one more puzzle piece that would help complete my picture.

Nearing the end of 2017, I submitted a DNA sample to 23andMe, Ancestry having already helped me identify my birth father. I thought, "Why not?" as I once again mailed in a vial with my saliva. When my results were returned, another close match was revealed. Actually, three close matches appeared—a maternal cousin and two of his children. He was someone of whom I was aware, but he was someone to whom I had not yet reached out. Using the results as motivation, I wrote to him early in December, and a week or so later, my cell phone rang, though I wasn't able to answer the call as I stood beside Linda's hospital bed where she lay after being returned from her second knee replacement. The voicemail began, "Hey, cuz, this is your cousin Paul calling."

Paul and I spoke later that evening. I told him about the search I had been on, what I had discovered, and he shared with me what he recalled and had heard about my birth mother. He told me that his mother, Eleanore, Genevieve's older sister by eleven years, and his father, Charles, older than my mother by fifteen years, had both been extremely protective of her. He told me about his father's enlistment and assignment to the Office of War Information during the Second World War and his deployment on dangerous overseas assignments. He mentioned also how his father had spent substantial time at the Paramount Studios in Astoria, Queens, which had been taken over by the Army Signal Corps during the war. I thought it interesting that my adoptive father had frequently joked about having fought World War II with the Signal Corps in Astoria before he returned to civilian life in 1945. Quite the coincidence; I wondered if they had ever crossed paths.

Months after my conversation with Paul, and a year after I had first guardedly asked my cousin what she knew of my adoption, Ann told me that she had recalled one more detail that she had been meaning to tell me. "You were named after Eddie Senz. He's the one who arranged your adoption." Though it had been decades, I immediately remembered Eddie Senz and his wife from when I was very young. They had a huge, black, standard-sized French Poodle appropriately named Horse and a maroon, open-top, wood-sided Willys jeep. Someplace in one of our carefully stored photo albums are pictures of me wearing a black vest with braided silver trim and a cowboy hat that he had taken in his studio. Eddie Senz and his wife were good friends of my parents. They had met in Astoria at the Signal Corps during the Second World War. Out of curiosity, I searched the internet for Eddie Senz's name and found the following:

> During World War II, Eddie Senz, a top New York makeup artist, was called upon by the U.S. Office of Strategic Services to visualize different ways that Adolf Hitler might disguise himself to avoid capture by Allied Forces

How the final details of my story fell into place became obvious to me. Everyone involved had returned to their everyday lives by the time I was born. But my father, Eddie Senz, and my cousin Paul's father, Charles, all had been at the Paramount Studios in Astoria during the same time period. My adoptive mother, father, and Eddie Senz were friends. Charles worked for the Office of War Information at the same time that Senz worked for the Office of Strategic Services, closely related government entities. Eddie knew my parents were hoping to adopt a child. It's apparent to me that he learned that Charles and his wife were shepherding my unwed mother through her pregnancy. Eddie Senz was the bridge, the final piece of my puzzle.

THE GIFT BEST GIVEN

PIECES OF THE PUZZLE. The paths of Charles Hans, above, and Eddie Senz, below, crossed at the Paramount Studios in Astoria, Queens, NY during World War II. Photo above courtesy of Paul Hans.

PIECES OF THE PUZZLE. Both Jim and Nina Di Gangi worked at the Paramount Studios in Astoria, Queens, New York, at the same time as Charles Hans and were close friends with Eddie Senz.

EPILOGUE
Orange County, North Carolina, Public Library

July 22, 2019

Monday morning, July 22, 2019, and I sit in the Orange County North Carolina Library at the same table that I've occupied for countless days and hours over the past months writing my story. Last night I finished compiling all the many pieces that I've written and then edited over and over again about the circumstances that led me, after sixty-seven years, to search out the woman who placed me for adoption at the time of my birth. I've written about my process of discovery, those I met along the course of this journey, and about the woman herself. Certainly, I've taken some liberties in recounting her story, but the timeline is accurate, the places authentic, and the telling of her life, given the few still alive who knew her and who could tell me otherwise, are true, to the best of my abilities.

Tomorrow morning—Tuesday—Linda, James, and I will depart our home in Hillsborough, North Carolina to drive six hours to Forsyth, Georgia, where my half-brother Ted lives. The day following that, Ted and his wife, Sheryl, along with my family and Kevin Fitzgerald, now a friend both to Ted and me and who has been part of this journey from early on, will travel the short distance from Forsyth to the City Cemetery in nearby Jackson. There, a wooden container built by Ted holding the ashes of Genevieve and Sebastian "Ted" Meza, her husband of forty years, will be placed into a niche in the east side of the cemetery's columbarium as Father Jose of the nearby St. Mary, Mother of God Catholic Church offers his blessing. The spirits of both have long ago found their way to the places destined for them, but it seems right that their earthly remains should at last rest in a sanctified place.

For a time, I had visions of Wednesday's interment serving as an opportunity for a reunion. Those who remain from Genevieve's family—grandchildren, nieces, nephews—have grown apart over the years. For the few who were invited, there were understandable reasons that prevented their attending. For others, it wasn't my place to reach out to include them. So, only the six of us, along with Father Jose, will stand before the crypt as it's closed, and that's all right.

This story of discovery that has given me so much began in another cemetery with only my wife and son around me. It seems only fitting that it will reach its completion, at least this chapter of it, again in a cemetery, again surrounded only by those closest to me. I find joy in believing that Genevieve and her husband, if they were not at peace before, soon will be.

ACKNOWLEDGEMENTS

This book is the unexpected by-product of a three year journey. Along the way, countless people helped me gather the details of my birth mother's and birth father's lives while others supported the writing of this book. I'm profoundly grateful to every one of you. Each of your recollections was a treasure and each of your suggestions made it possible for me to write this book. Fearful that I may unintentionally forget someone deserving of mention, I offer thanks to the following individuals.

Tobey Olson, purchased a box containing the memorabilia of a woman she knew nothing about at an auction one day. That woman would turn out to be my birth mother. Tobey and her husband, Dan, safeguarded those items until one day, a number of years later, I figuratively showed up on their doorstep. Their gifting those items to me threw open a window and allowed me to peer into Genevieve Norris' early life.

Chris Holaday, who has written about baseball, southern bread and classic local restaurants, possesses an amazing breadth of curiosity. He took an interest both in the memorabilia that came into my hands and the story that those items told. From the start, he repeated, "You need to write a book." I'm not sure that this is the book that Chris was thinking about, but I'm also not sure it would have ever been written had it not been for his urging.

Our paths ultimately crossed in different ways, but I've been blessed to meet and know both my paternal and maternal biological brothers. DNA suggests that each is my half-sibling. In my heart, you are brothers, pure and simple. Thank you for all you've shared about those who brought me into the world.

Each of my cousins, Neil and Wayne Cotiaux, Paul Hans and Jacqueline Sierakowski, have shed light on Genevieve and have made me feel part of the family. Wayne was the first to respond—warily—to my inquiries and then blessed me with Knorowski family photographs taken from his own albums. I'm lucky to have found you all.

The late Tex Harrison provided me with contact information for Kevin Fitzgerald who ultimately put me in touch with my brother, Ted. Were it not for these two, I might still be searching! Blessings to Tex and many thanks to you, Kevin.

Neil Cotiaux, Jeannette Santage, Bernadette Pavlis and Ann Tregear generously shared their time and their opinions when I asked them to read and comment on the first draft of my manuscript. Jessica Holland was responsible for editing my final manuscript, and her input, both on the technical aspects and with regard to its flow, made this a better book than it otherwise would have been. Thank you all.

To my friends with the Chapel Hill Writers Group and the Mebane Writers Block, thank you for your input, your support and your encouragement.

My birth mother left her home at the age of seventeen in pursuit of her dream to become a professional ice skater. I'm certain that she savored the good company of those with whom she performed. I want to offer my sincere thanks to all the members of that community who I have encountered who have shared their knowledge and offered their recollections. Special thanks go to the members of the Ice Follies Facebook group who have shared their smiles and their memories.

Finally, thanks to my wife, Linda, who has been involved with this project and supported me from the first. James, our son, was an unknowing witness to this story's genesis as we stood in the cemetery in Jackson, New Jersey in 2017. He again stood with us in 2019 as it came to a close in a Georgia cemetery—coincidentally, in the city of Jackson. I love you both.

About the Author

Edward Di Gangi is the author of several short stories. The Gift Best Given is his first book

Born in New York City, Edward now lives in Hillsborough, North Carolina with his wife Linda. Their son, James, and his wife Renee, live in nearby Durham.

Follow Edward at www.instagram.com/digangiauthor or www.facebook.com/digangiauthor or on his website at www.digangiauthor.com.

www.ingramcontent.com/pod-product-compliance
Lightning Source LLC
Chambersburg PA
CBHW020350080526
44584CB00014B/971